CULTURE HACKS

CULTURE

HACKS

Deciphering Differences in American,
Chinese, and Japanese Thinking

RICHARD CONRAD

LIONCREST
PUBLISHING

CULTURE HACKS

Deciphering Differences in American,
Chinese, and Japanese Thinking

ISBN   978-1-5445-0315-8 *Hardcover*

       978-1-5445-0314-1 *Paperback*

       978-1-5445-0313-4 *Ebook*

       978-1-5445-0316-5 *Audiobook*

For my parents

CONTENTS

PROLOGUE 11

INTRODUCTION 17

SECTION 1: JAPANESE THINKING

1. INTUITION AND INNOVATION......................................27
2. THE ORIGINS OF JAPANESE INTUITIVE THINKING 35
3. LEARNING INTUITIVELY THROUGH AIKIDO 43
4. ZEN AND MINDFULNESS IN JAPANESE CULTURE...........55
5. *STAR WARS* AND ZEN...61
6. THINKING FAST, THINKING SLOW, AND THINKING ZEN 71
7. THE LITERAL JAPANESE MIND 81
8. JAPANESE PERFECTIONISM..93
9. FAILURE AND SUICIDE 101

SECTION 2: CHINESE THINKING

10. CHINESE LATERAL THINKING....................................111
11. MY LESSONS IN USING LATERAL THINKING TO COMMUNICATE WITH THE CHINESE 123
12. USING LATERAL THINKING TO TURN DOWN DRINKS IN CHINA (A SURVIVAL SKILL)...............................131
13. THE CHINESE RELATIVE VIEW OF TRUTH..................137
14. THE IMPORTANCE OF NOT FOLLOWING RULES LITERALLY IN CHINA 149
15. THE CHINESE CHARACTERS.....................................159
16. FAMILY AND STATE 165
17. POWER, LAW, AND THE CHINESE DISREGARD FOR STRANGERS..181
18. INDIVIDUALITY, JOY, AND FRIENDSHIP IN CHINA........191

19. POOR TEAMWORK IN CHINA 203
20. FACE (面子) *MIANZI* 209
21. CHINESE FACE VERSUS JAPANESE HONOR 221

SECTION 3: AMERICAN THINKING
22. THE US AND THE BELIEF IN ABSOLUTE TRUTH 235
23. ALL OR NOTHING IN TRUTH, TRADE, HEALTH, AND LAW.............251
24. AMERICAN LINEAR THINKING 267
25. HOW THE US IS PERCEIVED FROM ASIA 281
26. WHO IS AN AMERICAN? 289

SECTION 4: COMPARISONS IN AMERICAN AND JAPANESE CULTURE
27. THE GROUP VERSUS THE INDIVIDUAL.......................295
28. BUSINESS IN JAPAN 309

SECTION 5: COMPARISONS IN AMERICAN AND CHINESE CULTURE
29. SIMILARITIES AND DIFFERENCES BETWEEN AMERICAN AND
    CHINESE CULTURE 329
30. RULE OF LAW VERSUS RULE OF POWER 345
31. BUSINESS IN CHINA 357
32. NEGOTIATING WITH THE CHINESE............................377

SECTION 6: THE JAPANESE AND CHINESE ECONOMIES AND FUTURE OUTLOOKS
33. THE JAPANESE ECONOMY 395
34. THE CHINESE ECONOMY..411
35. THE OUTLOOK FOR JAPAN 423
36. THE OUTLOOK FOR CHINA......................................431

CONCLUSION 441
ACKNOWLEDGMENTS...443
ABOUT THE AUTHOR 445

知己知彼，百战不殆

*Know yourself, know your enemy, and you
will not lose in one hundred battles.*

—SUN TZU, *THE ART OF WAR*

PROLOGUE

An incident in a small neighborhood grocery store in Japan changed the way I think about the world.

After unloading my basket of groceries, the cashier said I owed 6,543 yen. I was a bit slow counting the unfamiliar coins but was pleased with myself when I had counted out 6,542 yen. I was one yen short. The cashier counted it two times and then stared at me. I smiled back. She kept staring. I looked around the register for a dish of pennies, like we'd have in the US, but no luck. She kept staring. This wasn't a national chain, just a local mom and pop store. Surely, I thought, they wouldn't turn down a $50 purchase over less than a penny.

I finally realized we were stuck. I grabbed my money and groceries and got out of line. To the perfectionist and literal Japanese mind, one penny short was the same as $50 short. This was my first experience realizing that people from different cultures could think and view the world so differently.

When I was in college, it appeared as if—at least in economic terms—Japan was taking over the world. Americans didn't seem to understand Japan, so I moved there to learn the language and culture. While in Taiwan a few years later, I had an intuition that China could replicate Japan's success. I learned Mandarin and became a local student at a top Chinese university, where I earned a masters' degree in economics. For the past sixteen years, I've worked as an equity analyst researching and investing in Chinese and Japanese companies.

Over the past twenty-five years living, studying, and working in Asia, I've developed a framework to help understand the different ways Americans, Chinese, and Japanese think about and interpret the world. My experience was that most cultural misunderstandings and miscommunications were due to fundamental differences in the way we think. I title the framework *Linear, Lateral, Intuitive* because this phrase reminds me that Americans tend to think linearly, Chinese laterally, and Japanese intuitively. This book shows how and why each group thinks differently, how this impacts their societies and cultures, how to best communicate to bridge the cultural divide, and how this difference in thinking shapes each country's future economic outlooks. My goal was to write the book I wish I'd read when I first moved to Asia.

My understanding of different thinking styles evolved

when I was living in China and visited Tibet. Lhasa has an undeniable and palpable energy unlike any other city. It was very holy. I'm not sure how else to describe it. Lhasa presented a stark contrast to my experience in eastern China, where life was extremely pragmatic and just about the opposite of holy.

Tibet couldn't have been more different. From my perspective, Tibet was a place where people appeared to prioritize religious devotion completely. Folks were extremely poor and seemed completely detached from life. Their clothes appeared to be little more than old rags, and they would walk around all day, every day, chanting prayers and spinning small prayer wheels. Some Tibetans would prostrate themselves with every prayer. They would go face down no matter how dirty the ground, stand up again, and repeat, thus moving forward by a body length. It seemed madness to my American eyes. Yet, despite their material poverty, the Tibetan people I saw, to my wonderment, seemed no more or less happy to me than the average American.

I had a revelation while staring at a wrinkled old lady with long matted grey hair in a thick black wool dress that looked as though she had worn it every day for fifty years. She was spinning her prayer wheel over and over, repeating the standard Tibetan prayer of "Om Mani Padme Hum." And then it hit me: in the West, we believe that time began with the big bang 13.8 billion years ago (or that God created heaven and Earth and said "let there be light") and that time has moved forward ever since and will continue to move forward in a linear fashion as the universe ages. Having these set points allows Westerners to have fixed beliefs in absolute truths. Our linear logic came out of this belief in absolute truth and linear time.

Time for Asians, however, from India to Japan, is different. It is, always and everywhere, circular. Of course, Westerners view hours, minutes, and seconds on circular clocks and recognize cyclical seasons: winter, spring, summer, and fall. But when counting by years, we believe in a set beginning with time marching forward in a straight line. The Asian belief is that all time is circular. Universes come into and out of existence infinitely. Everything moves in a circular path with no set points on which to anchor.

With this perspective, Asians tend to view right and wrong, good and bad, as relative and not absolute. As the great Zen warrior Obi-Wan Kenobi said in *Return of the Jedi*, "Luke, you're going to find that many of the truths we cling to depend greatly on our own point of view." In my youth, I knew in my heart that Americans were good because we were democratic and anyone that was a communist was bad. This was a fixed belief I held with great faith. The Asian view on these absolute truths, however, would be that "it depends."

The German Chancellor Helmut Kohl tells a story about a conversation he had with Deng Xiaoping, the great modernizer of China. Helmut said, "If you take the facts into consideration, you are not really honest people. You maintain that you are communists, but in fact, you are much more Confucianist." Deng's pondered response was, "So what?"[1] In my experience, Chinese thinking eschews fixed truths and is much more lateral in its reasoning. Linear reasoning would expect a self-proclaimed communist to follow a communist system for politics and economics. But Deng's response, using lateral logic, was that the adoption of communism would not absolutely lead to a fully communist outcome. His idea of communism was flexible and could easily also include Confucianism and even capitalism (or market economics as he called it) even though this would appear contradictory to a linear logic thinker.

Differences in linear, lateral, and intuitive thinking can lead to unintended confusion, miscommunication, and misunderstanding. Constructive relationships among America, China, and Japan are only growing in importance in the twenty-first century, and it is vital that we work together with clarity. My hope is that this book helps us to all understand and communicate with each other better.

---

1   Lee Kuan Yew, *One Man's View of the World* (Singapore: Straits Time Press, 2013), 322.

INTRODUCTION

WHAT KIND OF THINKER ARE YOU?

How would you solve the problem of "The Village with Ten Cows"?

The "Village with Ten Cows" problem goes like this: Once upon a time, there was an idyllic village that had ten cows. The cows were healthy and happy and supplied the village with enough milk to fulfill the milk needs of one hundred villagers. However, the population of the village was 500, so 400 had to do without milk. If you lived in this village, what solution would you suggest to ensure there was enough milk to go around?

I believe you will solve this problem with the kind of thinking you were most accustomed to use. Therefore, to illustrate my theory on divergence of world views, I use three key areas of analysis to probe the distinctive difference in the way Chinese, Japanese, and Americans think:

- How do they solve problems or make decisions? Is their reasoning linear, lateral, or intuitive?
- Do they tend to interpret the world literally, abstractly, or somewhere in between?
- Do they view truth as relative or absolute? This is connected to their philosophical belief in time: is it linear and constantly moving forward, or is it endlessly circular?

Here is my basic framework applied to Japanese, Chinese and American thinking styles:

	REASONING PROCESS	MIND (ABSTRACT OR LITERAL)	VIEW OF TRUTH
Japanese	Intuitive	Literal	Relative
Chinese	Lateral	Balanced	Relative
Americans	Linear	Balanced	Absolute

The Japanese, for example, tend to reason using intuition, see the world in literal terms, and view truth as relative. This is very different from Americans and can make the Japanese challenging to understand. Of course, these labels are not absolute: linear thinking does happen in Japan, intuitive reasoning exists in the US, and abstract thinking occurs in China, but my focus is on the dominant forms of thinking and reasoning.

Most people do not usually make the distinction between abstract thinking and intuitive thinking. To make it easier to grasp, it is helpful to think of abstract thinking as the opposite of literal or concrete thinking, which concerns itself with the physical world. Whereas the opposite of rational or logical thought is intuition.

THE FIRST KEY DISTINCTION: LINEAR, LATERAL, OR INTUITIVE?

Americans are familiar with linear thinking, where one idea builds upon the other sequentially. This thinking underlies the scientific method and was behind the industrialization and modernization that came out of the West. Americans tend to believe everyone's logic is linear, but that some people are just better at it than others. In other words, Americans don't consider lateral or intuitive thinking to be logical and are generally not as aware of different types of reasoning.

Lateral thinking does not build from subject to object, but rather connects across subjects. The Chinese tend to be lateral thinkers.

One example of Chinese lateral thinking is the country's harsh punishment of crime. In the West, we follow linear logic and feel that the punishment should match the crime. The Chinese view this from a lateral perspective and punish criminals harshly and publicly.[2] This has the effect of scaring the rest of the population into better obey-

---

2   When a senior official goes to jail in China, an extra punishment is that they lose access to hair-dye. This way, the disgraced official is not only locked up, but also suffers the loss of face of appearing on TV with gray hair. This is an extra layer of humiliation.

ing the laws. This reasoning can be found in the Chinese idiom "Kill the chicken to scare the monkeys." By severely punishing a smaller person, large numbers of potentially more important people can be kept in line. Therefore, criminals not only receive punishment for their crime, but also an extra lateral punishment to scare the rest of society. This definitely infringes upon the rights of the punished individual, but the lateral impact is that it is much safer to walk the streets of a Chinese city late at night and alone than it would be in an average American city.

The Japanese tend to be intuitive, driven primarily by feeling and emotion with possible guidance by subconscious logic. The intuitive person often won't be able to easily justify or explain their motive because their idea or solution will not be the product of a straightforward cause-and-effect reasoning process, but rather a feeling or an insight that comes to them as a result of extreme focus and deep experience. What we call feelings can be very rational; it is just not readily deciphered in a step-by-step process. For example, I don't need to do a double-blind study to determine whether it's a bad idea to send money to that stranger who emailed me offering riches. My intuition is sufficient.

An example of Japanese intuitive thinking is that when a student joins the tennis team, they will not actually pick up a tennis racket for their entire first year. Linear logic thinkers would expect that learning tennis would begin with learning to swing the racket and hit the ball.

In Japan, the first year is spent picking up balls, watching, and generally being around people playing tennis to gain an intuitive understanding of how to play tennis. Only after one year of absorbing the lessons from observing tennis would they swing a tennis racket.

THE SECOND DISTINCTION: LITERAL OR ABSTRACT?

How does one's mind interpret, experience, and reflect back the world? How are these processes affected by cultural circumstances? Does one's mind see the world in literal terms, abstract terms, or balanced somewhere in between? For example, a tendency toward either literal or abstract thinking can influence a person's timeliness. If you arrange to meet someone at 5:15 p.m., the literal thinker will be there at precisely 5:15 p.m., while an abstract thinker may show up hours later.

Examples of preferences between the two perspectives:

LITERAL	ABSTRACT
Rules	Principles
Prose	Poetry
Concrete	Symbolic
Data	Theory
Lectures	Debate
Order/Structure	Change
Predictable	Spontaneous

Literal thinking is a key characteristic of the Japanese, so I will cover this more fully in the Japan section.

THE THIRD DISTINCTION: ABSOLUTE OR RELATIVE?

Does time move in a linear or circular path? This major difference between the West and the East leads to two big dissimilarities: the belief in absolute versus relative truth and the belief in the uniqueness of individuals and their roles.

In the West, with our fixed points of reference, we believe in absolute truths, that ideas or actions are immutably true or false, or even good or bad. In the East, where time is always circular, whether something is true or false, or good or bad, depends upon the circumstances, one's point of view, and the timing. Interestingly, a belief in circular time strips away the sense of individuality, because with infinitely circular time, I would have lived before and will live again in infinite iterations. There is nothing unique about me, which sharply de-emphasizes the ego and even the sense of individual rights, as we saw in the Chinese view of punishing crimes. This is in sharp contrast with the West where linear time means that I am a unique individual that will only exist once and I am defined by what makes me unique and not by what role I am asked to play in society.

People who believe time moves linearly have definite set points and, therefore, can maintain absolute truths and absolute judgments of right and wrong. Those who perceive time as circular, on the other hand, believe that everything is relative and evaluations of truth, or right and wrong, depend upon context and perspective.

Indian philosophy believes in infinite worlds and never-ending reincarnations. Interestingly, in Hindi, the word for "yesterday" and "tomorrow" is the same: *kal*. In a circular-time construct, both are the same, one day from today. This would generally be considered silly in the West, which is based on time always moving forward. The West has the concept of resurrection as opposed to reincarnation, but resurrection is a one-time event and the personality or soul survives the process. In the Bible, when Lazarus rose from the dead, he remained Lazarus. In an infinite universe with infinite worlds and infinite reincarnations, we are not unique snowflakes—our lives have existed before and will exist again.

When I am reincarnated in the East, I come back as a different person or even could come back as an animal. The process of becoming another person or animal is viewed as something like a change of clothes. I would never identify just with that particular pair of clothes, but rather with the immortal spirit that put on and took off those clothes with each reincarnation.

Since the belief in absolute or relative truth is a major difference between Western and Eastern thinking, I will cover this more fully in the US section.

MY ANALYSIS OF THE VILLAGE WITH TEN COWS PROBLEM

The **balanced-linear** person thinks we need to increase the number of cows from ten to fifty, so we have enough milk for 500 people. (Americans)

The **literal-intuitive** person thinks about how to increase milk output per cow through different feeding methods or stretch the current milk output with new milk fermentation methods to make a highly nutritious probiotic milk drink. (Japanese)

The **balanced-lateral** person looks to a large patch of grass on the other side of the villages on a steep hill and thinks goats could graze here and thus provide enough milk to supplement our cow's milk. (Chinese)

The **abstract-linear** person estimates the value of a cow at $3 per gallon of milk and thinks of the investment and man hours it takes to produce. They determine it is better for us to invest our money and time elsewhere and to buy the remaining needed milk from another village.

The **literal-linear** thinker organizes a framework to systematically breed bigger herds with larger and more productive cows that produce more milk than the village needs so we can sell the surplus to neighboring villages.

The **abstract-intuitive** person thinks, "Let's build a temple and offer our milk to the gods, and everyone can drink something else." If this last example doesn't make sense, I would suggest traveling around India and you can see for yourself the outcome of that style of thinking.

Which one are you?

SECTION 1

JAPANESE THINKING

CHAPTER 1

INTUITION AND INNOVATION

"I began to realize that an intuitive understanding and consciousness was more significant than abstract thinking and intellectual logical analysis."[3]

—STEVE JOBS

The Western idea of intuition is based on the concept that some information can be acquired without reason or observation: a gut feeling or a sixth sense that makes the person experiencing intuition feel one way or another. For example, "I had an intuition he was a liar," or "I felt that would be the right choice." This is different from Japan, where they cultivate their inner intuitive voice as their primary method of reasoning. This requires

---

3   Walter Isaacson, *Steve Jobs* (New York: Simon and Schuster, 2013), 35.

mindfulness, awareness, presence, and an undistracted, meditative mindset developed over one's lifetime.

I think we in the West look down on intuition because it is difficult to quantify. In the movie *As Good as it Gets*, Jack Nicholson's character is asked how he writes women so well, and his response is, "I think of a man, and I take away reason and accountability." A woman's intuition is spoken of negatively in the West, and I don't think we respect it for serious matters. Intuition gets looked down on as being unreliable and lesser than analytical reasoning.

To be clear, in general, Western women reason in a linear manner. Compared to Western men, however, Western women tend to be more in tune with their feelings and intuitions. The conclusions based on this kind of knowledge are deemed less reliable than cold hard facts and logic. In my experience, this is one of the reasons women are underrepresented in Western STEM (science, technology, engineering, and math) classes, the finance industry, and upper-level corporate management. It is based on bias and not on ability. And I believe this bias is a key reason that a country like Pakistan has had a female leader, but the apparently more advanced, more progressive, and more open-minded United States has yet to elect a woman president.

Steve Jobs helped to change this mindset somewhat through his success. I consider him a hybrid of sorts: a Western-trained, linear thinker with Western abstract creativity that was able to learn intuitive thinking and a Zen-like pursuit of perfection and apply that to his work. College friend Steve Kottke described Steve Jobs saying, "Steve is very much Zen. It was a deep influence. You could see it in his whole approach of stark, minimalist aesthetics, intense focus."[4] In his famous Stanford commencement address, Jobs gave some very Zen advice: "Your time is limited, so don't waste it living someone else's life. Don't be trapped by dogma—which is living with the results of someone else's thinking. Don't let the noise of others' opinions drown out your own inner voice. *And most important, have the courage to follow your heart and intuition.* They somehow already know what you want to become. Everything else is secondary."[5] (Emphasis mine)

Steve Jobs' accomplishments show how powerful intuitive reasoning can be even in the hypercompetitive Western business environment. It shows that linear analytical reasoning is not the only path to success and that intuitive reasoning can play an important role in our private as well as professional lives. Jonas Salk, who discovered the first effective polio vaccine, had a great quote: "Intuition will tell the thinking mind where to look next."

4   Walter Isaacson, *Steve Jobs.*

5   "'You've Got to Find What You Love,' Jobs Says," Stanford University, June 14, 2005, http://news.stanford.edu/2005/06/14/jobs-061505/.

"The theory of relativity occurred to me by intuition, and music is the driving force behind this intuition."

—ALBERT EINSTEIN

I believe it is a shortcoming in Western culture that we do not properly value intuition.

It has been my observation that the Japanese *do* value intuition, or a mindful and meditative reasoning process developed over long periods of time that relies not only on conscious awareness, but also taps into the power of the subconscious mind. They do not use intuition just for simple decisions and for quick judgments on how they feel about something.

The Japanese cultivate their intuition. They will focus on a single discipline for years or even decades, and out of that mastery, develop a deep intuitive understanding of a subject, much like how a chess master can develop an intuitive understanding of how to win a chess match without necessarily having the ability to logically explain each move in advance. Intuitive understanding takes years of intensive focus to develop and the Japanese cultivate intuition for their form of analysis and reasoning in contrast to the linear logic of the West. This difference in perspective highlights two key areas of potential misunderstanding: the Japanese are not creative, and the Japanese are robot-like in their thinking; logical, but without feeling.

It is my opinion that the Japanese are *not* creative, but

that they are fantastic innovators. To be creative, by definition, is to bring about something new that did not exist before. If something did not exist, then it would have to start off as an abstract idea. As the Japanese mind views the world literally, the Japanese tend not to be good at abstract thinking. Therefore, the Japanese have not been very successful in creating new things.

To wit: Japan had the world's second-largest economy before China recently surpassed them. Japan spent enormous sums of money on research and development both in the government and private sectors. Yet, the only big inventions to have come out of Japan over the past few decades have been the Walkman, ink-jet printing, the floppy disk, and LED lights. Note, these have nothing to do with the internet, machine learning, big data, the cloud, artificial intelligence, or any other part of the new economy.

Innovation, on the other hand, is very different from creativity. Innovation is taking something that already exists and making it better. The Japanese are fantastic at innovation. Early in Japan's development, they were known for low-quality knock-offs. Later, in the 1970s and 1980s, Japan started to get recognized for making superior quality, innovative products. Japanese TVs and cars took the world by storm, as they were coveted for their high quality, durability, and reasonable prices. Japanese innovation was based on continuous small improvements. For example, Japanese machining on auto parts became so precise, US auto companies didn't have measuring equipment sensitive enough to detect the difference between US and Japanese parts.

Westerners often hold the view that the Japanese workforce operates as unfeeling, robot-like worker ants. According to this stereotype, the rote education system of Japan didn't teach workers how to think. Japanese workers were successful at building cars or robots or high-speed trains because of superior dedication and their robot-like work ethic. What is interesting today is that despite the competition from Korea and China, who by hook and by crook are imitating or stealing any technology they can get their hands on, Japan still retains an edge in certain areas. What accounts for this difference? Intuition-based craftsmanship.

The front portion of a Japanese bullet train is made by hand. The gears from Japan's global leading high-end bicycle gear company are made by a couple of older craftsmen who work by hand and are the main bottlenecks in their manufacturing process. The production process of Japanese machine tools, the integration of parts into a Japanese hydraulic excavator or diesel engine, the material science in Japanese industrial motors, and the manufacture of small-sized robotic gears are all done by craftsmen. Their work is extremely difficult to imitate as Japanese production is art as much as science.

Far from being robotic, it is precisely the emphasis on using the intuitive part of the mind, the part that a computer cannot imitate, that makes Japanese companies so competitive at advanced manufacturing.

In an example of intuitive thinking in Japanese craftsmanship, Hajime Nakamura explains in the book *Ways of Thinking of Eastern Peoples*: "In the history of technology also the Japanese people have valued and still value intuitive perception (*kan*) more than scientific inferences based on postulational thinking." The Japanese emphasize one's judgment of craftsmanship over formulaic production methods. For example, Japanese swordsmiths never recorded the precise temperature for the water that quenched the red-hot steel. "Thus," Nakamura writes, "this temperature has been transmitted from master to disciple, as a secret which must be understood only through intuition."[6]

Today, Japan houses the only company in the world that can produce a nuclear core reactor vessel as a single unit with no welds. They produce it from a giant 600-ton ingot. This is as much art as science. If it were strictly science, the Chinese or Koreans could copy it. The material science behind this feat is based upon metallurgy knowhow developed by this company centuries ago in the art of forging samurai swords.

I would like to emphasize that this book is about tendencies. Japanese people tend to be literal-intuitive thinkers. But there are exceptions. Shigeru Miyamoto at

---

6   Hajime Nakamura, *Ways of Thinking of Eastern Peoples* (Honolulu: University of Hawaii Press, 1968), 575.

Nintendo created Donkey Kong, Mario Brothers, Legend of Zelda, etc. Satoshi Tajiri, also at Nintendo, created Pokémon. These two are undoubtedly creative and are definitely capable of abstract thought. But I would emphasize that these two are great exceptions in Japan.

In summary, the Japanese are not good abstract thinkers, so they are not creative. They are, however, excellent innovators and through focused, intuition-driven thinking using processes that are as much art as science; the Japanese take existing products and improve on them.

"Coming back after seven months in Indian villages, I saw the craziness of the Western world as well as its capacity for rational thought. If you just sit and observe, you will see how restless your mind is. If you try to calm it, it only makes it worse, but over time it does calm, and when it does, there's room to hear more subtle things—that's when your intuition starts to blossom and you start to see things more clearly and be in the present more. Your mind just slows down, and you see a tremendous expanse in the moment. You see so much more than you could before. It's a discipline; you have to practice it."[7]

—STEVE JOBS (EMPHASIS MINE)

The subconscious mind processes copious amounts of information beyond the scope of the conscious mind. An intense focus and a calm, effortless, and meditative mind-set better allows us to access insights developed subconsciously.

7   Walter Isaacson, *Steve Jobs*, 49.

CHAPTER 2

THE ORIGINS OF JAPANESE INTUITIVE THINKING

In Japanese society, the main emphasis is upon one's social position in relation to all other people; therefore, there are no one-size-fits-all rules. In *Ways of Thinking of Eastern Peoples,* Nakamura describes how this led the Japanese to avoid universal principles and logical thinking, but instead to focus on relationships and intuitive thinking.[8]

Without the expectation of universal truths, the only logic that mattered to the Japanese was that they could be understood in relation to their respective social system. Hierarchy and harmony were the key values in Japanese society. Cold, hard logic didn't fit when harmonious inter-

---

8   Hajime Nakamura, *Ways of Thinking of Eastern Peoples,* 531.

actions and the maintenance of relationships was always the top consideration.

Nakamura further pointed out that even Japanese mathematics lacked logical thinking, and the Japanese not only didn't develop the study of logic, they didn't even conceive of its usefulness.[9]

As Nakamura explains, the Japanese language also did not develop to fit logical thinking. In order to not risk offense, Japanese language is intentionally vague. In a typical sentence, it is not even clear if the subject is male or female, plural or singular, and, in fact, unless the subject is not intuitively obvious, it is simply omitted.[10]

Learning to speak Japanese is awkward at first for a Westerner because Japanese does not include the standardized English use of the subject. In a common everyday sentence such as "I am going to the store" or "What are you going to do tomorrow?", the Japanese would omit the subject of "I" or "you." Whereas in English, we would never just say "going to store" or "what are doing tomorrow" without the subject. To say "I love you" (which, incidentally, is an abstract idea that the Japanese rarely use), they would say (大好き), which means "big-like." In other words, *even in "I love you," the Japanese would exclude the "I" and the "you"!*

On the other hand, when the subject is not an everyday occurrence, the Japanese would definitely add it to

---

9   Hajime Nakamura, *Ways of Thinking of Eastern Peoples*, 549.

10   Hajime Nakamura, *Ways of Thinking of Eastern Peoples*, 535.

ensure the precise understanding no matter how obvious the situation. For example (and this is a case I witnessed), an elephant walks up and the Western person says, "That is huge." The Japanese person replies, "What is huge?" The Westerner says, "The elephant that just walked up to us." The Japanese person confirms, "Yes, that elephant is huge."

Nakamura explains this lack of use of the object in everyday cases by the lack of logic in Japanese expression. It would be logical to always include the subject to remove any confusion or to prevent misunderstandings, but this is not a point of emphasis for the Japanese.[11]

The Japanese language further loses its ability to manifest logical thinking by excluding the linking word "which." In English, the word "which" helps to link ideas and develop logical thinking. It is difficult to make clear connections in complex situations without using this word.[12]

For example, Newton observed that the apple fell, *which* was caused by gravity, *which* is an "attractive pull" based upon the relationship between the mass and distance of two objects, which can be mathematically calculated. This multi-connection sentence would be less clear in Japanese (or Chinese) because these languages lack the connecting word "which." Newton's linear connection of the pull of gravity and mass and distance led

---

11 Hajime Nakamura, *Ways of Thinking of Eastern Peoples*, 535.

12 Hajime Nakamura, *Ways of Thinking of Eastern Peoples*, 534.

to the development of calculus and modern physics. The ancients in the East certainly observed gravity a thousand years before Newton, but they never established the linear connection between gravity and mass and distance, the equation for calculating gravity mathematically, and the sequential connections that would have led to the development of the sciences of calculus and physics.

"Although the Japanese language...is unsuitable for logically precise expression," Nakamura writes, "it is well adapted to the expression of intuition and of individual emotion."[13] This orientation served the ethos of the samurai well. The samurai prized bravery and the lack of fear of death. Logical reasoning demands survival first and the samurai rejected this. This is explained in the samurai classic *Hagakure*: "Calculating people are contemptible. The reason for this is that calculation deals with loss and gain, and the loss and gain mind never stops. Death is considered loss and life is considered gain. Thus, death is something that such a person does not care for, and he is contemptible."[14] As such, if you used your calculating/rational mind, and developed a rational risk-reward framework fully cognizant of the long-term implications of any dangerous action in war, you would be far less likely to act bravely and would instead focus on self-preservation.

---

13   Hajime Nakamura, *Ways of Thinking of Eastern Peoples*, 551.

14   Tsunetomo Yamamoto, *Hagakure*, trans. Scott William Wilson (New York: Kodansha International, 1983),44.

In order to make the correct emotional decision, samurai were not encouraged to deliberate on actions. "In the words of the ancients, one should make his decision within the space of seven breaths...When your mind is going hither and thither, discrimination will never be brought to a conclusion. With an intense, fresh and undelaying spirit, one will make his judgments within the space of seven breaths. It is a matter of being determined and having the spirit to break right through to the other side."[15]

There is a story from *Hagakure* that illustrates this point. When asked about Buddhism, a priest replied that it is about eliminating the discriminating mind. The priest gave the example of the Chinese character for "cowardice" (憶) which is a combination of the radicals for "meaning" (意) and "mind" (忄), and that when the mind attaches to meaning and ignores instinct and duty, that is cowardice.[16]

When I studied Japanese, I learned the word for "cowardice" or "cowardly," "*okubyou*," was written as (臆病), but traditionally, (臆) and (憶) could be used interchangeably. Therefore, 300 years ago, they must have been referring to the writing of "*okubyou*" as (憶病). The meaning of the first character is "to remember or recollect." The second character means "sickness." What this meaning extends to is that cowardice is the sickness of

---

15   Tsunetomo Yamamoto, *Hagakure*, 47.

16   Tsunetomo Yamamoto, *Hagakure*, 146.

deliberate thinking and that bravery comes from acting spontaneously and fulfilling one's duty without applying the logical or rational mind.

In the famous (true) Japanese story *Chushingura*, or the *47 Ronin*, the ronin go to elaborate lengths for over a year to get revenge and kill the man who insulted their lord. After completing their task, all forty-seven ronin committed ritual suicide by disemboweling themselves with razor sharp swords. This would seem to be an honorable and successful mission, but in terms of the samurai worldview, the ronin came under a torrent of criticism for waiting so long to take action. The feeling was that they should have gone for their revenge immediately even though that meant they would have surely been cut down without fulfilling their duty of avenging their master. In my opinion, this is not easy logic to follow.

This focus on intuitive thinking and spontaneous bravery as opposed to linear logic is certainly one reason the Japanese were such ferocious fighters. But this quality also worked against them in WWII, as Ruth Benedict describes in *The Chrysanthemum and the Sword*. "...During the war the Japanese army had no trained rescue teams to remove the wounded under fire and to give first aid; it had no medical system of front line, behind-the-lines and distant recuperative hospitals. Its attention to medical supplies was lamentable."[17]

---

17 Ruth Benedict, *The Chrysanthemum and the Sword* (New York: Houghton Mifflin Company, 2006), 37.

Simple linear thinking would indicate that if you properly treat wounded soldiers, they can recuperate, return to duty, and boost the army's overall fighting power. The Japanese, however, felt that a soldier wounded in battle had failed and was dishonored, and were reluctant to treat them. This demonstrated their emphasis on the warrior spirit and the process of fighting heroically, but showed a complete lack of linear logic or focus upon the end goal of winning the war.

CHAPTER 3

LEARNING INTUITIVELY THROUGH AIKIDO

I feel that understanding Japanese Zen Buddhist thinking is helpful in understanding Japanese intuition. My journey in learning about Zen began with Aikido. Before going to Japan, my college Japanese professor gave me some great advice. He told me that interaction with the local Japanese was the best way to learn and that cultural fluency was just as important as language fluency. As one of the best ways to interact with a culture is to participate in local activities, I decided to learn Aikido.

Aikido (合気道) is a Japanese martial art which literally means "matching-energy-way." It is based upon samurai sword fighting techniques and includes sword work, but mostly focuses on hand-to-hand combat. There are no fighting competitions, per se, in Aikido. Every technique is practiced with usually one partner, sometimes more, and the move is generally predefined before being executed.

The first character in Aikido (合) means "to match." The first principle of Aikido is non-dissension. You never want to meet the opponent's force with force. Aikido is a self-defense martial art. The goal is to move along the line of the opponent's attack, match movements without conflict so as to become one moving entity, and then shift the center of the movement to your own center. Once you can shift the movement along a new line, you can maneuver the opponent into a submission or a throw.

The second character in Aikido (気) is more difficult to translate. It means energy or spirit, but must be understood intuitively. In Japanese, it is pronounced *ki* (like the word key). Some may be familiar with the Chinese pronunciation *qi* (pronounced like the first syllable in the word cheese) as in *qigong*. I studied *Ki*-Aikido as taught by Tohei-sensei, and every class started with repeating a *ki* saying. One of them was on the definition of "*ki*":

"We begin with the number one in counting all things. It is impossible that this one can ever be reduced to zero. Because just as something cannot be made from nothing, one cannot be made from zero. Ki is like the number one. Ki is formed from infinitely small particles, smaller than an atom. The universal ki condensed becomes an individual, which further condensed becomes the one point in the lower abdomen, which in turn infinitely condensed never becomes zero, but

becomes one with the universe. Thus, we understand the defi-nition of ki."

—TOHEI-SENSEI

The final character in Aikido is (道), which means "the way." In Chinese, it is pronounced *dao* as in Daoism and the Daoist philosophy. In Japanese, it is pronounced *do,* (sounds like doe, as in a female deer) though it can also be pronounced *michi,* in which case it means road. Japanese arts are generally described with a *do.* For example, *Judo* (柔道) is the soft-way, *Karate-do* (空手道) is the way of the empty hand, *Kyudo* (弓道) is the way of the bow, *Kendo* (剣道) is the way of the sword, *Sado* (茶道) is the way of tea ceremony, *Shodo* (書道) is the way of the brush or calligraphy, *Kado* (花道) is the way of flowers or ikebana, *Bushido* (武士道) is the way of the warrior.

Tanaka-sensei was the Aikido teacher in the local dojo I went to while living in a small town in Japan. He was a no-nonsense teacher who upheld one of the key aspects of the Bushido spirit: manliness. Sometimes he would be a little too aggressive when demonstrating techniques on students, who sometimes would get hurt. In those cases, Tanaka-sensei would laugh. But it was a most peculiar laugh. He would not smile at all. There was almost no expression on his face. His lips were turned down. He would just let out this *huh-huh-huh-huh* noise that sounded almost like a kid imitating a machine-gun. The laugh wasn't to indicate that anything was funny, and it was certainly not an apology, but was more like a recognition that the student had taken a hard fall. It was also a reminder that there would be no sympathy in the dojo.

One time in class, I finally executed a certain throw well and was so pleased with myself that I smiled. Big mistake. Tanaka-sensei pulled me aside and looked me straight in the eyes. He then almost imperceptibly shook his head. I stopped smiling. He kept staring at me. He always felt I didn't understand him. He took a deep breath and then said, "A samurai only smiles once every three years, and even then only with half of his mouth."

As D.T. Suzuki said in his classic book *Zen and Japanese Culture*, "To be alert means to be deadly serious, to be deadly serious means to be sincere to oneself, and it is sincerity that finally leads one to discover the Heavenly Way."[18] My smiling represented insincerity. I tried to never smile again in class. Many years later, I was watching TV in Japan and the Mongolian Sumo champion at the time had to miss a tournament due to injury, but he was being castigated because he had committed a major sin. What was his transgression? He smiled. Since he couldn't wrestle, he went back to Mongolia to visit friends and family, and, unforgivingly, a camera caught him smiling.

After WWII, Ruth Benedict noted that American POWs learned not to laugh in Japanese prison camps for fear of retribution as this was insulting the prison

---

18   Daisetz T. Suzuki, *Zen and Japanese Culture* (Princeton, New Jersey: Princeton University Press, 2010), 133.

guards.[19] An American laughing in a prison camp would make absolutely no sense to a Japanese person. How could they laugh while in such a shameful situation? In the West, we generally laugh when something is funny. *Remarkably, there is no native word for* funny *in Japanese.* It is not directly translatable. Instead one might say 面白い, *"omoshiroi,"* which means "interesting." Oddly, the characters mean "face-white." If a Japanese person laughs in a formal setting, it usually means they are uncomfortable or confused.

Tanaka-sensei's teaching style introduced me to Japanese intuitive thinking. As a linear thinker, one aspect of learning Aikido in Japan that always confused me was that the teacher never actually taught any of the techniques. I could not understand why the teacher would not teach and continued to feel like I was missing something. Tanaka-sensei would demonstrate on a student and then we would all bow and then bow to a partner, pair off, and practice that technique. We would practice over and over. If Tanaka-sensei felt we weren't getting it right, he would demonstrate again. If I got a technique right, he would very subtly push his lips together and push his jaw up. If I did a technique poorly, he would slightly scrunch his nose. I was almost like a dog watching its master, trying to read Tanaka-sensei's expressions.

What didn't make sense to me was that Tanaka-sensei never went into detail to describe how to do the throws or pins. The nonverbal clues and endless repetitions were

---

19   Ruth Benedict, *The Chrysanthemum and the Sword,* 37.

the way class was taught, which is the direct opposite of the linear West where the teacher would explain the important aspects of each technique step by step. As it turns out, this indirect teaching method was a key aspect of intuitive learning as opposed to the more linear explanation method I was used to in the US.

Joseph Campbell, the great expert on mythology, wrote on intuitive understanding: "...the first doctrine of Buddhism [is]: it cannot be taught. No experience can be taught. All that can be taught is the way to an experience."[20] It was a surprise to me when I finally realized that Tanaka-sensei was intentionally not teaching us. He was only demonstrating and then we would practice over and over. Eventually, we would come to an intuitive understanding of our own of what the correct technique was. It was a much slower way of learning, but also much deeper. It was experiential and after any of the amazing "I finally get it" lightbulb moments, I would highly value and never forget those lessons. This is the teaching method underlying Zen Buddhism in Japan. As D.T. Suzuki wrote: "What is performed by spiritual teaching is to point out for you what you have within yourself. There is no transference of secrets from master to disciple."[21]

Suzuki underlines a key difference in belief systems in the East and West. In the West, we believe in absolute

---

20   Joseph Campbell, *Myths of Light: Eastern Metaphors of the Eternal* (Novato, California: New World Library, 2003), 123.

21   Daisetz T. Suzuki, *Zen and Japanese Culture*, 435.

truth. There is one path to truth. While a Westerner may choose the modality, be it the various sects of Christianity, Judaism, Islam, etc., Westerners tend to believe there is one vehicle for truth. We do not mix and match, and generally believe our faith is the one true way to understand the world. This is very different in the East. They believe there are many different paths to the mountain top. I've been in Buddhist temples in Japan, and within the temple, there is a Shinto shrine. That would be like a Catholic church having a small shrine in the corner dedicated to Norse gods or Greek gods. Totally unthinkable in the West.

Easterners believe that the truth itself is the mountain top. The mountain top cannot change, but the path to the truth must be your own and there are many paths to the top. The teacher cannot explain the techniques because their path to the mountain top may be different from yours. The goal for the disciple, therefore, is not to pursue what the master had learned, but rather to pursue what the master was pursuing.

In discussing the process of learning swordsmanship, Suzuki describes how the deepest lessons must come from within to be genuine. He remarks that spiritual training similarly cannot be learned out of a book, "but the culmination is to realize the mystery of being, and *the realization is from within yourself*, for it cannot come from anywhere else. If it does, it is not yours but someone else's."[22] (Emphasis mine)

---

22 Daisetz T. Suzuki, *Zen and Japanese Culture*, 135.

At a deeper level, if a technique were taught, then it would reside in the mental sphere. To use the technique in a fight, the practitioner would necessarily need to think through the proper moves for defense and attack. This would cause delays. By learning experientially, the body and muscles learn the moves and they can be reproduced without conscious thought. This would be described in the West as being "in the zone" or in a "flow state." The Japanese train for this flow state. Again, from Suzuki: "When the ultimate perfection is attained, the body and limbs perform by themselves what is assigned to them to do with no interference from the mind."[23]

It took me a long time to understand the Japanese intuitive way of learning, but what confused me for even longer were the Zen stories Tanaka-sensei would tell during or after class. Some of the stories made sense to me, but I really struggled with others. I couldn't understand their underlying message using my linear thinking. Tanaka-sensei's Zen stories ultimately showed me how the Japanese use intuitive reasoning to solve problems.

Here was one such story:

Once there was a father who was a thief. He was getting old and his son wanted to learn the trade. The father agreed to accommodate his son's desire and took the boy along with him on his next outing. While inside the targeted house, the father surprised the boy and locked him inside a chest in the main

---

23   Daisetz T. Suzuki, *Zen and Japanese Culture*, 100.

bedroom. The boy banged on the chest, but the father just ran away and left him there. When the homeowners returned and opened the chest, the boy had to run and jump out a window to escape. They chased after him. The boy saw a well and dropped a stone down the well to make a noise. The pursuers focused their search on the well and the boy was able to escape. When he got home he was very angry at his father. The father very calmly explained that the son now knew everything required to be a thief. The father couldn't teach the boy how to be a thief. He could only show him how to learn for himself and gain his own intuitive understanding.

This was the same way Tanaka-sensei was teaching us. Tanaka-sensei told other Zen stories. He retold one to me over and over when he learned I was moving to China. *A boat bumps into another boat. The driver of the first boat is furious, but then he notices no one is in the other boat. He has no one to get mad at so his anger dissipates. To avoid fights, be an empty boat.*

My interpretation of Tanaka-sensei emphasizing this story for me was that a fight requires two angry parties and that if I could stay calm and without emotion, like the empty boat, then I could avoid fights. This turned out quite helpful during my first month in China. I was riding my bicycle to class and accidently knocked a man off of his bike as I was turning into the main gate. The man jumped up, screaming at me. A crowd quickly gathered as these incidents often turned into entertaining fights.

The man called me "*gandu*" Shanghaiese for "moron." I mistakenly thought he was calling me "*ganbu*" which is "party official" in Mandarin Chinese. Channeling my best empty boat spirit, I thanked him for being so kind as to call me a "*ganbu*," but that I was just an ordinary person. Everyone around laughed and laughed. I kept thanking the man. He kept calling me "*gandu*," but had no one to fight, so he got back on his bike and rode away.

Another Zen story: *A man comes down the road on a fast galloping horse. A person on the side of the road asks, "Where are you going?" The man says, "I don't know. Ask the horse."* Make sure your linear logical mind isn't taking you places your true self doesn't want to go.

This story hit me one night five years later sitting alone in my dorm room in China. I was surrounded by Chinese language, history, and economics texts as well as various job applications I was filling out. I suddenly had an epiphany. I was alone and pursuing the wrong goal. The girl I was in love with was in Japan, and she didn't know how I felt. I dropped everything, poured out my heart to her in a letter, and three short years later we were married.

Another story: *A professor visits a Zen master. The Zen master pours tea for the professor, but keeps pouring and pouring until the cup is overflowing. The professor tells him to stop. The Zen master says this tea cup is like you—all full of opinions and views, there is no room for anything from me to go in.*

This story hit me hard as a typical know-it-all, twenty-three-year-old American at the time, and this was a strong reminder not to presuppose, or assume, or judge. It was a reminder to accept that there was much I didn't know, so that I could make space for learning. Ultimately, this story helped me to stop criticizing what I didn't understand as a foreigner in Japan and to develop an attitude of wanting to learn other points of view. In new situations, I always remind myself to be an empty cup.

And: *A tree grows, but it is crooked and not straight. It is an ugly tree. Its wood does not produce a nice smell. It is a useless tree so it never gets cut down and grows quite tall and provides nice shade.*

This is actually a Daoist story from ancient China. The deeper point for me was to not judge value too quickly. Something may seem less positive at first, but can possess its own beauty or usefulness, and what appears to be a deficiency may actually turn into a strength. This recognition may not come from a simple linear logic perspective.

Finally, there was one story I just could not understand: *A man is being chased by a tiger. He climbs off a cliff and hangs by a vine to escape the tiger. Two mice start to chew the vine. If he climbs back up, the tiger will devour him. If he hangs on, he will plunge to his death. Just then he notices a strawberry right next to him growing on the side of the cliff. He eats it. The strawberry is delicious.* After telling this story, Tanaka-sensei looked me in the eyes with his expressionless face. He then asked in his gruff voice, "Do you understand?" He looked at my blank expression and then answered his own question, "Probably no." I did not. This story and my subsequent confusion pushed me to learn about Zen.

.

CHAPTER 4

——

ZEN AND MINDFULNESS IN JAPANESE CULTURE

The word Zen (禅), as you may realize, is a Japanese way of pronouncing a Chinese word, "ch'an." And the Chinese word "ch'an," is a Chinese way of pronouncing a Sanskrit word, which is "dhyana," and "dhyana" means "contemplation." Contemplation of what one ought to be contemplating, namely the divine presence that inhabits all things.[24]

—JOSEPH CAMPBELL

The Japanese believe there are multiple paths to the truth and so their society concurrently follows various religions. It is said, and not inaccurately, that Japanese are Shinto at birth, Christian when they get married, Confucian in their day-to-day lives, and Buddhist when they die.

Zen Buddhism, which originated in India, is abstract.

---

24   Joseph Campbell, *Myths of Light: Eastern Metaphors of the Eternal*, 91.

The original religion in Japan is Shinto (神道), or "the way of the gods," and it is very concrete. Shinto is a nature religion based on physical objects and this philosophy forms the foundation of Japanese society.

In addition to Shinto, Confucianism came to Japan in the sixth and seventh centuries from China. Confucianism is not really a religion per se, but rather an ethical system that resonated in Japan with its emphasis on loyalty and hierarchy. (In the China section, I'll touch upon the key differences between Confucianism in China and in Japan.)

Buddhism also made its way to Japan from China around the sixth and seventh centuries, but really took off from the twelfth century with enthusiastic adoption by the warrior class.

Even though Zen Buddhism is not widely practiced in Japan, it still has a major impact on the culture. People that practice Zen in Japan are highly specialized. Zen requires decades of disciplined training and is for the select few. The Japanese as a people, however, are deeply influenced by Zen throughout their lives. Simplicity of design, finding contentment with less, the importance of mindfulness, being in the moment, and learning intuitively all deeply permeate Japanese culture. Zen philosophy is learned through the arts in Japan such as: tea ceremony, flower arrangement, calligraphy, bonsai, and martial arts.

Suzuki describes the no-mind state of Zen as follows:

"In Japan, perhaps as in other countries too, mere technical knowledge of an art is not enough to make a man really its master; he ought to have delved deeply into the inner spirit of it. This spirit is grasped only when his mind is in complete harmony with the principle of life itself, that is, when he attains to a certain state of mind known as '*mushin*' (無心), 'no-mind.'"[25]

This "*mushin*" or "no-mind" is critical in understanding Zen, but I feel it often gets misunderstood. In 無心 (no-mind), the first character means "emptiness" as in a void. The second character means "heart," but not literally or figuratively the heart as we would define it, but rather the mind. And not just the logical mind in the head, but the entire mind of the body. The word literally means "empty heart" or "empty mind" and gets interpreted as completely emptying one's mind: a type of "mind-less-ness." This is a mistaken interpretation. The correct translation would be "mind-full-ness," a concept which has become quite popular in the West lately.

The *mushin* meditative mind is a state of activating and accessing different parts of the brain. It can be accomplished if one relaxes the mind. In attempting to clear the mind the practitioner quickly finds the mind jumping around from thought to thought. This is the so-called "monkey mind." With enough training, however, the mind learns to tame the monkey and clear itself of all of the distractions. The mind then becomes like

---

25   Daisetz T. Suzuki, *Zen and Japanese Culture*, 94.

the proverbial calm surface of a pond at night, clearly reflecting the moon. In this state, the idea is not mind-less-ness. The goal is mind-full-ness. And in this state of mindfulness, the world can be perceived as it is.

Mindlessness is a passive state, while mindfulness is an active state. *Mushin* is an active state with a cleared mind. Not a comatose state devoid of thought. For this reason, meditation is done in a seated position. If the clear mind is accomplished while lying down, the person would quickly drift into sleep. The seated position prevents sleep and allows the mind to fall into a relaxed state and to stay there. If one practices enough meditation, this state may be maintained even while actively engaging in the world.

The famous Japanese haiku of Matsuo Basho captures this mindful meditative state. "The old pond, the frog jumps in, the sound of water" (古池や、蛙飛び込む、水の音). It seems like a nice haiku. It relaxes the mind. But it must be understood intuitively at a deeper level as it is actually a profound idea. The old pond represents eternity. The action of the frog jumping in is a temporal action. The sound is the flash point where life exists. It is where time and eternity are one. This is similar to the imagery of the cross, where the temporal and eternal meet.

Our Western linear minds think eternal means a long time. Eternity would be time stretching forward forever. For circular-time cultures, however, eternity goes beyond the concept of time. It shuts time out. When the mind is contemplating that which is beyond contemplation. That is eternity.

Another area this circular-time concept can be seen is in Japanese or Chinese art. The picture within the frame in traditional East Asian art is not fully filled in as it would be in the West. There is always a white area, a space for blankness. A Chinese painter may show majestic mountains and a river, while the detail-oriented Japanese painter may depict three frogs or a specific crane, etc. What they will both have in common is a large part of the painting around the main scene that remains white and empty. This white area represents the void or the eternity from which life comes and back into which it goes.

When the Chinese or Japanese paint a frog or a duck, those are not specific frogs or ducks. The written Chinese character for frog or duck can refer to *any* frog or duck. Their symbolism is as an eternal representation of frog or duck. In a circular-time framework, all frogs or all ducks are not personalized individual frogs or ducks. This lack of individuality also holds true for people, and this is the belief system behind letting go of the ego and acting in accord with the way of nature. This lack of focus on the ego is the key reason for the emphasis upon the group and not the individual in Eastern societies.

In a linear thought framework, as in the West, every frog, every duck, every person, every moment is unique. So, in our Western paintings there is no place for the eternal and every inch of the scene is filled in. This tendency can be correlated with a strong Western emphasis on the ego and the uniqueness of the present moment, which is strongly de-emphasized in the East. Zen meditation helps the practitioner to clear their mind and gain an intuitive understanding of their relationship with the eternal, as well as their proper role in the universe.

CHAPTER 5

─────

STAR WARS AND ZEN

After learning a little bit about Zen, I realized that my original introduction to Zen philosophy, though I didn't know it at the time, was from *Star Wars*. The original *Star Wars* movie was a smash hit. The movie spoke to audiences of all ages on a deeper level. I believe I can elucidate the tenets of Zen thought in this iconic film.

Obi-Wan Kenobi was based on a traditional samurai warrior. His clothes were folded left over right, in the Japanese style. His Jedi beliefs eschewed laser guns for the far more elegant lightsaber from a more noble age, echoing the samurai sword. Furthermore, even his name has a samurai resonance: an "*obi*" in Japanese is actually the sash worn around a kimono.

Obi-Wan is not the only nod to samurai culture. Darth Vader's helmet is clearly modeled after a samurai helmet. Yoda is a standard Japanese name. When Yoda spoke, he didn't use Japanese grammar exactly, but he did switch subject, object, and verb around, and often finished sentences with a verb, as is done in Japanese. Such as when he said to Luke, "Mud hole? Slimy? My home this is!" or "Found someone, you have" or "It is the future you see." Yoda, however, does not represent a traditional samurai warrior. He harkened back to a much earlier incarnation of Zen, namely the old rogue Chinese Daoist priest. He had retreated from life and lived in the midst of pure nature and laughed far too much to represent a samurai warrior.

Campbell highlighted the difference between these two types: "In China, the ideal is really the old rogue, the old fellow who's got wisdom in him, a kind of comical character through whom life just flows. The ideal in Japan, however is this samurai discipline, the discipline of life in form."[26]

In *The Empire Strikes Back*, Yoda emphasized one of the key principles of Japanese Zen Buddhism: staying in the present. When Luke asked Yoda to train him, Yoda said, "Ready are you? What you know of ready? For 800 years I have trained Jedi. My own counsel I will keep on who is to be trained. A Jedi must have the deepest commitment, the most serious mind. This one a long time have I watched. *All his life he has looked away...to the future, to the horizon. Never his mind on where he was.* Hmm. *What he was doing.* [Yoda poked Luke with his cane.] Hmph! Adventure. Heh! Excitement. Heh! A Jedi

---

26 Joseph Campbell, *Myths of Light: Eastern Metaphors of the Eternal*, 133.

craves not these things. You are reckless!" (Emphasis mine)

Similarly, the Buddha said, "The past is already gone, the future is not yet here. There's only one moment for you to live, and that is the present moment." He also said, "Do not dwell in the past, do not dream of the future, concentrate the mind on the present." From the 300-year-old book on the samurai ethic *Hagakure*: "There is surely nothing other than the single purpose of the present moment."[27]

The story about the man hanging perilously on the vine and eating the delicious strawberry was ultimately about the precarious nature of life. That we must ignore depressing thoughts about the past or fearful thoughts about the future and dedicate ourselves to keeping our focus on the present.

In *Myths of Light,* Campbell relates a sword master story from Japan with the same lesson of focusing on the present. He tells of a wager that a fencing master gave to his students: if any of them could manage to catch him by surprise—in any way—he would bow before them. Days went by with all the students trying to discover ways to trick him, but to no avail. One particular day, the fencing master had been out in the mud in his bare feet, and he asked his ten-year-old student for a basin of water to wash his feet. The little boy brought a basin of warm water, and when the master tested the temperature, he found it too

---

27 Tsunetomo Yamamoto, *Hagakure*, 68.

warm. He told the boy to bring a basin of cooler water. The young student returned and set the basin of water at the master's feet. Without looking, the master set his feet in the basin—and instantly recoiled from the steaming hot water. He promptly gave the little boy a deep bow.[28] The lesson was that even a little boy could keep his focus on the present and that even the master can sometimes learn from the youngest of students.

The concept of the Force in the original *Star Wars* movies was also very close to the concept of *ki* in Japanese (気) or *qi* in Chinese. In *The Empire Strikes Back*, Yoda said, "Size matters not. Look at me. Judge me by my size, do you? Hmm? Hmm. And well you should not. For my ally is the Force, and a powerful ally it is. Life creates it, makes it grow. Its energy surrounds us and binds us. Luminous beings are we, not this crude matter. You must feel the Force around you; here, between you, me, the tree, the rock, everywhere, yes. Even between the land and the ship." D.T. Suzuki defines "*ki*" (気) as "something imperceptible, impalpable, that pervades the entire universe. In one sense, it corresponds to spirit, it is the breath of heaven and earth."[29]

Intuition is another key aspect of Zen that came up in *Star Wars*. In *Star Wars: Episode IV A New Hope*, Obi-Wan Kenobi puts a blast helmet on Luke so he is essentially blind during his lightsaber training. Obi-Wan then tells

---

28   Joseph Campbell, *Myths of Light: Eastern Metaphors of the Eternal*, 87.

29   Daisetz T. Suzuki, *Zen and Japanese Culture*, 149.

Luke, "I suggest you try it again, Luke. This time, let go your conscious self and act on instinct." Luke replies, "With the blast shield down, I can't even see. How am I supposed to fight?" Obi-Wan responds, "Your eyes can deceive you. Don't trust them. Stretch out with your feelings." *Star Wars* is only a movie, so Luke learns intuitive thinking in only a few short lessons from Obi-Wan and Yoda. A true samurai would dedicate his life to learning how to cultivate his intuition.

When talking about Zen, swordsmanship, and intuition, Suzuki says if one tries to think in a sword fight, they are dead. "Everything he does must come out of his inner mechanism, which is not under control of consciousness. He must act instinctually and not intellectually."[30] Zen, therefore, is about deep inner experiences and not following scriptures, or lectures, or other outside formulaic teachings. Zen is intuitive and experiential.[31]

Because Zen is rooted in inner experience, it eschews external teachings. One is not meant to strictly adhere to the sayings of Buddha, or to rigidly follow ascetic training. In essence, there is no higher being to look to than oneself. The Japanese concept of *satori* (悟り, meaning "awakening or enlightenment"), is rooted in intuitive understanding.[32]

Yoda gives a separate lesson on using the intuitive

30 Daisetz T. Suzuki, *Zen and Japanese Culture*, 218.

31 Daisetz T. Suzuki, *Zen and Japanese Culture*, 218.

32 Daisetz T. Suzuki, *Zen and Japanese Culture*, 218.

mind and not the rational mind in *The Empire Strikes Back*. Luke asks Yoda how he will know the good side from the bad. Yoda responds, "You will know—when you are calm, at peace, passive. A Jedi uses the Force for knowledge and defense. Never for attack." Luke responds, "But tell me why I can't..." Yoda exclaims, "No. No! There is no why." In a true Zen story, at that point, the teacher would sometimes strike the student to get them to stop trying to understand with their rational mind what needs to be understood intuitively. "Zen upholds intuition against intellectualism, for intuition is the more direct way of reaching the truth."[33]

Campbell tells another story that touches upon this aspect of intuitive learning for a Japanese swordsman. A disciple will often have to contend with surprise attacks by their sword master at any time of day, even when doing the most mundane of daily tasks. There is no way to always be consciously on guard, so the key lesson is, *"You have got to be in a state of absolute centeredness and spontaneous response.* That is the basic lesson of the art of fencing (*Kendo*)."[34] (Emphasis mine)

Another aspect of Zen is that the practitioner must be dedicated and committed. In *The Empire Strikes Back*, when Yoda said his famous line to Luke, "Do or do not... There is no try." This was echoed by another great Zen teacher, Mr. Miyagi in *The Karate Kid*. Daniel-san said,

---

33   Daisetz T. Suzuki, *Zen and Japanese Culture*, 61.

34   Joseph Campbell, *Myths of Light: Eastern Metaphors of the Eternal*, 87.

"I guess so," when asked if he was ready to start learning karate. Miyagi-sensei responded, "Either karate you do *yes* or karate do *no*. You do karate *guess so*, (makes a squishing motion with his hands) just like grape."

Without intense focus, concentration on the present, and complete commitment, intuitive thinking does not develop. The Eastern masters say that the mind needs to be still like a pond at night; only then can it properly reflect the image of the moon. An agitated or disturbed surface of the pond would distort the image of the moon. Similarly, only with the mind still and clear and not distracted or racing from thought to thought can the subconscious mind effectively communicate with the body and the conscious mind.

One aspect of Zen intuitive learning is to learn without consciously learning. This came up in the *Karate Kid*. Mr. Miyagi was a Zen teacher. He had Daniel-san waxing his car and sanding the floors and painting the fence. Daniel-san was learning instinctively how to defend himself, but he didn't know he was learning. That way, the moves became ingrained into his subconscious. He could do them without thinking.

In fact, he could do them even better without thinking because when he was learning, his conscious mind didn't know what they were for. The student is learning and practicing without intentionally trying to learn or practice. This is important because the conscious mind is deliberate and would react much slower than a subconscious or intuitive response. The conscious mind is also vulnerable to stress and fear, so a trained reflex is far more reliable in a fight than a decision or action that needs to be processed by the conscious mind.

Another interesting aspect of Zen that came out in the *Star Wars* movies was that truth is relative. In *Return of the Jedi*, there is an interesting exchange between Luke and Obi-Wan:

> Obi Wan: So, what I told you was true...from a certain point of view.

> Luke: A certain point of view?

> Obi-Wan: Luke, you're going to find out that many of the truths we cling to depend greatly on our own point of view.

Buddha said, "Nothing exists entirely alone; everything is in relation to everything else."

One big source of consternation among my generation of *Star Wars* fans was that George Lucas went back and changed the scene in the original *Star Wars* movie where Han shoots at Greedo first. He tried to turn the story into a simple one about good and bad, right and wrong, with simplistic morals that match a linear-logic, absolute world of good and bad. The Zen and Eastern view of life is much more in line with the original scene. Han Solo had good and bad in him, as we all do.

In Tibetan art, there are horrific monsters. Those monsters are inside all of us. As Nietzsche said, "Be careful in casting out your demons, lest you get rid of what is best in you." Zen teaches us that we must learn to balance the good and bad in our nature and live a life that brings out our best qualities.

Lucas went back to simplistic Western absolute thinking in having Greedo shoot first. But that is not who Han was. Han shot Greedo first precisely because he was a survivor focused on saving his own skin. Because Han was this type of person, his decision later in the movie to go back and save Luke was precisely the reason why his action was so heroic. The positive influence of Luke's attitude of self-sacrifice evoked the heroic part of Han's nature.

CHAPTER 6

———

THINKING FAST, THINKING SLOW, AND THINKING ZEN

I've been asked many times how I would describe Zen thinking to a Westerner, and to do so I've unearthed a few examples of Zen-like practices in Western culture.

Most people learn to type and then practice for years or for decades even without the express goal of getting better at typing. They are writing essays for school, or reports for work, or emails to friends, and over time they improve at typing without ever having attachment to this goal.

I believe many in the West use a Zen mind when they are typing. Their mind is not consciously telling each finger which letter to press on the keyboard. The fingers know where to go. In fact, it is much faster when you don't think about what you are doing with the controlling conscious mind. Imagine trying to type with the conscious mind saying out each letter as you type each word. That would be *much* slower. While typing, ego is not involved. The mind is acting intuitively beyond conscious control, and the focus is on the present; yet, the action is happening with the true focus elsewhere.

To truly understand the Japanese Zen mind, try to imagine typing sixty words per minute while someone is holding a samurai sword over your head threatening to decapitate you if you typed too slowly. Concentrating and typing without thinking about the letters or the sword hanging over your head would be the Zen mind. Imagine living your whole life in that mindset, removing the ego and control.

Zen thinking might also occur during activities we might not otherwise associate with meditation. When cutting up food with a sharp knife, the mind has no choice but to be in the present and to forget all of the worries from the past causing one to be depressed, or concerns about the future that would cause anxiety. Anyone that has played baseball knows that the conscious mind would take way too long to react to hit a baseball. The pitch comes in too fast. The body must intuitively react, in the way it was trained, to successfully swing the bat and hit the ball. This is the Zen mind. The jazz greats also remind me of Zen thinking. They dedicate themselves for decades to their instruments and became innovative masters playing out of their spontaneous centers in the true sense of Zen.

As Suzuki explains, the practice of Zen philosophy is to learn and master a technique so that you can take the next step, which is to forget the technique and become immersed in a subject. Then we can transcend the obvious and get in touch with the deeper mysteries of life, which helps make one a true master or artist.[35]

In the West, we are starting to realize there may be something to intuitive thinking. A 2012 *BBC* article titled "The Second Brains in Our Stomachs" pointed out that there are over 100 million brain cells in the human gut, as many as there are in the head of a cat.[36] This means that significant cognition occurs not only in the head but also in the gut, and that there is more to it when we say we "trust our gut" or "I have a gut feeling." The Japanese recognized this traditionally. The Japanese say (腹を割る—"cutting one's belly open") to mean *to speak openly and frankly*. Or they would say (腹を読む—"to read one's belly"), usually in the negative, to mean *it is difficult to know what someone else is thinking* or *I can't read his belly*. (腹芸) or "belly-art" means the intentional expression of meaning from one person to another without using words. To be resolved or calm and collected would be *the gut is ready* (腹ができている). If someone is very angry,

35 Daisetz T. Suzuki, *Zen and Japanese Culture*, 220.

36 Michael Mosley, "The Second Brain in Our Stomachs," BBC TV, July 11, 2012, http://www.bbc.com/news/health-18779997.

it means (腹が立つ) or *their belly is standing up.* Someone deceitful would have a *black belly* (腹が黒い), and a despicable person would have a *rotten stomach* (「腹が腐ってる」). When the Japanese commit *Seppuku*, or ritual suicide, the sword cuts the belly, as this was considered the seat of the soul.

A 2017 article on Quartz.com, "Your Intuition Is More Powerful than Your Intellect, and Just as Easily Expanded," details a variety of ways in which intuition supersedes logic.[37] For example, the article discussed an experiment having two decks of cards with one side rigged to be better than the other. It took subjects about fifty cards to figure out the decks were different and eighty cards to figure out the difference. But it only took about ten cards for their palms to start sweating when they reached for the weaker deck. The subjects' nervous systems were registering the information faster than the conscious mind. The author concluded, "The science is clear: intuition is a powerful force of the mind that can help us make better decisions. Fortunately, intuition is a skill that can be honed by practicing the habits of highly intuitive people."

Those habits are:

· Slow down and listen to your inner voice

---

37 Travis Bradberry, "Your Intuition is More Powerful than Your Intellect, and Just as Easily Expanded," *Quartz*, January 10, 2017, https://qz.com/880678/intuition-is-more-powerful-than-intellect/.

- Be intuitively aware of what others are feeling
- Practice mindfulness, or stay in the moment
- Nurture creativity
- Trust your gut
- Analyze your dreams for clues

In his brilliant book *Thinking Fast and Slow*, Daniel Kahneman gives a wonderful description of the difference between "the intuitive System 1, which does the fast thinking; and the effortful and slower System 2, which does the slow thinking, monitors System 1, and maintains control as best it can with its limited resources."[38] This framework makes sense from a linear logic standpoint, but I believe it omits Zen intuitive logic or meditative thinking. Perhaps in the future, someone could write the book *Thinking Fast and Slow and Zen*.

In his book *Thinking Fast and Slow*, Kahneman recognizes intuitive thinking but, for him, it is part of his thinking fast framework and happens "in a fraction of a second," "immediately," and "automatically."[39] This intuition is part of his System 1 thinking. He doesn't recognize intuition as possible in System 2 slower thinking.

Kahneman does recognize the value of intuition, but with the very large caveat that: "Valid intuitions develop when experts have learned to recognize familiar elements in a new situation and to act in a manner that is appropriate

---

38   Daniel Kahneman, *Thinking Fast and Slow* (New York: Farrar, Straus and Giroux, 2011), 408.

39   Daniel Kahneman, *Thinking Fast and Slow*, 416.

to it"[40] and "If the environment is sufficiently regular and if the judge has had a chance to learn its regularities, the associative machinery will recognize situations and generate quick and accurate predictions and decisions. You can trust someone's intuitions if these conditions are met."[41]

Kahneman uses chess as a classic example for intuitive thinking, where after the prerequisite 10,000 hours of concentrated practice, the chess master can understand the best move with just a glance at the board.[42]

Japanese intuitive thinking is in accord with this example. One must be immersed in, and a master of, a subject for intuition to be reliable. The difference is that the Japanese not only recognize intuitions that come quickly or at a glance, but the Japanese also use slow, deliberate, and meditative intuitive thinking, where the correct feeling may not come right away, but could come after hours, days, or even years of deep, concerted effort. In other words, Kahneman only recognizes "intuition" as thinking quickly. I believe this misses slow and deliberate Zen intuition.

ZEN THINKING SLOW

Deliberate and concentrated Zen intuitive thinking wouldn't fit Kahneman's *Thinking Fast and Slow* frame-

---

40 Daniel Kahneman, *Thinking Fast and Slow*, 12.

41 Daniel Kahneman, *Thinking Fast and Slow*, 243.

42 Daniel Kahneman, *Thinking Fast and Slow*, 238.

work. Kahneman wrote of slow thinking, "the process was mental work: deliberate, effortful, and orderly."[43] This presupposes that intuitive thinking as he refers to it cannot be deliberate, effortful, and orderly. As the Japanese do not, in general, reason linearly, their slow thinking is also done intuitively. In fact, Japanese System 2 intuitive thinking is done with intense focus.

When one focuses on ikebana flower arranging (or *shodo* calligraphy, or bonsai, or tea ceremony), the actions are done with slow, deliberate, concentrated, intuitive thinking. Similarly, the Japanese engineer that has spent decades of their career working on small diesel engines or industrial robot algorithms or precision vision sensors can make innovative breakthroughs using concentrated intuitive thought. These engineers never learned logically how to build a diesel engine or hammer out the front of a bullet train. Instead, they became expert craftsmen over decades of immersive practice and learned to feel what the correct method was.

I think an interesting example of this dichotomy is the great Indian mathematician Srinivasa Ramanujan.

His mentor G.H. Hardy famously said that Ramanujan's ingenious solutions were "arrived at by a process of mingled argument, intuition, and induction, of which he was entirely unable to give any coherent account."[44]

---

43 Daniel Kahneman, *Thinking Fast and Slow*, 20.

44 John Woodcock, "The Man Who Knew Infinity," May 14, 2016, https://johnwoodcock.com. au/2016/05/man-knew-infinity/.

Bruce C. Berndt, professor of mathematics at the University of Illinois and author of *Ramanujan's Lost Notebook*, has noted that Ramanujan's work is finally being recognized and appreciated in the fields of modern mathematics and physics, as nearly all of his theorems have been proven correct over the past forty years.

Surely, the brilliant intuitive thinking of Ramanujan cannot be described as quick or lazy. He was an exceptional intuitive thinker, but along with other nonlinear thinkers, he was unable to show linear proofs of his theorems. This lack of linear proofs prevented others from learning step by step how to reach these great conclusions. This inability of others to replicate the same path is the reason that nonlinear-thinking countries fell so far behind during the Industrial Revolution that propelled the West to the leading position in the world development-wise.

I certainly do not mean to contradict Kahneman's *Thinking Fast and Slow* thesis. It remains extremely valid for Western linear thinkers. And, of course, the various biases that plague our thinking that he highlights remain valid for everyone. Thinking slow is much more reliable than thinking fast, and "intuitive reasoning" in a Western context remains unreliable in the absence of the prerequisites as highlighted by Kahneman, namely, "a sufficiently regular and predictable environment and sufficient time and experience to learn these regularities."[45]

There are no shortcuts to intuitive thinking. On the

---

45   Daniel Kahneman, *Thinking Fast and Slow*, 243.

other hand, I am encouraged that if a Western linear thinker works at intuitive thinking, much like the afore-mentioned Steve Jobs, they can improve, and their intuition can become a rich source of inspiration, guidance, and new ideas. Further signs that this might be possible in the West are the recent resurgence of meditation, as intuitive insights are one of the great benefits of this largely Eastern practice.

What I learned from Japanese intuitive thinking was to find clarity of thought or insights on difficult questions by listening to my inner voice and by taking notes of ideas that came to me right after waking up. For example, I got stuck on various concepts in writing this book and would invariably use the practice of focusing on that specific issue while falling asleep and then seeing what solutions came to mind upon rising, when the mind was most fertile. Some of my best writing was done in my head lying in bed. The key was to get those words onto paper before the distractions of the day took over and I forgot them.

CHAPTER 7

THE LITERAL JAPANESE MIND

Undoubtedly, the Japanese are a unique people. Japan is an island nation that purposefully closed itself off from the world for over 200 years. From 1640, the Shogunate enacted the *Sakoku* policy, which meant "closed country." Japanese were not allowed to leave, and foreigners were not allowed to visit. A small trading enclave the Dutch were allowed access to for trade was the one exception. The net result was that from around 1640 to 1850, Japan developed with very little influence from the outside world and is a key reason the Japanese feel their culture is so different from other countries. As Karel van Wolferen wrote: "It is almost an article of faith among Japanese that their culture is unique, not in the way that all cultures are unique, but somehow uniquely unique..."[46]

---

46   Karel van Wolferen, *The Enigma of Japanese Power* (New York: Vintage Books, 1990), 14.

I believe that one aspect of this Japanese uniqueness is their literal-intuitive mode of thinking. I have been fortunate enough to have worked with people from all over the world, but I have never met other literal-intuitive thinkers and it appears that the Japanese people have this distinction alone.

I have, however, met other literal thinkers. I once worked for a Swiss-German company and found them to be literal thinkers, but literal-linear and not literal-intuitive. My Swiss-German boss was so literal that he would scream at me if I missed a comma on line six of page eight of a document he would dictate to me. The attention to literal detail was astounding. As an American, I always wanted to focus more attention on the main point he was trying to make with the document, but he wanted perfection. It explained why the Swiss were so good at precision manufacturing such as high-end watch making. In one year together, I do not recall one time he ever tried to be funny. This extreme focus on detail and lack of humor reminded me of the Japanese.

To elucidate the singularity of Japanese literal thinking, we need only retell the story of the Japanese WWII surrender. Toward the end of the war, there was a great worry that the Japanese as a nation would not surrender in 1945 and would fight to the bitter end. As Ruth Benedict pointed out, "In a hopeless situation, a Japanese soldier should kill himself with his last hand grenade or charge weaponless against the enemy in a mass suicide attack.

But he should not surrender."[47] Fortunately, loyalty to the Emperor trumped their duty not to surrender. Van Wolferen highlighted the difference when he wrote, "To begin with, Japanese loyalty is directed solely at a group or person, not a belief or abstract idea."[48] At the end of WWII when the Emperor went on the radio to announce Japan's surrender, everyone took his order literally, laid down arms, and surrendered with remarkably little fuss. In a wonderful case of Japanese understatement, the Emperor said in his surrender statement, "The war situation has developed not necessarily to Japan's advantage."

The example of Japanese literal thinking going too far can be found in the story of a soldier by the name of Hiroo Onoda. He was fighting in the Philippines in WWII and never heard about Japan's surrender. So, what did he do? He kept fighting in the Philippine jungles for the next twenty-nine years! Eventually, a Japanese hiker ran into him and explained that the war ended almost thirty years ago. To Hiroo Onoda's literal mind, that wasn't good enough. He was a soldier at war and he had never been relieved of duty, so he kept fighting. Ultimately, Japan had to dig up his original commanding officer, put him back into his army uniform, send him to the Philippine jungle, and give the direct verbal order to Onoda to surrender. Only then did Onoda lay down his arms.

There is another popular story showing the Japanese

---

47   Ruth Benedict, *The Chrysanthemum and the Sword*, 38.

48   Karel van Wolferen, *The Enigma of Japanese Power*, 169.

literal mind. Perhaps the story is urban legend, but I suspect it is true. In the 1980s, a US company made an order to a Japanese company for a component and specified a defect rate of 0.03 percent. The Japanese couldn't understand the request, but went ahead and delivered 10,000 of the components and three separately marked faulty components as defects. This story gets told to show Japanese perfectionism, but I think it is a much better example of their being so literal. What the US company meant was that they wanted a less than 0.03 percent defect rate. But what they asked for specifically was a 0.03 percent defect rate, which the Japanese took literally, though they had no idea why the US company would want defective parts.

The Japanese take the world as they observe it and therefore emphasize individual events and cases as opposed to universal rules. This type of thinking rejects the supernatural and only recognizes the physical world.[49] Typically, what exists outside the realm of the observable world is god and religion. God is the ultimate abstract concept. The Japanese have no abstract god like we do in the West, but they do have tens of thousands of nature gods that could be identified in visible objects. They also do not believe in heaven after death, because it is another abstract concept.

Seeing the world in literal terms means the Japanese are not good at abstract thinking, but the Japanese language is not completely without abstract concepts. As

49   Hajime Nakamura, *Ways of Thinking of Eastern Peoples*, 350.

Hajime Nakamura points out, the Japanese do not express these abstract ideas in the native Japanese language. They use two-character *kanji* words as borrowed from the Chinese. Japan does not have native words for Western philosophical ideas, but they do have imported words that are made by combining Chinese characters.[50] The two examples Nakamura gives are the word for "concept" *gainen* (概念), and "reason" *risei* (理性).

Nakamura continues on the Japanese literal mind: "At least, it is historically true that the neglect of logic is one of the salient features of traditional Japanese ways of thinking. Concrete intuitions are favored much more than abstract concepts devoid of any tangible connection with the humanly perceived world."[51] Suzuki also makes this point: The Japanese are not into meticulously developed theoretical abstractions or deep philosophical debates. Instead, the Japanese focus on the world as it is.[52]

I believe this literal aspect of the Japanese mind is why they are so strong at manufacturing, yet so weak at finance. As anyone that has dealt with Japanese companies can tell you, Japanese managements struggle with concepts such as the cost of capital, time value of money, return on equity, or return on invested capital. Some of the most ferociously competitive and profitable manufacturing companies in the world are in Japan, yet these

---

50 Hajime Nakamura, *Ways of Thinking of Eastern Peoples*, 532.

51 Hajime Nakamura, *Ways of Thinking of Eastern Peoples*, 543.

52 Daisetz T. Suzuki, *Zen and Japanese Culture*, 230.

same companies will destroy a lot of value every year through huge cash hoards that earn far below their cost of equity. Japanese companies are also world class at literal functions such as quality control, but notoriously weak at more abstract functions such as forecasting.

Apart from the exactness to the single yen when dealing with money, there are other interesting aspects of Japanese literalness that are striking for foreigners. The first is that in the middle of the night, with absolutely zero cars on the road, a Japanese person will not walk across the street against a red light. Common sense would say it is fine to cross, but the Japanese will wait for the light to turn green. Foreigners also quickly learn to appreciate that Japanese trains run exactly on time. And this exactness was even maintained prior to the digital age. We notice that Japanese trains run on time to the minute, but internally, Japanese trains are scheduled to the second!

Another aspect of Japanese culture's literalism is that everyone in a family often gets called by their specific role. Therefore, a husband will call his wife "mother" the same as the children will call her as she is the mother in the family. I must say that this is, psychologically speaking, strange for an American married to a Japanese person. Calling one's wife "mother" is generally not considered such a good idea in the West.

It has been my experience that the Japanese are also notoriously bad at learning foreign languages. I believe a key contributing factor to this struggle is that their literal minds hate to make mistakes. If the meaning would get through, but they literally don't get the words or grammar correct, they would rather not speak. So, they end up stuck in the catch-22 of not wanting to speak until they are proficient, but they are very slow to gain proficiency because they don't practice speaking nearly enough. This also makes learning Japanese difficult for foreigners. Making mistakes is critical to the learning process, but the Japanese have little patience for a foreigner that speaks Japanese poorly. They believe literally that since you are not Japanese, you should not be speaking Japanese.

Unlike Chinese with its very simple grammar, Japanese grammar is terribly complex. Japanese expression is vague, as preserving harmony in relationships takes top precedence, but grammar is quite precise. Chinese doesn't actually have tense, so it is not clear from the Chinese verb whether it takes place in the past, present, or future. That would be intolerable to the literal Japanese mind. For example, the word *to eat* in Chinese, always and everywhere can be expressed with the single Chinese character: 吃.

Here are some of the conjugations I could think of for the word "to eat" in Japanese:

食べます (eat formal)、食べました (ate formal)、食べる (eat informal)、食べた (ate informal)、食べています (eating formal)、食べていました (was eating formal)、食べている (eating informal)、食べていた (was eating informal)、食べられます (to be eaten formal)、食べら

れました (was eaten formal)、食べたい (want to eat)、食べたかった (wanted to eat)、食べさせます (make to eat formal)、食べさせました (was made to eat formal)、食べさせる (make to eat informal)、食べさせた (was made to eat informal)、食べられます (can be eaten formal)、食べられました (could be eaten formal)、食べられる (can be eaten informal)、食べられた (could be eaten informal)、食べながら (while eating)...I could go on and on.

If you are speaking English with a Japanese person and ask them "How are you doing?" or "How was your weekend?" watch closely because their minds will freeze up. They are thinking of an answer because they are taking the questions literally.

Another literal feature of Japanese society that jumps out to the foreigner is the exact calculation they use to recognize and repay nonmonetary debts or favors. Japanese culture has a strong focus on obligations. *Gimu* (義務) is the biggest or most serious obligation. This is what they must unquestionably perform for their country, company, or immediate family. In that order. *Gimu*-level obligations are sometimes difficult for a Westerner to understand at first because they are unquestioned and take absolute priority over any personal considerations. Kamikaze are the classic example, where pilots flew off to their certain death to fulfill their *gimu* obligation to their country. As Benedict points out, these obligations have no limits and can never be fully repaid.

Here is a hum-drum example of *gimu* in modern Japan: say you've purchased airplane tickets and booked hotels for your once-a-year overseas vacation, but the day before you leave, your boss calls to say you need to stay and work. Because of the *gimu* obligation and the priority of the company over the family, the Japanese worker would have no choice but to cancel their vacation. Arguing or pleading their case with their boss would not even be considered as an option.

The next level of obligation is *giri* (義理). These are obligations they have to fulfill even though they may not want to. "These debts are regarded as having to be repaid with mathematical equivalence to the favor received and there are time limits."[53] In a traditional Japanese community, the village head would literally track and record every favor done so that it could be repaid appropriately and proportionally.

I have a great friend who told me an interesting story in this context. She is an American that married a Japanese man and lived for decades in a small town in Japan. When she first moved to Japan, she understood gifts and reciprocity, and tracked very carefully to whom she owed gifts and favors. Japanese people clear these *giri* "debts" twice a year. Once in the summer with the *Ochugen* gifts and once in the winter with the *Oseibo* gifts. My friend collected apples from a local orchard, made applesauce, and packed it in elegant glass jars sealed with wax and

---

53   Ruth Benedict, *The Chrysanthemum and the Sword*, 116.

a delicate bow attached. When she gave the applesauce to her neighbors, they had no idea what it was. They had never seen it before. Their literal minds couldn't attach a literal value to her gifts, making them essentially worthless for clearing her debts. She said, "I might as well have given them jars of poo."

There is a classic child's story popular in Japan that also illustrates the absurdity of the literal focus on gift equivalence. A new family moves into a village, and the next-door neighbor gives them a welcome gift. The new family returns the favor with a gift of their own. The next-door neighbor gives a new gift to repay that gift. This goes on and on until they have swapped literally everything in their houses and eventually they end up swapping even their sons: a ridiculous example of how this literal exactness can go too far.

I attended a recent speech from a Japanese politician from the ruling party. He made some stunning comments about how Japan needed to rethink its relationships with the US and China. This politician stated that Japan had major revolutions every ninety years or so. The first was with Commodore Perry and the Black Ships in 1853 leading to the Meiji Restoration. The next was in 1945 with Japan's defeat at the end of WWII. He felt Japanese society was ready for another such major transformation.

What struck me was a comment this politician made about whether or not Japan could still trust their alliance with the US. Apparently, President Trump made the statement that "the US would stand behind Japan." This politician, and I'm sure many others in Japan also, took this statement literally. He asked, "Why would the US stand behind Japan. Why not stand side by side or in front?" It made it sound like Japan was a mere pawn on a chessboard out in front protecting the US. The interesting point is the term "stand behind" in American culture means to support, back up, or encourage. I would urge my fellow Americans, particularly those in government and high office, that when communicating with the Japanese, to be very careful in their phrasing as the Japanese will tend to interpret statements literally!

CHAPTER 8

JAPANESE PERFECTIONISM

Among the global expatriate crowd, a common topic is cultural affiliation. For example, if someone is Japanese, but moved to the US at a young age, are they more American or Japanese? If I had to determine if someone were Japanese or American and had to boil it down to one single test, I would give them the "wrapping the present test." If they were meticulous to the millimeter with the present, wrapping paper, and tape all perfectly parallel and aligned, that precision would indicate to me they were Japanese. If it looks anything at all like a present I had wrapped, then I would know they were more American. In the US, we often say "don't let perfect be the enemy of the good." The philosophy in Japan is the opposite. *Don't let good be the enemy of the pursuit of the perfect.* When doing even mundane tasks such as folding clothes, putting away shoes, wrapping presents, etc., the Japanese always pursue perfection (though they would probably prefer this to be phrased as the pursuit of excellence).

I believe there are three sources of Japanese perfectionism: their environment and culture, the influence of Zen Buddhism, and their literal minds.

Originally, Japan was a rural village society, with rice as the staple food. Wet paddy rice farming is intensive and mathematical, and requires the strict following of a planting-harvesting process. Rice is a sensitive crop. Seedlings must start out in a seed bed and later get transplanted into a perfectly flat rice paddy that has been flooded with careful and controlled irrigation. Lack of water, even for a short amount of time can ruin the crop. The nutrient needs of rice also change over time. On top of the timing of different types of fertilizer, the farmer needs to pull weeds and control pests, and at harvest time the rice needs to be cut, threshed, and cleaned. Attention to detail is key in rice farming.

I also believe that the climate and terrain of Japan plays another role in Japanese perfectionism. Japan has rich volcanic soil along with plentiful rainfall, which provided abundant crops, which in turn, provided a lot of time for the pursuit of craftsmanship and the arts. Japanese were also confined in small rooms for months at a time through the long winter. Living space was limited and idle time abundant, so they became very detail oriented and experts at miniaturization. This all led Japan to develop what they call their *shokunin* (職人) society or *mono-zukuri* (物作り) culture, which is craftsmanship.

As a volcanic island, Japan suffers from frequent earthquakes. (When I lived there, it was not uncommon to feel an earthquake at least a few times every year.) This required Japanese carpentry and building to be extremely quality focused. Japan has a temple in Nara that is over 1,300 years old and made completely from wood. It is five stories tall and is the oldest wooden structure in the world and has survived despite the area's frequent earthquakes. The wood is designed to sway in an earthquake and return to its original position. Even more impressively, this five-story wooden structure was built without any nails. This type of construction, not using nails, requires extreme precision in fitting the various pieces of wood together. I feel this regularity of earthquakes was another key factor in Japanese perfectionism: if a house or other structure were built poorly, the consequence could be fatal.

Harmony also developed as a top virtue in Japan and is a complement to perfectionism. The main responsibility of an individual in village life was to fulfill their responsibility and to not let the others down. When society and relationships are the top priority, morality develops to emphasize dedication to the group over the individual.[54] The implications were serious. If one shirked their responsibilities and expressed an unrepentant attitude, they could be expelled from the village. As no other vil-

---

54   Hajime Nakamura, *Ways of Thinking of Eastern Peoples*, 414.

lage would accept a stranger, this was virtually a death sentence. The Japanese are famous for their phrase (出る杭は打たれる), *the nail that sticks out gets hammered back in*. Part of not sticking out was fulfilling one's duty to the best of one's abilities.

Zen Buddhism was another factor in Japanese perfectionism. On Zen, Campbell writes, "The fundamental principle of Zen would seem to be: 'Do what you have to do perfectly, and without reservations.'"[55] In his book *Sake and Satori*, Campbell also quotes a paper by Rev. Phillip Eidmann: "In Japanese Zen, the concept is especially strong that somehow salvation comes by the performance of one's duty perfectly."[56] This pursuit of perfection can be seen in the meticulously laid out Japanese Zen gardens or the extreme attention to detail in the Zen-influenced arts of Japan, such as tea ceremony or flower arrangement.

In *Hagakure, the Book of the Samurai*, the author writes: "All professions should be done with concentration."[57] This is concentration of the mind and also concentration of efforts to only focus on one thing. In Japan, someone who is a multitasker is referred to as *nagara-zoku*, which literally means you belong to the tribe of multitaskers and is very much a derogatory term. It also says in *Hagakure*, "Throughout your life advance daily, become more

---

55 Joseph Campbell, *Sake & Satori* (Novato, California: New World Library, 2002), 86.

56 Joseph Campbell, *Sake & Satori*, 131.

57 Tsunetomo Yamamoto, *Hagakure*, 27.

skillful than yesterday, more skillful than today. This is never-ending."[58] This can be represented today in *kaizen*, which means continuous and never-ending improvement. *Kaizen* is credited with Japanese success in manufacturing and, like *sayonara* or *ichiban* or *tsunami, kaizen* has also entered the Western lexicon.

I would say the final source of Japanese perfectionism is their literal thinking. I have witnessed that Japanese don't get bored easily even when doing a repetitive task. Linear and lateral brains are always looking for the next step. Literal-intuitive minds are open and can always find something new in the same thing. They don't get bored in the quest for perfection.

I had an interesting conversation once with a leading chef in Japan that I feel illustrates the Japanese view on perfection. Japan is famous for having many Michelin-starred restaurants. Of the cities in the world with the most Michelin-starred restaurants, Tokyo is number one, Kyoto number two, and Osaka number four. I met with the owner and head chef at a two-star Michelin restaurant in Kyoto. The owner didn't introduce himself as "the owner," that would be too crass. Instead, he introduced himself as (料理長) or "head chef." He started at eighteen and worked eight years as an (奉公) apprentice. He was a chef at his first job for four years and then the head chef at two other restaurants for another twelve years. He then

---

58   Tsunetomo Yamamoto, *Hagakure*, 27.

left and opened his own restaurant and has been running that for thirty years.

I asked him if he had grown bored, making the same Kyoto-style food for over fifty years. Apart from looking at me for a few moments like a completely clueless foreigner that asks nonsensical questions, he spent some time thinking and responding thoughtfully to my question.

He used a harsh, but sympathetic tone. He said, "How could I be bored? It is all constantly changing. The seasons change, and the ingredients change. I change every year. When different conductors play Beethoven's ninth, they pursue what Beethoven was trying to pursue when he originally created that symphony. Yet, every conductor will produce a different version. It will never be the same. They will reinterpret. The orchestras are different. The conductor's minds will be different. So even though it is the same symphony, it will always be different. For my restaurant, I need to think about which ingredients to buy. Then which seasonings to use. It is like painting a picture. But anyone can add flavor. To pursue my thoughts of perfection, I need to decide when not to add seasoning and when to use the natural flavors of the food. It is much harder to not add seasoning. And much riskier. I could be accused of not doing my job or perhaps the flavor isn't as good."

He continued: "Anyone can follow the directions of a recipe, but even if the recipe is good and the ingredients are good, blindly following the recipe just makes high-end *esa* (餌) [*esa* is a word used to describe food that is given to an animal]. That will not move people's hearts. It must be done with (真摯に) *utmost sincerity and effort.* The goal is to create cuisine that will satisfy all of the senses. It must look good, it must taste good. The mouth feel (食感) must be good. It must smell good. The sound should be good. And all of these factors need to be in harmony. To accomplish all of this, I need to go back to my childhood, when I was completely carefree and happy. Before you learn the hardships of life. And use that child-like mind to create new dishes and a symphony of a meal."

The Japanese use the word "*kan*" (感) to describe gut feel. "*Kang a ii*" (感がいい) means someone has a good gut feeling or good intuition. For chefs, it can take decades to develop this *kan*. Sushi chefs can take up to ten years of training before they are allowed to even start slicing fish. Kyoto food is well defined. It has a long history and is a combination of court food from when Kyoto was the capital city of Japan, and also Buddhist food from the long Zen Buddhist tradition in Kyoto. This chef was very Zen in his thinking of when not to add ingredients. When doing nothing was the best thing to do. (Unimaginable, for example, in Chinese cooking.) He mentioned the childlike and intuitive mindset that was required. He was also innovative in the sense that within the strict confines of Kyoto cuisine, he was able to create new dishes, new ways of making traditional dishes, and new ways of combining the dishes into a full meal.

After fifty years, he was clearly a master chef, and yet, was still extremely passionate about the pursuit of perfection in his cooking. There have been many complaints that the Michelin judges were too generous in awarding stars in Japan, but how many countries can boast such a plethora of chefs that have dedicated their heart and soul for fifty years to produce just one kind of cuisine? I don't believe there was any favoritism.

CHAPTER 9

FAILURE AND SUICIDE

Japanese people and Americans have a completely different view of failure. In the Japanese educational system, students are sorted and weeded out with rigorous and unforgiving entrance exams at the grade school, high school, and college level. As a Japanese student, once you fall behind, there is virtually no way to catch up. There are no second chances in Japan. Students learn to fear failure. This is very different in the US where if you do well in school, that is good, but not necessary. If you're American and don't get into a good college, you can make up for it by working hard and getting into a good grad school or perhaps by just doing well out in the real world. Americans believe everyone deserves a second chance.

We often say in the US that "A" students teach "B" students to work for "C" students. This would make no sense to a Japanese person.

Americans think failure can be good. In fact, if you

haven't failed, you aren't trying hard enough or aren't taking enough risks. When trying to invent the light bulb, Thomas Edison famously said, "I have not failed. I've just found 10,000 ways that won't work." Edison also said, "Negative results are just what I want. They're just as valuable to me as positive results. I can never find the thing that does the job best until I find the ones that don't."

This is striking from the Asian point of view. Lee Kuan Yew remarked: "...America has a culture that celebrates those who strike out on their own. When they succeed, they are admired as talented entrepreneurs and accorded the social status and recognition they rightly deserve. When they fail, it is accepted as a natural intermediate stage, necessary for eventual success, so they pick themselves up and start afresh."[59]

Lack of entrepreneurialism is a major weakness in the Japanese economy relative to the US. The Japanese fear risk-taking and dread failure. The Japanese ideal is to find life-time employment by joining a large leading company or becoming a government bureaucrat. Contrast that with these comments from Silicon Valley entrepreneur Naveen Jain from a podcast with Dave Asprey: "Dream so big that people think you're absolutely crazy. When people ask you what is it that you're doing and you tell them what you're doing, and if they don't think it's crazy, you're not thinking big enough. Think big and never be afraid to fail. As an entrepreneur, you only fail when you

---

59   Lee Kuan Yew, *One Man's View of the World*, 79.

give up. Everything else is just a pivot. That means if things are not working, you change, you adapt and you pivot, and then, until you give up, you have not failed. Every idea that does not work is simply a stepping stone to bigger success."[60]

I didn't fully understand the extent to which the Japanese experience failure and fear taking risks until I became friends with the middle-aged lady who lived across the street.[61] One winter night during a big snow, I helped her shovel her very long walkway. I was young and enjoying the snow and felt a surge of neighborly friendliness. Unexpectedly, my kindness became a burden of obligation to her. She repaid it by inviting me over to dinner sometimes or bringing leftovers for me to eat. She also introduced me to her son and we became friends. Her son introduced me to another neighbor's son and we occasionally all went out drinking together. The neighbor's son, compared to me, seemed wealthy and happy. He bought a new car and was always dressed fashionably. I was a poor English teacher that rode around on a "mama-san" bicycle and had very little in the way of spending money. I admired his success at such a young age. He was about twenty-six.

---

60 Dave Asprey, "The Microorganisms in Our Body That Keep Us Alive— Naveen Jain—#382," *Bulletproof Blog*, https://blog.bulletproof.com/ the-microorganisms-in-our-body-that-keep-us-alive-naveen-jain-382/.

61 When you live in a foreign country, it is important to find conversation partners, such as middle-aged women who love to talk and to have someone to talk to. They are the best friends of a language learner.

One day, my neighbor came over with shocking news. Her son's friend had committed suicide. I couldn't believe it. He was so young and full of life, and seemed to be doing so well. Apparently, he lost his job at work, and in the shame of it, killed himself. After learning this news I couldn't sleep. I kept thinking, *why wouldn't he just go find a new job?* I found the answer in Benedict's great book *The Chrysanthemum and the Sword*: In a relative truth society, such as Japan's, the success of a peer or falling behind a peer can be seen as a failure and sometimes this makes the Japanese work harder, but in some cases, it leads to a deep depression.[62] The boy felt he had shamed his family.

Amazingly, everyone's reaction was not what I was expecting. Of course, they were sad. But I didn't sense any despair. There did not seem to his Japanese friends and neighbors anything unnatural about his decision to commit suicide. As a Westerner, I was raised to believe suicide was a sin. But somehow, the Japanese can find a sort of beauty or at least understanding in the choice of suicide to redress one's shame. Benedict also helped explain this: Suicide is not seen as a sin in Japan. In fact, suicide, done in the right way, clears away shame and can restore one's lost honor.[63]

The Japanese view on suicide, and death in general, is difficult for Americans to understand. Like cherry blossoms that are beautiful while they bloom, but do not

---

62   Ruth Benedict, *The Chrysanthemum and the Sword*, 153.

63   Ruth Benedict, *The Chrysanthemum and the Sword*, 166.

hold on to the tree tightly and easily fall at the first stiff wind, the Japanese will also hold lightly on to life. With a nature religion at the base, death is viewed as just part of nature. The book *Hagakure* emphasized that: "The way of the samurai is found in death."[64] Suzuki also explained the Japanese view of death. Zen does not make a sharp distinction between life and death. Therefore, the inevitabilities of life should be accepted with equanimity. Death is included and should be viewed objectively and dispassionately.[65] Additionally, "The Japanese may not have any specific philosophy of life, but they decidedly have one of death, which may sometimes appear to be recklessness."[66]

The boy's actions seemed to me to be reckless. What I didn't understand was that often when a Japanese person feels shame, such as when they fail an important exam or lose their job or fall deep into debt or disappoint their families, they will choose suicide. If one is torn between duty and human compassion (what the Japanese call *giri* and *ninjo*), suicide is a way out and can be viewed heroically. Therefore, suicide in Japan is not uncommon. But the Japanese have also become numb to it. When someone kills themselves by jumping in front of a subway train, they call it a (人身事故) or "human accident." It happens so regularly that the people stranded in the station will

---

64 Tsunetomo Yamamoto, *Hagakure*, 17.

65 Daisetz T. Suzuki, *Zen and Japanese Culture*, 82.

66 Daisetz T. Suzuki, *Zen and Japanese Culture*, 85.

actually be annoyed at the train delays, and the station-master will pass out notes so people can explain why they were running late. The family of the deceased then has to pay for the cleanup and inconvenience caused, which can run in the tens of thousands of dollars.

The friend from the neighborhood killing himself made me consider my own experience in relationship to risk taking and success. After college, I decided to go to Japan to try and find an English teaching job and to learn Japanese. I didn't know a soul in Japan and I only had $500 in my pocket. I stupidly didn't even bring a credit card. I didn't speak Japanese, I didn't have any interviews, much less a job, lined up. I didn't even know where I was going to stay the first night I arrived. Despite this, I wasn't worried at all. I felt that I could figure it out.

The day I left home, my dad shook my hand and said, "Good luck." That was it. No more support from my parents. Unfortunately, I ran out of money before I could find a job, so I called home to ask for help. Instead of sending cash, my mom mailed me a copy of George Orwell's classic book *Down and Out in Paris and London*. After leafing through the pages and not finding any money, I realized the tough love message: you're an adult, figure it out. I was on my own.

My experience would have been very different in Asia. If I failed, as an American, I felt I could always go home. I never in a million years would have felt bad about taking the chance and failing. I grew up believing "nothing ventured, nothing gained" or that "you can't steal second base with your foot still on first base." My shock and complete lack of understanding at why this friend gave up and had killed himself led me to start really looking into how different people can have different value systems and even different views on life and death. It felt so incomprehensible at the time and still does today.

SECTION 2

CHINESE THINKING

CHAPTER 10

CHINESE LATERAL THINKING

In contrast to the orderly and homogenous society of Japan, China is a cacophony: messy, vibrant, and varied. From a distance, China appears to be a single, unified entity; but from up close, it is as diverse as Europe and is as much a confederacy of provinces as a single nation state. The languages of Guangdong province and Heilongjiang province are as different as Greek is from Swedish. Still, over 90 percent of Chinese identify themselves as Han Chinese with 5,000 years of shared history, so we can make some useful generalizations about its people overall, beginning with their lateral thinking style.

The modern Chinese word for logic (逻辑—*luoji*) is a foreign borrowed word that was created because it sounds like the English word "logic." As foreign as the linear process of logic is to Chinese minds, the Chinese style of lateral thinking—which draws on diverse relationships between ideas to solve problems—can be difficult for Western thinkers to grasp. Western thinking tends to move linearly toward a point or a conclusion. It is something like prose or a narrative, while Chinese thought is more like poetry.

Chinese thought is based on relationships and refers to ideas, processes, and capabilities. In a business setting, Westerners like to start with generalities and then move their way toward specifics. Westerners will often get thrown by the way the Chinese will jump from broad generalizations straight to the minutest of details. The focus of Chinese lateral thinking is on outcomes, not on the path to resolution specifically, as circumstances are always changing. Most importantly, Chinese thinking highlights context and relationships. As Western humor evolves toward a punch line, Chinese humor creates a humorous context.

As Hajime Nakamura describes, Chinese thinkers value particulars and what could be perceived by the senses, the myriad and diverse details of the observable world, presented in concrete terms. Because they root their thinking in tangible sensory information, they are drawn to complexity over simplicity, diversity over similarity, and their thinking draws on the physical world rather than abstract laws and ideas.[67]

In short, the Chinese believe the world is far too

---

67   Hajime Nakamura, *Ways of Thinking of Eastern Peoples*, 217.

complex for simple linear logic. Rather than focusing on unifying rules or patterns, Chinese thinking became as complex as the perceived world. As Nakamura contends, this influenced the development of Chinese reasoning, which centered around practical, everyday living. By contrast, the study of logic was considered impractical, as its abstract unifying concepts were not directly related to concrete details.[68]

Lucian Pye, an expert on Chinese negotiation styles, pointed out that the Chinese tend to avoid the "middle level of generalization" that characterizes Western cultures rooted in logic and scientific inquiry. Instead, Chinese thinkers tend to vacillate between concrete, observable details and very high-level generalities. This does not mean the Chinese have no development of "middle-level concepts"—for example, their political literature makes clear distinctions between goals, strategy, and tactics, three mid-level abstractions—but the focus of their attention tends to be more polarized at either the very directly observable level of detail or the very high level of moral abstraction. This has an impact on their negotiation styles, as avoiding this "middle level" can also mean avoiding discussions of strategy.[69]

China was saved in 1978 by the common sense of

---

68 Hajime Nakamura, *Ways of Thinking of Eastern Peoples*, 234.

69 Lucian W. Pye, *Chinese Negotiating Style—Commercial Approaches and Cultural Principles* (Westport, Connecticut: Quorum Books, 1992), 62.

Deng Xiaoping. Prior to Deng's leadership, China was an authoritarian, communist country with a socialist economy. The results were disastrous. China's growth miracle began from Deng's "Reform and Opening Up" policies in 1978. Prior to that, the Chinese economy lacked market mechanisms and private businesses. The Chinese government historically did an awful job allocating capital, producing goods, and assigning jobs. GDP per capita in 1978 was only $156. That was below even India at the time. Today, China has the second biggest economy in the world and a GDP per capita of over $9,000.

Deng needed capitalism to grow the Chinese economy. The problem was that "capitalism" was a bad word and completely unacceptable in communist China. Deng got around this by simply changing the name of the proposed system from "capitalism" to "market-based economics with Chinese characteristics" (有中国特色的市场经济). The truth did not matter to Deng. As long as it could catch mice, it was a good cat. There was no way to change China to a capitalist country, so Deng used his common sense and lateral logic to change the perception into something acceptable. It may not have been logical for a socialist country to have capitalist economics, but it sure made a lot of sense. Deng said that "being poor is not socialism" (贫穷不是社会主义), and that resonated with the Chinese people.

Lin Yutang said that an educated Chinese person should be reasonable and follow moderation, restraint, and common sense while avoiding being too logical or theoretical.[70]

Because of this lack of linear logic, the Chinese have always been comfortable with contradictions. The word for contradiction in Chinese is (矛盾), a spear and a shield, which is based on an ancient Chinese proverb. In that story, a man was selling spears, claiming they could pierce any shield and also shields that could block any spear. The people asked what would happen if one of his spears met one of his shields in battle. The man had no answer and that became the Chinese idiom to describe a contradiction.

The Chinese often feel one can find truth in contradictions. The world is full of contradictions and is constantly changing, so the Chinese tend to embrace contradictions. One moment a Chinese person will explain that Taiwan is an inviolable part of China and the next talk about Chinese exports to Taiwan or categorize investment from Taiwan as part of Foreign Direct Investment. The Chinese are comfortable with this contradiction as Taiwan is, of course, a part of China, but at the same time, it is effectively a separate economy.

Another big contradiction facing China was their communist system, where wealth should be shared equally. But Deng Xiaoping adopted capitalism, which is great for growth, but not equal at all in terms of wealth distribution. Deng got around this apparent contradiction

---

70   Yutang Lin, *My Country and My People* (Oxford, England: Oxford City Press, 2010), 104.

with his creative lateral solution that they would let some people get rich first (先让一些人富起来). This acceptance of contradictions does not lead to good scientific thinking, but it does create a more tolerant attitude, allows substantial room for compromise, and can lead to finding creative solutions not possible with linear thinking.

To show how Westerners experience Chinese lateral thinking, I'll use the example of Mao Zedong from the viewpoint of Henry Kissinger from his fascinating book *On China*. Kissinger described meeting with Mao: "Most political leaders present their thoughts in the form of bullet points. Mao advanced his ideas in a Socratic method. He would begin with a question or an observation and invite comment. He would then follow with another observation. Out of this web of sarcastic remarks, observations, and queries would emerge a direction, though rarely a binding commitment."[71] There was not a linear process to Mao's thinking; only the direction would emerge.

Kissinger also describes Mao's thinking with such phrases as "his apparently meandering dialogue,"[72] "In Mao's typical paradoxical style,"[73] and "It was always difficult to sum up Mao's elliptical and aphoristic comments and sometimes even to understand them."[74] That

---

71   Henry Kissinger, *On China* (New York: Penguin Books, 2011), 257.

72   Henry Kissinger, *On China*, 258.

73   Henry Kissinger, *On China*, 280.

74   Henry Kissinger, *On China*, 312.

sounds just like a linear thinker trying to understand a lateral thinker.

Kissinger highlights a great example of Mao's lateral thinking: When facing the twin superpowers of the US and the USSR, Mao not only didn't follow convention and seek support from one of them—he threw theory on its head and took them both on.[75] It would make no logical sense for China to pick a fight with either the more powerful US or Soviet Union. Mao went even further by picking fights with both of the major superpowers and at the same time. Mao did this because he knew the main concern for the US and the USSR was each other and the defeat of China would throw this out of balance, forcing them both to ultimately support China.[76]

Another example of Mao's lateral thinking manifested itself in 1955, when Mao decided to start shelling the Taiwanese islands of Quemoy and Matsu—an action that could have led China into nuclear war—despite having zero intention of actually taking the islands. According to Kissinger, the Soviets couldn't believe Mao would risk nuclear war for an action with no tangible benefit.[77]

Not all of Mao's lateral logic was positive. As if the disastrous experiment with pure communism in the Great Leap Forward wasn't enough, Mao had to complicate it with some strange campaigns based on dreadful lateral

75   Henry Kissinger, On China, 149.

76   Henry Kissinger, On China, 149.

77   Henry Kissinger, On China, 157-158.

thinking. He proposed that the Chinese should melt down all of their metal items into low-quality pig-iron so that Chinese steel output could catch up with England. However, melting down their metal farm equipment severely hurt harvests the following year and of course in no logical way was this a sustainable method for producing steel. More bizarrely, Mao had his "Four-Pests" campaigns and at one point mobilized the entire country to kill all the sparrows. People would bang drums until the birds would fall from the sky, dropping dead from exhaustion. This campaign to kill these grain-eating birds led to a massive overgrowth in the locust population, which was absolutely disastrous for agricultural output. There was not even a scent of linear logic at work there.

Chinese lateral thinking can also be found in their writing, music, and popular culture. For example, the first impression of a Westerner of Chinese writing is the tendency toward incredibly long run-on sentences. As they try to tie together a large number of factors at once, they create much longer sentences than any in English would ever be. Notes for traditional Chinese music cannot be scored on a Western system. Much of the music occurs in between the standard Western notes.

Chess is popular in the West. It is a linear game. The Chinese, on the other hand, developed *weiqi*, a far more lateral game. It was much more difficult for linear thinking computers to master *weiqi* (or *go* as the Japanese call it). Computers beat the reigning world's chess champion for the first time in 1997. Only through developments in supercomputers and advanced AI was a computer able to beat the reigning world's *weiqi* champion in 2016. I've heard *weiqi* has more potential moves than there are atoms in the universe. In such a game, an intuitive mind is required much more than an analytical mind.

Medicine is another good area to explore the difference in Western and Chinese thinking. Western medicine is very linear. Chinese medicine is lateral. In Western medicine, we treat the disease. In Chinese medicine, however, they believe the disease is a symptom of an imbalance in the person's body, mind, or even life. The goal is instead to try to restore the imbalance and to allow the body's immune system to naturally cure the disease. The Chinese believe every person has a different body type and, through diet and supplements, the goal is usually to try to control the balance of the five elements: wind, water, fire, earth, and metal. Once in balance, the body can naturally heal. In Chinese foot massage, lateral thinking is evident in their belief that the big toe relates to the brain, the arch to the stomach, and the heel to the tailbone, etc.

The first time I went to see a Chinese doctor, I had diarrhea. After discussing my symptoms, the doctor did nothing for my stomach. Instead, she put acupuncture needles in my wrists, ankles, and neck to rebalance my energy. After that, she put glass cups over a flame to create a vacuum and then stuck them to my back to draw out the bad energy and excess heat. It didn't fix my stomach, but I must admit that I felt better afterward.

Another interesting aspect of Chinese lateral thinking is that some of the famous quotes we know in the West from China don't actually exist in Chinese. They were clever lateral translations and the challenge with lateral thinking is that these phrases would then translate back into Chinese as something different. For example, a famous Chinese phrase that was never actually said was the so-called curse, "May you live in interesting times." This appears to have been a lateral translation from the phrase (宁为太平犬，莫作乱世人) which means "I'd rather be a dog in times of peace than a human in times of upheaval."

Deng Xiaoping never actually said, "To get rich is glorious," but he was credited with this after his famous 1991 Southern Tour when he further opened up the Chinese economy. It was actually a standard government slogan at the time, and I suspect the Chinese used this phrase as a lateral translation of Deng's comments to explain his message for a Western audience.

Another case is the phrase for trying to get things done in China "问题不大，但是有一定的困难," which means, "the problem isn't big, but there will definitely be difficulty." A brilliant, lateral thinker translated this instead into English as the more famous phrase, "In China nothing is impossible, but everything is difficult." Due to the lateral nature of the translation, it cannot be retranslated back into Chinese to the original phrase.

One example of lateral thinking that always made me shake my head was the situation at a contract manufacturer's Chinese factories. Overworked, underpaid, and clearly desperate employees were increasingly jumping from their dormitory rooms to commit suicide. Instead of applying Western linear logic and trying to figure out why these workers were committing suicide and addressing the core problem, the company applied some good lateral thinking. They installed nets around the workers' dorms to catch anyone that tried to jump!

A fun recent example of Chinese lateral thinking is a new business in China to rent boyfriends during Chinese New Year. Chinese single working women get a lot of pressure from their parents and, often even more so from other relatives, to get married. Filial piety indicates they must go home and spend Chinese New Year with their family, but if they aren't married or don't have a boyfriend, the pressure and criticism can be intense. The solution to this conundrum was the creation of dating services, where attentive young men will pretend to be boyfriends for the week-long Chinese New Year holidays. Linear thinkers would explain to their parents and other relatives that they currently didn't have boyfriends and their career had priority. Or they simply wouldn't go home to protest the unwanted pressure. The lateral thinking single Chinese working woman can now get around this problem by pretending to have a boyfriend for a week, returning to life as normal once the holiday was over with her relatives none the wiser.

Another aspect of Chinese lateral thinking that always stood out for me was the tendency of Chinese companies to carry three separate sets of accounting books. I've interacted with a number of people that have bought companies in China. Some of these people made normal private equity investments, some created mergers, and some bought distressed assets. What they all told me was that you need to see the "real books." Using good lateral thinking and a relative view on truth, Chinese companies will often have one set of books for public investors to see, one set for the government and tax authorities, and then the real set of books. I've even heard of a fourth set of books for the rating agencies. What is interesting is that if you ever have a frank conversation with a Chinese entrepreneur, they don't seem to think there is anything wrong with keeping three sets of books. They believe in different truths for different audiences.

CHAPTER 11

MY LESSONS IN USING LATERAL THINKING TO COMMUNICATE WITH THE CHINESE

In 1993, soon after becoming president, Bill Clinton bluntly told the Chinese not to conduct any more nuclear weapons tests. Given that President Clinton said this to the Chinese publicly, the only way they could save face and show that they weren't in a subordinate position to the US, was by publicly testing another nuclear device. To make their point abundantly clear, the Chinese conducted two nuclear tests. I thought this was a good case of an American not understanding how the Chinese think and communicating incorrectly. I'll get into the importance of "face" in Chinese culture in later chapters, but to understand the blunder Clinton made it's crucial to know that the Chinese prize face above all else, and will sacrifice money, honor, and their own health to gain it. In addition to understanding these values, lateral logic would have been required to accomplish Clinton's goal. Linear logic only made things worse. At the time, I was very new to thinking about China, but I knew President Clinton needed a different approach.

The first time I learned to use lateral logic successfully to my advantage, I was a student living in the foreign student dorms at Fudan University in Shanghai. I was living on the third floor of dorm A. Unfortunately, my room was directly across the street from the kiln where they burned the trash every day from the Chinese undergrad girls' dorms. Twice a day, my room smelled like an oven where you smoked meats. The thick toxic fumes were unbearable. Two Belgians in the room next door complained to the admin folks in charge of housing and got nowhere. I decided to take a different tack because I saw their appeal to reason was ineffective.

Concurrent to the trash burning situation, the building had another problem. We had shared bathrooms and there were students on the fourth floor from a specific country I won't name, but, for reasons known only to God, they would sometimes defecate all over the Western-style toilet seat. (So, I quickly learned how to use the Chinese-style squat toilet.)

Instead of going to the admin office, I found some

of the janitors and asked them to help. I never mentioned to them about the intolerable smoke. Instead, I told them about the unhygienic toilet seats. The janitors were responsible for cleaning those bathrooms, so they were immediately sympathetic to my plight. They reacted to the toilet issue and didn't bother to point out that I lived on a different floor from the toilet problem. Instead, they found an empty room on the fifth floor of dorm C (to which they had a key) and immediately helped me move over all of my stuff. I then went to the admin office and explained that I had already moved. The admin folks had no choice but to give me a new key and change their records and I enjoyed the rest of my time in the smoke-free building.

Soon after, I was in an old Chinese bus hurtling down a raised highway at dangerous speeds. One of my fellow American passengers asked the driver to slow down. This only caused him to drive faster. I thought about it. Linear logic would assume that if we asked the driver to drive slower, the driver would slow down. But this didn't work with lateral logic. Asking the Chinese driver to slow down would mean we didn't trust his driving, so he was driving faster to save face and show us what a good driver he was. Instead, I applied lateral logic. I told him this was my first visit to Shanghai and that he was driving so fast that I was missing my chance to view this magnificent city. The message worked, and he slowed down right away.

I learned to make comments that made no logical

sense in context, but the Chinese, with their lateral minds, would relate to my comments and conclude that I was a reasonable person. Seeing me as a reasonable person greatly improved the quality of our communication and interaction.

If you speak any Chinese (or are with someone that does) try this trick. Say, "Hangzhou is a nice place" (杭州好地方). The Chinese, reflexively, will almost always repeat back enthusiastically that Hangzhou is a nice place. All of a sudden you have instant common ground and have built good rapport. Hangzhou certainly is a nice city and West Lake is beautiful. But there are other beautiful places in China. For whatever reason, I found that virtually any Chinese person I said this to would always resonate with "Hangzhou is a beautiful place."

I suspect what happens is that the Chinese lateral minds conclude I must have visited Hangzhou, I liked Hangzhou, I must like China, I'm a friend of China, and therefore we are friends (or something along those lines).

After the 2004 Athens Olympics, I had a good line that was very helpful. Whenever a Chinese person would tell me they couldn't do something or something couldn't be done, my reply would have nothing to do whatsoever with the issue at hand. Instead I would say that I saw a Chinese man run faster than any other man in the world. The person would immediately say, "Liu Xiang." He won China's first track and field gold medal with his winning performance in the 110-meter hurdles at the Athens

Olympics. He was a hero in China. The lateral logic implication from me was that if a Chinese athlete could be the fastest runner in the world, then this person should have no excuses as to why they couldn't do something. Their pride for Liu Xiang was so strong, that I would say this technique worked more often than not.

I had a funny incident once where I was trying to explain Chinese lateral thinking to an American, but it didn't work. I joined some friends for their dinner in Shanghai. I arrived late. The table was covered with food and it was clear everyone looked full. I was sitting next to an American named Bill. He was the senior member of the group and was mad at the younger Chinese man named Fong, who had over-ordered. Bill found it wasteful. He finally reached his boiling point and said loudly and clearly to Fong, "Do not order any more food!"

I had just arrived but could tell this was a mistake because Bill was causing Fong to lose face. I explained to Bill under my breath that he was using linear logic. There was too much food already, so the linear logic was self-evident: don't order any more food. But Fong was Chinese and would interpret it differently. He would think that Bill was saying he is no good at ordering food or that he hasn't liked what Fong has ordered so far. To prove otherwise, Fong had almost no choice but to order more food.

Bill couldn't believe his ears. He kept shaking his head. I said, "Trust me, I've lived here a long time and have some insights on Chinese culture." Bill asked what he should have said. I replied something like, "This food was so delicious and I ate so much, that if you order any more I'm going to get too fat and my wife will get mad at me." Bill thought this was utter nonsense and knew better how to solve the problem. He stood up and said loudly and rather slowly to Fong, "DO NOT ORDER ANY MORE FOOD!" Fong went away as though to the bathroom. Less than ten minutes later another round of dishes was coming to the table. Bill went apoplectic. He started screaming and turned bright red. The more he screamed, the happier Fong seemed to get, and the angrier Bill got. It was too late to help.

Through this experience, I realized another advantage long-termers in China have is that we've gone through our blow-up phase and can shrug our shoulders and move on when these mini culture clashes erupt. The Chinese don't take these incidents personally and the long-term foreigners learn to do the same.

Another case of linear clashing with lateral thinking occurred when I was in a car leaving from the downtown Shanghai office of a big Northern European company. I was in the car with the global CEO. We were going to visit their production factory on the outskirts of Shanghai. The car and driver both belonged to this company. Using good lateral thinking, the driver didn't have a map. Instead he relied on asking people along the way. He knew roughly where the factory was and that was good enough for him.

After stopping around three times asking for directions, the CEO had seen enough. How could the driver for his company not know how to get from their office to their own factory?

The CEO lost his cool. He started screaming at the driver that as soon as they got to the factory, he would be fired. The CEO told me to translate. I said to the driver that the boss needs to use the bathroom but can't use a public Chinese bathroom. So, we needed to get to the factory quickly. There was no way I was going to tell him he was going to be fired. God knows where he would have driven us. The CEO was turning purple with rage. I was worried the man would have a heart attack.

Using some lateral thinking myself, I suggested we hire a local motorcycle taxi and have them lead us to the factory. The locals always know best. The driver agreed, and we were led to the factory in about ten minutes. I have no idea what ultimately happened to the driver. When we arrived, the CEO started screaming at the local Chinese bosses. But to the CEO's further consternation, they barely considered it a noteworthy issue. China was growing so quickly no map could keep up with all of the new roads.

Another communication technique I adapted to my linear thinking is that under no circumstances will I criticize the Chinese. I will always take their side no matter what my true view is. Sometimes I'll take their side on an issue to the extreme and then the Chinese will start to debate the issue themselves. For example, as a student in China, I would always say how socialism was better than capitalism because there was less of a wealth gap and society was more just. I would also argue that the lack of wealth prevented a lot of crime and corruption and other social problems. Some of my classmates would tell me how I didn't understand anything and start explaining all the problems with socialism and planned economics, while the more politically correct students would have to argue along with me on socialism's merits. I learned a lot listening to them argue. If I have no choice and must criticize China, I always stick with something the Chinese also universally agree is a problem, such as: the pollution in China is terrible, China has an overpopulation problem, or that Chinese society is changing so fast it is disorienting for the average Chinese person. This way, the harmony and the rapport in our relationship is maintained as I'm not saying anything to make the Chinese lose face.

CHAPTER 12

USING LATERAL THINKING TO TURN DOWN DRINKS IN CHINA (A SURVIVAL SKILL)

When I was still relatively new to China, I was invited to a dinner with some former students from my department. The most successful businessman sat at the head of the table and toasted me with a drink of fiery *Maotai*. The glass was about half the size of a standard shot glass, so I figured it was harmless enough. A big mistake to say the least. I was the foreign guest, so the second person at the table then toasted with me. Then the third. This proceeded to go around the table. I couldn't turn any of them down because it would have been a terrible loss of face to drink with one person, but then not another. Later in the meal, we took another turn around the table with everyone toasting me. Basically, I had sixteen drinks of *Maotai* while everyone else had two.

(This would never happen in North China. They are hard drinkers in the north and would have gone drink for drink with me. But this was Shanghai and let's just say that barbarian invasions always came from the north, so the people that remained in North China were hale and hearty, while the more intellectual types moved south.)

That night I went back to my dorm sick as a dog and with the worst headache of my life. It felt like someone had a wooden board pressed against my head and was hitting it with a rubber hammer.

The lesson from that experience was that if I could turn down the toast from the top person at the table, then it was no problem turning down a toast from anyone else. Drinking in China at these banquet dinners is all or nothing. I should be grateful for that experience because I quit drinking that night and have been on the wagon for over twenty years now.

The challenge then was how to turn down drinks in China. Linear logic arguments such as *I don't drink,* or *I don't like drinking,* or *I have a health issue* don't work. The Chinese will persist and say, "Just drink a little, a little bit will be fine." They will be *very* persistent. Saying *it is my religion* also leaves a bad taste in the air and some awkward conversations. In the US, I just put two hands in the air and make a motion like I am driving, which always works instantly, but this technique barely fazes the Chinese.

After a while, I developed a repertoire of lateral excuses that didn't make any sense logically, but always got me out of drinking and left everyone in a happy mood. I still use these excuses to great effect. One of my favorites is to quote the phrase "If you don't smoke, and you don't drink, then your life is worth less than a dead dog's." (不吸烟，不喝酒，死了不如一条狗) It rhymes in Chinese.

Humor in Chinese is context driven, so the context of a *laowai* (foreigner) saying this very local Chinese phrase already throws them off balance. Of course, it makes no logical sense to say that I won't drink because not drinking makes my life worth less than a dead dog. But it works using lateral logic. It is a big insult to myself. This completely humbles me in their eyes while simultaneously boosting their own status, which I suspect is one reason it works so well. Perhaps paradoxically, putting myself down in such a way expresses such a sense of self, I am also communicating that I won't bend to pressure. Usually, everyone laughs and they don't offer me any more drinks. Another phrase I use is: (不喝酒，摆在市长走), which means "If you don't drink then you will have no success doing business at the market."

Sometimes I tell a full joke, which also always seems to work for the same reasons as the phrases above. My go-to joke to get out of drinking is this: A rich man is on his way home and tells his driver to stop because he sees a beggar at the side of the road. He opens the window to talk to the beggar, but the rich man realizes he's forgotten his wallet, so he has no money. He grabs a pack of cigarettes and offers them to the beggar. The beggar apologizes and says he doesn't smoke. He then offers some liquor, but the beggar doesn't drink. He feels really bad for this man and offers to take him to the bath house for some time with a young maiden. The beggar apologizes again and says he doesn't do such things. The rich man very excitedly then tells the beggar to get in his car. The beggar asks why. The rich man says he wants to take the beggar to his home to show his wife what a man that doesn't drink, smoke, or fool around looks like.

Another joke that works well uses historical figures: Lin Biao didn't drink or smoke and lived to age sixty-three. Zhou Enlai drank, but didn't smoke and lived to seventy-three. Mao Zedong smoked, but didn't drink and lived to eighty-three. Deng Xiaoping drank and smoke and lived to ninety-three. Zheng Xueliang not only drank and smoked, he was also a womanizing, gambling, glutton and he lived to 103.

Again, there is no logical sense from this story as to why I don't drink or wouldn't drink with them. In fact, it argues logically that I *should* drink with them. But it always makes my Chinese companions laugh and shows what lengths I'll go to not to drink. Of course, I always do it with a smiling and silly manner to keep the atmosphere light.

If I had to sum it up, I would say that the trick to effective communication with Chinese people is to not think logically about what you are trying to accomplish. Instead, think about your relationship to the person you are talking to, what their position and capabilities are, what their motivations are, their "face" or social standing, and what you can say to motivate them to help you achieve your desired outcome. Specifically, find common ground, something they believe, some way to lift their social standing, or something that they will agree with that will give them a positive emotional response.

CHAPTER 13

THE CHINESE RELATIVE VIEW OF TRUTH

"This brings us to the problem of Chinese logic, which is based on the Chinese conception of truth. Truth, according to Chinese, can never be proved; it can only be suggested."[78]

—LIN YUTANG

In addition to lateral logic, another defining aspect of Chinese thinking is their view that truth is relative. The Chinese belong to the Eastern world, where time is circular, and there are no fixed absolute points. Truth is always relative. Seasons come and go. Dynasties rise and fall. The circle is a recurring motif: the *feng shui* map, the Chinese Wheel of Fortune, the Chinese Zodiac, and the *Yin-Yang* symbol were all mapped out as circles that revolve around infinitely.

---

78 Yutang Lin, *My Country and My People*, 83.

The *Yin-Yang* symbol is a circle and the interacting black and white "fish" inside are in motion circling each other endlessly. The Chinese often talk about the wheel of fate spinning around. During tough times, they will say to be patient because the wheel of fate will spin in your favor again. There are actually no fortune cookies in China. They were an American invention. But the Chinese are big believers in the ebb and flow of fate and fortune, which can sometimes register as superstitious.

Some of this belief system can be seen in their (风水) *feng shui* philosophy, where the elements in the environment need to be in proper balance in accordance with Chinese beliefs about the natural world. *Feng shui* was always mapped out as a circle, and I was told that the circular magnetic compass was originally invented by the Chinese for use in *feng shui*.

Some *feng shui* advice includes: fish are good near the entrance of a home to swish away bad luck with their constantly moving tails. Don't put a mirror near the entrance of a house as that can reflect away all the good luck. A home with a straight corridor from the living space to the front door is bad luck because money will flow straight out. A house with a mountain to its rear is considered secure. Water can represent wealth, so a small fountain in the house or near the entrance can bring wealth flowing into the house, but also remember to keep the toilet cover down, so wealth doesn't get flushed away.

My favorite *feng shui* story was of a Japanese developer

who was building the 101-story World Financial Center in Shanghai. The original design had a large circular hole at the top. Supposedly, the building was so tall, it needed this hole to allow the wind to flow through without rocking the building too much. The building also had a design where it twisted as it rose into the sky. A local *feng shui* expert declared that this building with the circle on the top was going to represent a Japanese dagger stabbing into the heart of Shanghai and would bring much bad luck. The circle on the top looked just like the Japanese flag. So, the Chinese insisted the design be changed. The plans were modified and the circle was replaced with a rectangle. The Chinese now say the building looks like a giant bottle-opener.

The Chinese zodiac is another circle with twelve animals representing time in twelve blocks. Inside of that circle are the five elements: water, wood, fire, earth, and metal. The five elements repeat every five years. So, someone could be born in the year of the water dragon, twelve years later it could be the fire dragon and twelve years after that the metal dragon. The total cycle takes sixty years and then starts over again from the beginning. The Chinese believe one's personality and fate depend upon which element and in which zodiac animal year one is born. Couples are judged to be lucky or unlucky, fated to have happy lives together or to be a bad match depending on their specific zodiac symbols. Weddings are often scheduled for fortuitous times. Births will rise and decline depending on the year. Dragon is lucky, but Chinese will go out of their way to avoid having Sheep babies as they are thought to be too passive to succeed in China's hypercompetitive society.

Every point in a circle is relative to every other point. Truth is always relative to where one stands. Chinese law reflected this belief in relative truth, so the Chinese legal system has ended up very much based upon power as opposed to the absolute concepts of truth and justice.

There was a joke around the time of the Tiananmen incident that captures this. A student was arrested for screaming out "I oppose the Communist Party" and was sentenced to two years in prison. Another student screamed out that "Li Peng is an idiot." He was sentenced to twenty years in prison. He asked why his sentence was so much harsher and was told that he was guilty of revealing state secrets.

This arbitrary nature of crime and punishment further pushes the Chinese away from the idea of self-evident truths such as life, liberty, and the pursuit of happiness. Life in China was traditionally much more about survival and hoping for a good fate.

As Sydney Shapiro, author of *The Law and Lore of China's Criminal Justice* wrote, "The man in the street was the victim, not the beneficiary, of the law in feudal China. Penalties were severe for even minor infractions. A person who stopped an official on the road to petition for redress from wrong had to be beaten first. Only then could he submit his complaint. The law was meant to suppress the citizenry, not afford them any rights. A man could be executed for 'behavior not in keeping with the times.' This was interpreted to mean that anyone who was critical of the regime, who was not a docile subject, who had a bit of pride and self-respect, was considered 'a greater danger than thieves and robbers.'"[79]

This all led to a very flexible attitude toward right and wrong throughout Chinese history. Lin Yutang compared Chinese justice to an art rather than a science, and contended that a Chinese judge, rather than apply an abstract and absolute law to all similar cases of crime, would apply rulings personally and individually.[80] The law was flexible to individual events and circumstances. Outside of law, Lin writes, personal opinions follow a similar ambiguity. "A typical Chinese judgment is: 'A is right, and B is not wrong either.'"[81] I may be right from my point of view and you may be right from your point of view or you may be right at a different time under different circumstances. It is all very fluid.

The great ancient Chinese story of the *Old Man and His Horse* (塞翁失马, 焉知非福—translated as, "the old man loses his horse, how to know if it is or is not good fortune") sums up the philosophy well. As the story goes,

79 Sidney Shapiro, *The Law and Lore of China's Criminal Justice* (Beijing, China: New World Press, 1990), 30.

80 Yutang Lin, *My Country and My People*, 76.

81 Yutang Lin, *My Country and My People*, 104.

one day a horse runs away from the home of an old man. The villagers all come by to commiserate, saying what bad luck. The old man says, *"How do you know?"* The next day the horse comes back with three wild horses. The neighbors congratulate the old man saying what good luck, but he just replies, *"How do you know?"* The next day the man's son falls off of one of the wild horses and breaks his arm. The neighbors come by to express sympathy at the old man's bad luck. The old man says, *"How do you know?"* The next day the army arrives at the man's home to conscript young men, but the old man's son couldn't go because of his broken arm. The neighbors come to congratulate the old man on his good fortune. The old man again replies, *"How do you know?"* As is made clear in the story, in a world without absolute truths, it is impossible to judge if something is good or bad. This world is far too complex, unpredictable, and dynamically changing to judge in absolute terms. What appears good may actually turn out to be bad and vice versa.

For an American, this Chinese flexibility toward truth can be a little disorienting at first. When I was looking for a summer internship during my time as a graduate student in China, I asked my professor to write a letter of recommendation. He told me to write it myself and then he would sign it. I thought I heard him incorrectly, but my classmates told me this was standard in China.

Concurrent to that (and not to claim I am without sin) as a student in a Chinese university, it was stunning to see the level of cheating, particularly by the male students. They explained to me that it was no big deal. The big challenge in China was to pass the University Entrance Exam. Competition is incredible, and the students kill themselves to do well on that test. If they succeed and enter a good university, they have already proven themselves, so no reason to overly stress about college or graduate-level work. Anyway, they justified it by saying that the cheating techniques they were using would be useful out in the real world.

Foreigners sometimes look at the Chinese and wonder how they can so shamelessly steal technology through reverse engineering, patent infringement, corporate espionage, or cyber theft. The Chinese consider this retribution for their undeserved and unforgivable century of humiliation at the hands of Western imperial powers. Much of Japanese industrial technology came originally from licensing US technology and then improving on it and canceling the license. East Asian companies aren't great at compensation, so retired workers can be lured with high-paying consulting jobs to reveal manufacturing secrets. Korea actively recruited retired Japanese engineers to teach them technological secrets. The Chinese, in turn, actively recruit retired Japanese and Korean workers. All is fair in love and war and business in Asia.

My favorite story of the Asian flexibility toward truth was when a large Japanese steel company suspected a large Korean steel company was stealing their high-end steel-making technology but couldn't prove it. However, that same Korean steel company decided to sue an ex-employee for allegedly stealing their technology and selling it to a large Chinese steel company. Turns out the technology the Chinese company allegedly stole from the Korean company was actually stolen first by the Korean company from the Japanese company![82] *How dare you steal the technology I stole!*

One of the first phrases and concepts that a foreigner learns in Chinese is (得看你的标准是什么), which means, it depends what your standards are. If you are judging something as good or bad or right or wrong, it always depends. The Chinese rather consider everything as a (过程) or a process. I've often seen Americans criticize Chinese human rights (which are, more accurately, civil rights). The Chinese understand this issue as a process that must be put in context. While Chinese human rights today may compare unfavorably to US or European standards, these countries are in different stages of development. China's fast growth over the past few decades took hundreds of millions of people out of poverty. That is an incredible accomplishment in their eyes in the process toward improving human rights. Of course, they know they have problems and still need to improve. But the Chinese recoil at being judged by the absolutist

---

82   Kosei Fukao, "Posco Missteps Pay Off for Nippon Steel in Tech Theft Case," *Nikkei Asian Review,* October 8, 2015, http://asia.nikkei.com/magazine/20151008-SEA-CHANGE/Business/ Posco-missteps-pay-off-for-Nippon-Steel-in-tech-theft-case.

standards of people with completely different cultural backgrounds. With this view, it is inappropriate for people from countries with a much higher stage of development to criticize the Chinese in such final terms.

One of the challenges of China's lack of belief in absolutes and having never cultivated linear logic was that it prevented the development of scientific thought. From the seventh to the ninth centuries during the Tang Dynasty, China was the peak civilization in the world. But China fell behind in the following millennium because their thinking prevented them from indigenously developing science.[83] As Lin points out, the Chinese imported mathematics and astronomy from other cultures, and they never created a system of grammar. Development of larger, abstract concepts (Lin lists benevolence, kindliness, propriety, and loyalty as examples) was also hindered, because discussions of these concepts were so general that these terms remained vague.[84]

This lack of development relates back to the weight the Chinese put on direct perception. In *The Ways of Thinking of Eastern Peoples*, Nakamura argues that by valuing specific, concrete details in the real world—especially

---

83 I find it notable that China in the Song Dynasty, a thousand years ago, was the biggest economy in the world and possibly accounted for over 50 percent of global GDP. Unwisely, that dynasty adopted the custom of the foot binding of women. China then had a terrible millennium where they spent large periods of time under foreign control, and their economy fell to only a few percent of the global total. Mao Zedong abolished foot binding, and ever since, China has been in ascendency and is back on track to become the largest economy in the world again. The lesson is that the binding of women's feet is a bad custom!

84 Yutang Lin, *My Country and My People*, 81.

in the form of visual information—the Chinese became more concerned with particular circumstances, and far less interested in forming universals.[85]

This type of thinking just led to more confirmations of observations as opposed to finding patterns and using that to develop theories. Without developing theories, Chinese scientific scholars had no way to build upon each other's work. Today, China overcomes this through imitation. They are dedicated learners and have deeply studied and copied Western technology as well as the scientific method. The Chinese belief in relative truth held back its development for centuries, but that era is now over. China now has the tools necessary to catch up with the West.

There is not much to say on the topic of Chinese people being balanced thinkers. Similar to Americans, the Chinese can think in literal or abstract terms, but are generally somewhere in the middle. The Chinese don't view the world in literal terms like the Japanese do. Fall one penny short on a purchase in China, and the Chinese wouldn't even bat an eye. If a Chinese soldier were abandoned in the Philippines for twenty-nine years, he most likely would've started a family and a business.

Unlike the Japanese, the Chinese are capable of abstract thought. Historically, the Chinese have contributed many notable inventions and ideas. For example, the Chinese had the four great inventions of the ancient

---

85   Hajime Nakamura, *Ways of Thinking of Eastern Peoples*, 185.

world: gun powder, the compass, paper making, and printing. I wouldn't have guessed it, but the Chinese also invented ice cream and restaurants. The Chinese, however, have not contributed much to the modern world and modern areas of abstract theory such as finance or political philosophy. Their government is nominally communist (a European idea) and their economy is partly socialist, but primarily capitalist (also Western ideas). I'll echo Lin, who described Chinese thinking as synthetic, concrete, personal, and full of common sense. The Chinese shy away from abstractions but embrace proverbs.[86]

---

86   Yutang Lin, *My Country and My People*, 76.

CHAPTER 14

THE IMPORTANCE OF NOT FOLLOWING RULES LITERALLY IN CHINA

In *My Country and My People,* Lin Yutang tells a great story about following rules. He describes a government order from Nanking, issued by the Central Kuomintang government, that prohibited the Chinese officials from having offices in foreign concessions. Parts of Shanghai were among these foreign concessions cut out by various foreign powers prior to WWII. At the time, this meant that offices that already existed in Shanghai were effectively being told to shut down. This presented a problem for the ministers who lived in Shanghai, as well as the government employees at those offices who were poised to lose their jobs. The decision seemed impossible to repeal, because requesting to stay in Shanghai would require expressing a desire for a foreign post, which would be considered unpatriotic.

The Nanking ministers from Shanghai did not argue with the decision. They did not point out that the change would be inconvenient, impractical, and costly. Instead, they arrived at a far more clever and inexpensive solution. They purchased door plates, and each Shanghai office hung a new name on the face of the building: Trade Inspection Bureau. Everyone kept their jobs, and their honor.[87]

In a contrasting example of compliance with the rules, Lin tells the story of mission schools that were pressed by the government to institute three new policies in order to be registered. First, the schools were expected to cut religious instruction from the curricula. Second, they were required to hang a portrait of Sun Yatsen, the president of China at the time, in the assembly hall. And last, they were instructed to hold Monday memorial meetings. The missionaries could not accept these changes, and in contrast, the Chinese officials viewed these as simple regulations that should be easy for the mission schools to implement. Some of the missionaries made plans to close their schools. One school complied with the new policies, but the Western principal, out of a sense of stubbornness and honesty, kept a single line in the school's literature, expressing that religious instruction was one of the school's aims. The school was denied registration.

---

87   Yutang Lin, *My Country and My People*, 66–67.

Lin's perspective on this scenario was that the school should have implemented all the changes and "proceeded *a la chinoise* with the rest."[88] *A la chinoise*, of course, is a French expression meaning "like the Chinese."

I had a somewhat similar situation personally when I was a fully local student (not an exchange student) in a Chinese university. Every student was required to write an essay and fill out a form declaring their support of the Chinese Communist Party with Jiang Zemin at its core. My advisor was concerned because if I didn't fill it out and sign it, I couldn't graduate. He recommended I just fill it out and not think about the meaning of any of it.

I didn't feel conflicted signing the pledge, however, as I had seen enough of Chinese behavior to realize that this country absolutely required rule with an iron fist. Only a few weeks prior, I had watched about a hundred migrant workers tip over a bus with the driver still inside because he wouldn't open the door. The migrant workers all wanted to get a seat and they tried to board the bus first while it was pulling up to the bus stop. The driver kept waving them away from the door as the bus was still moving. It was a mad scramble. Workers jumped in front of the bus, forcing the driver to stop. The driver wouldn't open the door as he was still in an intersection and needed to pull forward about thirty feet. The migrant workers then all rushed to one side of the bus and started pushing. Much to my amazement, the bus started rocking

---

88   Yutang Lin, *My Country and My People*, 67.

farther and farther back and forth, and in one big push, they were able to topple the bus.

Which is only to say, I saw the need for strict rule and a strong central government. Also, I was a huge admirer of Deng Xiaoping and his Reform and Opening Up policies. Deng was still alive at the time, and there was no arguing the massive improvement in human rights in China through the hundreds of millions of people China was pulling out of poverty. I happily said I support the Chinese Communist Party bringing stability and development to the Chinese people. My professor did not care if I did or did not support the Chinese Communist Party, he just wanted me to fill out the form and sign it. The truth of my actual opinion was irrelevant.

The situation is the same today. China makes certain rules but does not expect perfect compliance. Legalistically-focused Western firms have trouble not following explicit rules even if the Chinese do not expect them to be strictly followed. This works most of the time in China. The one caveat is that Chinese authorities will take advantage of this lax attitude and will use this rule breaking to go after an "offending company," even if all of their competitors are doing the same thing, as retribution for some other undefined transgression. A recent example of this was the large fine GlaxoSmithKline (GSK) had to pay in 2014 for their bribery scandal. The rules on sales of pharmaceuticals in China is a grey area—a *very* grey area. GSK got in trouble and was punished, but what they did was not different from most or even all of their competitors. Their true transgression must have been somewhere else.

The Chinese say 上有政策, 下有对策, "the policies come from above and then the counter policies come from below." A funny example of that was during Xi Jinping's anti-corruption drive that started from the end of 2012, when the party banned officials from staying at five-star hotels. The countermeasure (and an example of good Chinese lateral thinking) was that the popular five-star hotels changed their rating to four stars. Equally the "Four dishes and one soup" campaign sought to rein in extravagant banquets by party officials. However, restaurants just started providing four giant plates filled with various dishes spread across each plate. As the Chinese say (山高, 皇帝远), "the mountains are high and the emperor is far away."

One story I heard highlighted for me the Chinese motivation to not strictly follow rules, a tendency that follows the culture's adherence to lateral thinking. I spent Chinese New Year in the home of a classmate in Jiangsu Province. He lived in a small town, but his grandmother was from Nanjing. Given her age, I couldn't help but ask if she was in Nanjing in WWII. She was, so I asked her to tell me about her experience. She told a story that even her family hadn't heard. She was pregnant when the Japanese army arrived. There were Chinese in front of the advancing Japanese troops with loudspeakers shouting (别跑, 别跑), "Don't run away, don't run away!"

I asked, "What did you do?"

She said she ran away.

I asked, "What happened to the people that didn't run away?"

She said they were all killed by the Japanese. She said she ended up giving birth in a field by herself and had to use a rock to cut the umbilical cord. I was shocked. I didn't know what to say. I finally muttered, "*That must have hurt.*"

She gave me a look as though I were the single dumbest person on God's green earth. It reminded me that given China's history, the instinct to not follow rules is strong.

Instead of linear logic, the Chinese resonate with common sense. Lin describes the tendency to follow common sense as saner than following logic. In following logic, one must look at a truth analytically, dissecting it into its various parts. This keeps an individual from seeing the whole of the truth, as well as the natural tendencies and influences that contribute to the unique circumstances where the logic is being applied. Common sense, however, "seizes the situation as a living whole," and this allows the Chinese to factor in observation, reason, and human nature.[89] As a Westerner, I had difficulty understanding this, but learned my lesson on a bus ride in Shanghai.

A master's degree takes three years to earn in China

---

89   Yutang Lin, *My Country and My People*, 85.

and the final year is spent mainly on writing a thesis. Many students take advantage of this time to find an internship and gain work experience. I found an internship with a Western bank. Every day, I traveled three hours back and forth to work by bus. The roads were congested, the pollution was a nightmare, while the winters were frigidly cold and the summers scorchingly hot.

One summer day with the temperature well over 100°F and near 100 percent humidity, I got on the bus and sat in the back. A migrant worker got on and was smoking a cigarette, but China had just mercifully passed a law against smoking on trains and buses. We were the first stop and the bus was still waiting to leave. The doors were still open. The man was smoking right in front of the bus driver, but he just got on, so it wasn't a big deal. Then, to my surprise, as the bus doors closed and we started driving away, the man lit up a new cigarette. He was sitting right below a sign saying "No smoking." The bus driver called to me, but I refused to pay the one RMB (about twelve cents) for a ticket. I said that man should not be smoking on a public bus. She said, "What does that have to do with you?" I said, "He is breaking the rules and ruining the air for everyone in the bus." She told me again to pay for my ticket. I asked if it was a rule to pay for the ticket. The bus driver emphatically replied yes. I said, "Is it also not a rule to not smoke on the bus?" The bus driver was fed up with me and collected money from everyone else.

When his cigarette was finished, the migrant worker came back and confronted me. He was barely five feet tall so I just stayed in my seat and listened as he lambasted me. His accent was thick, so I had a hard time understanding him, but one insult I did catch was that I was the one that carried the night soil back in my home country. He went back to his seat. The bus driver insisted I pay. I told her that the *xiao liu mang* (which means scoundrel and is not a nice thing to say) was not to blame, but that the bus driver was better educated and should know better—she was not enforcing the laws of the People's Republic of China. She yelled at me that I was an idiot. I said that she "didn't take responsibility" which is also a powerful insult in Chinese. I felt bad and sort of came to my senses and paid for my ticket.

I thought I was in the right and would get some sympathy from the other passengers, particularly as I was standing up for their interests. Their reaction was the exact opposite. The well-dressed man in front of me explained how I was completely in the wrong and didn't have a lick of common sense. He said that China had only recently changed the law so it was unreasonable to expect everyone to follow it right away. It was a process of improvement. Only one person on the bus smoking was great progress. I had to agree. In the past, half the bus would light up. I saw his point. I asked, "But isn't this the Chinese law?"

He said, "Yes, but why would you insist on American enforcement of Chinese laws, when China requires Chinese enforcement of Chinese laws? You are not the world's policeman." Everyone around us agreed. I thanked him for explaining that to me.

I realized I was in the wrong. As I walked off the bus, I apologized to the bus driver and to the migrant worker. Before the doors could close behind me, the migrant worker jumped up and screamed at me, "The Chinese will not easily be bullied."

I thought this was funny. I wasn't trying to bully anyone. So, I said back. "The Chinese will not easily follow their own rules."

As the bus drove away, about half of the folks were waving their arms out of the windows screaming insults at me. I learned to stop applying my standards to their country. I also decided to splurge and take a taxi for the next few days.

Yes, I was the ugly American, and I had no excuse for my behavior, except this: Shanghai was in the middle of a heat wave and the temperature was over 100°F every day for a month. Humidity was fierce. I can't do justice to describing what it was like spending up to three hours a day in those packed buses on those dreadfully polluted roads. It was so hot, I couldn't sleep at night. It felt like trying to sleep in an oven. I lost a lot of weight. I felt I was losing my mind. I even ended up getting shingles despite still being in my twenties.

Only the poorer students that couldn't afford the

train ticket home would remain in the dorms for the summer. I was hanging out with a few such classmates one sauna-like evening. Word came that a student at a different university in Shanghai got so tired of his room-mate snoring at night that he used a three-inch fruit knife to cut his head off. He then went back to sleep. When the police showed up the next day, he readily admitted his crime and said he just wanted a good night's sleep. We heard that he was executed that very same day and a bill was sent to his parents to pay for the bullet. What left an impression on me at the time was that when we heard this news, sitting around sweating through our T-shirts and almost panting, we all just kind of shrugged our shoulders. It was certainly a horrible crime, but we could also see how it happened. It was so hot that the boy's crime didn't surprise us. I was lucky, perhaps, to have only argued with the bus driver and migrant worker.

CHAPTER 15

THE CHINESE CHARACTERS

When Emperor Qin (Qin Shi Huang) unified China in 220 BCE, he did not get China to unify the hundreds of Chinese spoken dialects, but he did get them to use one character system for writing. This writing system has survived all of China's wars, upheavals, dynasties, invasions, and other calamities. It represents Chinese culture in its essence.

Chinese is monosyllabic. Each character has one sound and in Mandarin there are four tones: flat; rising; dipping down and then up; and falling. Every word is represented by a character. Each character is a pictograph. Nakamura points out that the Chinese use of pictographs is congruent with the emphasis on directly perceptible details. Through these symbols, the Chinese can gain an intuitive understanding of what is meant, and they are also able to convey abstract concepts through concrete images.[90] If we wrote English in the same way: #1=♥≠$ would mean "number one is love and not money" or "love is more important than money." Every word and every phrase in Chinese is written this way. More complicated words are formed by joining two or more characters together.

For example, the character for woman is 女. The original character was a pictograph of a woman bowing or kneeling. If you combine the character for woman with a child (好), the meaning is *good*. In English, the word good refers to the abstract concept of good. In Chinese writing, using lateral thinking, anything good is associated with the good image of a mother with her child. In other words, a mother with her baby is the representation of all that is good to the Chinese mind. The character for *bad* today is (坏) "land" and "no." So, having no land is bad. Chinese characters have evolved a lot over the ages particularly with Mao's big efforts to simplify the characters to help with rural literacy. The original character for bad was (壞), which means "land" and "stolen." You can see how much easier the newer version is to write. Some complained that much history and meaning and depth was lost with the simplified characters, but this was necessary to make it easier for the masses to achieve literacy.

As radicals are added together, new words can be formed. For example:

---

90   Hajime Nakamura, *Ways of Thinking of Eastern Peoples*, 181.

- A woman with a roof over her head (安) means *peace*.
- A woman with a broom (妻) is *a wife*. (These may come across as quite sexist, but in China's defense, many of these characters were created thousands of years ago.)
- A woman plus a hand (奴) is *a slave*.
- A slave plus power (努) is *effort*.
- A slave and heart (怒) is *anger*.
- If a roof is over a pig (家), that means *a home*. (In ancient times, a pig was kept under the house to eat all of the human waste and excrement. A very efficient recycling system.)
- If a woman were added to home (嫁), that would be the verb for a *woman to marry*.
- *Man* (男), incidentally, is "rice paddy" plus "power."

Not all characters retain their original meaning, but it is easy to understand how 3,000 years ago the idea of putting a rock (石) together with skin (皮) would mean *to break* (破). And it is always interesting to contemplate the lateral thinking that occurred for the image for *beauty* (美) in ancient China to be a big (大) sheep (羊).

More complex words are created by putting, usually, two characters together.

- Peace (安) followed by complete (全), means safe (安全).
- Peace (安) plus heart (心) would be (安心), or calm.

- A big (大) house (家) means everybody (大家).
- People (人) and house (家) means other people outside the family (人家).
- Old (老) person (人) house (家) means older person outside the family (老人家).
- China (中国) is, of course, the middle (中) kingdom (国).
- Japan (日本) is sun (日) and source (本).
- America (美国) is the beautiful (美) country (国).
- England (英国) is the heroic (英) country (国).
- Germany (德国) is the moral (德) country (国).

Most country's names have no meaning. For example, *Italy* is (意大利), which oddly translates as "meaning-big-profit" but doesn't intend to mean anything about profits. They use it because it is pronounced *yi-da-li*, which sounds like Italy. To make a sentence, you just string characters together. So for example, *I (*我*) love (*爱*) you* (你) is (我爱你—*wo-ai-ni*). Chinese is actually very similar to English with the subject-verb-object. To say *I don't love you*, just add a (不) which means no or not, so (我不爱你—*wo-bu-ai-ni*) or *I not love you*.

One word I'll never forget learning is "thing" (东西). It is a combination of *east* and *west*. If you said "East-West" in a linear logic context, it would refer to geography or orientation. But using lateral Chinese thinking, it means *thing*. Since China is the Middle Kingdom, between heaven and earth, anything that exists in the people's world from east to west is a *thing*.

I was walking home one morning after doing Tai Chi. In front of me, there was an old man riding a three-wheel bicycle and also two younger ladies walking home together. For some grievance or another, he would ride up like a dive bomber in attack mode and scream insults at them and then when they would try and respond, he would ride away preparing for another loop back. After about three rounds, one of the ladies screamed at him in a shrill voice, (你算什么东西), which means "you count as what thing." I didn't know the word at the time, so I ran home to look up *dong-xi* (东西) in my dictionary. I was fascinated to learn that it meant "thing" and that the lady went beyond the normal insult of asking "who" are you or "who" do you think you are, and tried to demean him further by asking "what" thing are you?

Learning the required 2,000 or so Chinese characters takes years of dedicated study. There is no way around it, but my strong recommendation to any student of Chinese is to make the effort. The characters contain the essence of Chinese culture and one needs to think in characters in order to think like a native Chinese speaker. Ultimately, every word in the Chinese language has a character representation. Therefore, every thought and idea gets expressed through its lateral association to a pictograph image.

CHAPTER 16

FAMILY AND STATE

The family system in China is extremely broad. Chinese lateral thinking dictates that your brother's wife's cousin's classmate's little brother could be included in your family circle. It is far wider than family would be considered in literal Japan, which extends little beyond immediate family. The belief in relative truth means that Chinese behavior is VERY different when directed toward those within one's circle versus toward those outside your group.

I believe it is no exaggeration that the extended family or clan is the most important institution in China. It has endured through the ages and is the top priority for each individual. As Lin said, the family system is the basis for all of the institutions and social constructs in China, including "face, favor, privilege, gratitude, courtesy, official corruption, public institutions, the school, the guild, philanthropy, hospitality, justice, and finally the whole government of China."[91]

---

91   Yutang Lin, *My Country and My People*, 167.

The family gained this importance due to Confucianism and the unreliability of the government in a large country often struggling with internal disorder and external invading powers. The family is what is great about China, but also the source of major societal problems. In essence, guided by relative truth, China has one set of rules for conduct within the extended family or clan group and a much different set of rules for those outside of the group.

One of the key distinctions between China and Japan is that the imperial family in Japan, though not directly ruling, has remained in place unchanged for almost two millennia. This is very different from China, which had many dynastic changes and successful peasant revolutions. It depends how you define it, but China has marked roughly twenty to thirty-six dynastic periods.

With each change in dynasty came turmoil. The family was the one constant throughout all this time. In *The Enigma of Japanese Power*, Karel van Wolferen explained, "Whereas Chinese emperors were expected to be benevolent and maintain justice in order to keep the 'Mandate of Heaven,' their Japanese counterparts, as direct descendants of the sun goddess, were not in need of heavenly endorsement; they were themselves assumed to be in perpetual possession of benevolence."[92] By having an Emperor that didn't actually rule, there was no threat that the Emperor could ever make a mistake or

---

92   Karel van Wolferen, *The Enigma of Japanese Power*, 192.

fall out of favor. Therefore, the institution of the Japanese Emperor could survive changing forms of ruling government underneath. In China, the Emperor *did* rule and when they fell out of favor or power and lost the mandate of heaven, they would get replaced.

I read once of the confusion when the Manchu-ruled Qing dynasty was in its final days and Sun Yatsen's Republic was taking control. The Manchurians required all Chinese men to have *bianzi,* or the front of their head shaved and long braided hair way down their back. (Business in front, party in the back, but taken too far.) Anyway, the Manchu forces would cut off the head of any man they found without a *bianzi.* The Republicans, on the contrary, would decapitate any man that refused to cut his *bianzi* on the spot. The great stress for the common man was that he would constantly fear for his life either way. This is a situation that almost never happened in the far more stable Japan.

The other difference apart from political continuity is that until 1945, Japan was never successfully conquered by foreigners, whereas the Chinese built the Great Wall specifically to keep the barbarian invaders from the north out. Unfortunately, as Patton pointed out, "Fixed fortifications are a monument to the stupidity of man."[93] The Great Wall couldn't keep the invaders out and served mainly just to keep the Chinese in. The Chinese were

---

93   William Weir, *50 Military Leaders Who Changed the World* (New Delhi, India: Pentagon Press, 2007), 173.

under pressure from these foreign forces for a millennium and, in fact, over the past 750 years, China has been ruled by foreign powers for about half of that time. The Yuan Dynasty from 1271 to 1368 signaled Mongolian rule of China. The Qing Dynasty from around 1640 to 1912 was ruled by the Manchurians. (This doesn't even include the devastating and humiliating invasions from the Western powers and Japan in China's so-called century of humiliation from 1839 to 1949.)

Mongolians attempted to conquer Japan two times, but their invading fleets were swept away by typhoons, the so-called "*kami-kaze*" or "divine winds." The people of China, on the other hand, learned to absorb and assimilate these foreign conquering rulers. They also learned to fend for themselves as foreign rulers would have their interests in mind much less. The family was consistently the only reliable institution to fall back on.

Confucianism also fostered the Chinese focus on family. The broad definition of Chinese family includes friends as well, and with this in mind, Lin points out that only one of the "five cardinal relationships" for the Chinese is a bond outside of family: the relationship between king and subject. All moral conduct stems from these five cardinal relationships, and so the social fabric is dictated primarily by relationships between family: between father and son, between husband and wife, between brothers, and between friends.[94] These four relationship factors

---

94 Yutang Lin, *My Country and My People*, 170.

form the circle within which Chinese interact. Family, friends, extended family, introduced friends, classmates and colleagues, etc., fill out the inner circle—and then there is everybody else.

Another part of the social ladder was merit based. The Imperial Examination system was set up by Confucius, and any student who did well could become an official. This title brought power, money, and influence. The Chinese say that wealth cannot last past three generations (富不过三代). As Lin said: "The society, rather than any hereditary class, is the social unit. These families go up and down kaleidoscopically."[95] This meritocratic system brought two great benefits to China. Firstly, it put a massive emphasis on education, as any student that did well on the Imperial Examinations could rapidly move up the social ladder. Secondly, the social mobility fostered a strong entrepreneurial and risk-taking spirit in the Chinese. (The Japanese have an equally strong focus on education because it is their duty, but Japan lost out on the entrepreneurial and risk-taking spirit.)

Lin points out that over eighty years ago the concept of society did not exist in China and it is noteworthy how weak it remains today, despite the best efforts of the Chinese government.[96] An example of this can be seen in the Chinese character for "society." Lin first notes the similarity between the characters for family (家) and

---

95   Yutang Lin, *My Country and My People*, 182.

96   Yutang Lin, *My Country and My People*, 164.

state (国) where the character for family is contained and organized by the state. "Society," then, is (国家), or "state-family." Common Chinese sayings affirm the relationship between state and family: "Put the family in order and rule the state in peace."[97]

As I will cover later in a chapter on teamwork, this concept of "people inside my circle and outside my circle" hurts China's ability to cooperate on a large scale. This is a big negative aspect. Contrarily, Chinese people are extremely cooperative within the family circle. They work together to pool resources or to help people within their circle in a way that extends far beyond the levels that would occur in Japan or the US.

This Confucian emphasis on the family developed very differently in Japan than in China. The Japanese wanted the country to be the top priority, whereas for the Chinese it was the family. In *The Enigma of Japanese Power*, van Wolferen explains that the Japanese adopted Confucianism, but then changed it so that loyalty to the Emperor took precedence over loyalty to the family.[98]

As Robert Bellah pointed out in *Tokugawa Religion*, in China "if one chose to join the official rank, one had 'to transform filial piety into loyalty to the sovereign': but... when these two virtues seriously conflicted, it was the duty of the son as the son that should receive first consideration. This is further evidence that the family system

97 Yutang Lin, *My Country and My People*, 164.

98 Karel van Wolferen, *The Enigma of Japanese Power*, 256.

was the foundation of traditional Chinese society and filial piety the basis of its moral principles."

The Japanese worried about the tension between the state and the family, so to prevent the same situation as existed in China, no one in Japan outside of the nobles and the samurai had last names. (Japanese were all given last names only with the Meiji Restoration in 1868.) Without a last name, allegiance would only go to the immediate family and mainly to their *daimyo*, or lord.

The larger political construct of the clan, as it existed in China, could not develop in Japan. In Japan, one's in-laws are referred to as literally *giri*-relations. "*Giri*" means "duty," so the mother-in-law is referred to as the *giri*-mother or duty-mother. The word indicates a person to whom an outside, reciprocal, and time-limited obligation is owed. Interestingly, in Japan not only are in-laws considered *giri*-relations or outside the family, but even blood relatives one layer away—such as aunts or uncles—are considered "outsiders." Even a daughter, once married, is considered outside of one's family. This is in sharp contrast to China where cousins, or nieces, or nephews, etc., would be considered "inside" family members.[99]

In China, everyone had a last name, and there are only a limited number of last names despite the massive population, so the pool of potential relatives could be quite large. Regular people in China are referred to as

99   Ruth Benedict, *The Chrysanthemum and the Sword*, 137.

Laobaixing (老百姓) "the old one hundred names." And there really are only roughly one hundred core last names in China. The Chinese census determined that over 14 percent of the population was surnamed *Wang* or *Li*. So, if you were curious, that does mean there are over 90 million Wangs in China.

This web of family connections extends to cultural and political attitudes of protectionism. The Chinese draw stark distinctions between who is in and who is out of their family or clan, and this affects their attitudes around political borders.

I believe we misinterpret the meaning of the Middle Kingdom. I had a revelation during a kung fu class with my *Shifu* Master Wang. He always said, "We have heaven, we have earth, and only then could we have us people in the middle." He was saying that our bodies came out of the earth and our spirits from the heavens, and they combine in our life here. The Middle Kingdom is this human kingdom between heaven and earth. This resonated with everything I learned living in China. It is Western arrogance to think the Chinese meaning of the Middle Kingdom is China as the middle country and we foreigners are non-middle countries around it. The historical view in China was that the people around China were barbarians, less than fully human. But China isn't a kingdom in the middle of these barbarians. The barbarians are incidental. China is the Middle Kingdom of the Chinese people in between heaven and earth.

The message from the Manchu King in 1795 to King George III of Great Britain illustrates well the superiority that the Chinese felt over the barbarians:

"Swaying the wide world, I have but one aim in view, namely, to maintain a perfect governance and to fulfil the duties of the state. Strange and costly objects do not interest me...I have no use for your country's manufactures...

...It behooves you, O King, to respect my sentiments and to display even greater devotion and loyalty in the future, so that by perpetual submission to our throne, you may secure peace and security for your country hereafter...Our Celestial Empire possesses all things in prolific abundance and lacks no products within our borders. There was, therefore, no need to import the manufactures of outside barbarians in exchange for our produce...

I do not forget the lonely remoteness of your island, cut off from the world by the intervening wastes of sea, nor do I overlook your excusable ignorance of our Celestial Empire...tremblingly obey and show no negligence."[100]

The point is that the Chinese believe China is a special kingdom for their special race. What other nation has ever constructed anything like the Great Wall of China

---

100 Adda B. Bozeman, "Politics and Culture in International History," in *Oriental Mythology: Masks of God*, Joseph Campbell (New York: Penguin Books, 1962), 384.

to keep other people out? When Zhang He, the great Chinese mariner, voyaged across Asia all the way to East Africa in the early 1400s, he went giving gifts and sharing China's technologies, and receiving tributes. His ships were multiple sizes bigger than Christopher Columbus' ships. But Zhang He had no desire for military conquest or colonizing new lands because China already possessed everything it needed and couldn't possibly learn anything from the barbarians.

While they may feel superior, the Chinese are, however, paranoid about defending their country, as the Great Wall can attest. China took over Tibet because they were worried about the so-called Great Game between Britain and Russia in the nineteenth century as they vied for control of Afghanistan, central Asia, and Tibet. China also worried that India would rule Tibet. The fear was that Tibet could be used as a strategic launching pad for invading China from the west. The Chinese have a perception that what territory made up China in the past still belongs to them. They want that territory back, and they want whatever territory is around China that will create a buffer zone and help them defend China from any potential invasion. No doubt, China will wait however long it takes and do whatever is necessary to get Taiwan back.

China's foray into the South China Sea should also be understood in this context. China feels surrounded with Japan and South Korea to its east, Russia to its north, a potential Islamic militant threat from the west, India to its southwest, Vietnam to its south, and Taiwan to its southeast. China wants to break that encirclement. China knows that its power in Asia is rising inexorably and it has a major advantage over the US in terms of distance and commitment. They are extending their reach into the South China Seas by constructing man-made islands as military outposts. This is not to create a base for future Chinese expansionism. Rather, this should be viewed as a new Great Wall of China. It is a new buffer China is hoping to add to separate themselves further from potential outside invaders and to weaken the US's ability to encircle China.

China wants to maintain their position as a united country with a secure Middle Kingdom. There is one area apart from Taiwan, however, where the Chinese do want to expand—though peacefully—and that is in the far southeast of Russia. Vladivostok was part of China once. Most people may not realize that, but the Chinese certainly remember. The interesting aspect is China's plan to retake this territory: in a funny example of Chinese lateral thinking, waves of Chinese immigrants are heading to southeast Russia and peacefully diluting away the limited Russian population.

One of the negative consequences of the one-child policy is that China's ratio of males to females under fifteen years old is around 117 boys for every hundred girls.[101] This is due to China's traditional preference for

---

101 "The World Factbook," Central Intelligence Agency, 2018, https://www.cia.gov/library/publications/download/download-2018/index.html.

boys. The time-honored Chinese belief is that the more boys you have, the wealthier you are (多子多福—*more boys, more wealth*). In a country like China that lacks a good social safety net such as a reliable social security system and health insurance system, parents rely on children to take care of them in old age. The one-child policy means parents would only have one child to rely on. A boy picks a wife (娶), but a girl marries off to another family (嫁). Like we say "don't cry over spilled milk," the Chinese will say "don't cry over spilled water, or a daughter that has married off and gone away" (嫁出去的女儿, 泼出去的水). Since the daughter marries off to the boy's family, parents need a son that will stay around to support them in their retirement. With ultrasound, parents could choose to abort baby girls, sometimes resorting to infanticide if ultrasounds were unavailable. This practice of selective abortion of girls led to China having an excess of around 30 million boys today.

One lateral solution to this excess is that boys are marrying women overseas in large numbers. Uganda has complained about the number of Chinese men marrying locally.[102] Chinese men are also actively seeking brides in eastern Russia.[103] When I visited that region, I was surprised how many Chinese men were living there. I

---

102 "The World Factbook," Central Intelligence Agency, 2018.

103 Olga Gertcyk, "We've Come for Your Women: Chinese Men Seek Siberian Brides," *The Siberian Times*, October 11, 2016, http://siberiantimes.com/other/others/features/f0261-weve-come-for-your-women-chinese-men-seek-siberian-brides/.

spoke to some locals, and apparently the Russian women were fed up with the excess vodka drinking of the local men. By contrast, the diligent and hard-working Chinese men presented themselves as much more reliable partners. As a result, an increasing number of Russian women in the region were marrying Chinese men. Russia already has a demographic challenge and the Russian far east has a population of only around 6 million. By stealth, China is using their excess male population to slowly but steadily move back into what they consider rightfully Chinese land.

Chinese people also prioritize family above nation. The family is the one institution the Chinese would be willing to die for, but unlike the country, the family would never ask for that. The Chinese have a famous idiom describing how they would not want their sons to join the army and fight. "They hate war, and will always hate war. Good people never fight in China. For 'good iron is not made into nails, and good men are not made soldiers.'" (好铁不打钉，好汉不当兵)[104]

"The Chinese are the world's worst fighters because they are an intelligent race, backed and nurtured by Taoist cynicism and the Confucian emphasis on harmony as the ideal life. They do not fight because they are the most calculating and self-interested of peoples."[105]

—LIN YUTANG

---

104 Yutang Lin, *My Country and My People*, 58.

105 Yutang Lin, *My Country and My People*, 56.

Chinese common sense dictates that dying for a cause is a bad outcome for the individual and their family. When talking with Chinese people, one often hears the phrase "we only have this one life" (只有这一条命). The meaning is to treasure one's life and be careful with it and not lose it due to acting recklessly or carelessly. Another phrase I heard frequently was (好死不如赖活), which means "a good death is not as good as a bad life." According to the famous "Thirty-Six Stratagems" of ancient Chinese military strategies, running away is number thirty-six and is called *the best strategy* (走为上策). "From the Chinese point of view, pacifism is not 'noble'; it is simply 'good' because it is common sense," Lin writes. "If this earthly life is all the life we can have, we must try to live in peace if we want to live happily."[106]

Let me try to make the case in more modern terms: compared to the massive and aggressive nuclear arsenals of the US (with an estimated 6,800 nuclear warheads) and Russia (with an estimate 7,000 warheads), China only has around 260 nuclear warheads. The Chinese have just enough to discourage anyone from attacking China.

The rise of China is inevitable, but this does not mean conflict with the US is inevitable. In fact, the Chinese genuinely want to avoid conflict. They do, however, have a fervent desire to avoid invasion and will fight to build a sufficient buffer around China to make them feel safe. They will fight if they feel their sovereignty is challenged.

---

106 Yutang Lin, *My Country and My People*, 56.

The challenge over the next fifty years will be for the US to accommodate China's rise. It will be a delicate balance as the US continues to promise the security of allies while at the same time building a strategic relationship with the Chinese. The US will eventually have to accept increased and even dominant Chinese influence in Asia. The challenge will be getting from a unipolar world of US dominance to a bipolar world with equivalent US and Chinese power. This will be a difficult process. The US will not willingly cede power while the Chinese will not be stopped from retaking what they consider their rightful place in Asia.

CHAPTER 17

POWER, LAW, AND THE CHINESE DISREGARD FOR STRANGERS

In contrast to the Chinese, who feel obligations to individuals and family, the Japanese are much more obligated to entities such as society or their company. The behavior of the Japanese people after the devastating 2011 earthquake and tsunami demonstrated for the world how orderly, courteous, and socially minded the Japanese are in even the most extreme of circumstances. Similarly, when Japanese workers go on strike, they show their civil spirit by actually continuing to work at full speed. They will only wear a black arm band to indicate their displeasure, as they would not want their selfish demands to damage the overall Japanese economy. For the Chinese, the family is the top consideration, above the country or society, and this has positive and negative aspects. I will touch on the positive aspects later and certainly do not want to diminish them.

The negative outcomes of China's focus on the family include a terrible tendency by the Chinese toward rent seeking, an ingrained proclivity against teamwork with those from outside their family, indifference toward the suffering of others, and official corruption as the idea that one is stealing from the state or the masses in order to help one's own family and is therefore a virtuous act.[107]

Despite his emphasis on family, Confucius forgot to include the relationship of people toward strangers. He did partially cover this with his famous saying (己所不欲, 勿施于人), "Whatever you don't want done to yourself, don't do to others." But this lacked the weight of being included in the five key relationships and also it was stated in the negative. Five hundred years later, Jesus updated this idea with his guidance in the positive to "treat others as you would want them to treat you." So not only don't do what you don't want done to you, but on top of that, do what you would want done for you. Traditional China never got this lesson.

In 2011, video footage from Guangdong Province emerged when a two-year-old girl was run over by a truck.

---

107 Rent seeking is a type of behavior where you game the system to take more than your fair share—basically, when someone only thinks of their own needs or their family's needs and not the needs of society as a whole. A classic example is that Chinese toilets typically don't have toilet paper. If they do have toilet paper, the rent-seeking Chinese that get to it first will take it all home for their private use and with no consideration for anyone that comes later.

Eighteen people passing by failed to stop to help the little girl. Another truck came by and she was hit again. She later died from these injuries. It became a sensation on the Chinese internet as everyone questioned how these people could be so callous.[108] The Chinese debated this incident for months after it occurred. The main issue was whether morals were changing for the worse. However, Lin Yutang wrote about this indifference over eighty years ago, arguing that indifference arises out of the absence of the rule of law.[109] Unfortunately, China never had the parable of the good Samaritan and this attitude of indifference to strangers existed historically and remains true to this day.

Anyone living in China for a while will witness fistfights. With 1.4 billion people and a large number of riding bicycles, it is inevitable that some bikes crash into others. If the two riders are male and face prevents either one from apologizing, a fight will sometimes break out. (Apologies also express guilt and liability, so to be fair, face is not the only reason the men won't apologize.) Usually, it starts with insults. A crowd will form around the two, pulling out their cell phones to film the melee. Eventually, the insults will go too far, someone will get called a turtle egg (王八蛋), someone will get pushed, and a fistfight will

108 Richard Hartley-Parkinson, "Yue, the Girl Who Shamed China, Is Dead: Two-year-old Run Over TWICE as Dozens of People Ignored Her Lying in the Road Succumbs to Her Injuries," *Daily Mail*, November 5, 2011, http://www.dailymail.co.uk/news/article-2051679/Yue-Yue-dead-Chinese-girl-Wang-Yue-2-run-bystanders-watch-dies.html.

109 Yutang Lin, *My Country and My People*, 44.

start. As a tall foreigner, I witnessed many such fights. I never, ever saw anyone break up any of these fights. Why risk yourself for a stranger?

Before going to China, I imagined that the average Chinese person would know kung fu and would be a great fighter. Reality couldn't have been further from the truth. I was expecting crane-style versus praying mantis-style, but instead the fights more resembled a contest between pugilistic six-year-olds. The other takeaway was that the bigger guy always won. The crowd was almost always happy. At first, I thought it was like free entertainment for people passing by. But later I concluded that because of the face issue, the pain and struggle of the fighters brought the spectators schadenfreude-like happiness that someone was doing worse than them and, however infinitesimal, it raised their standing in society overall.

One of the funniest complete-lack-of regard-for-strangers incidents I ever saw was in Jiangxi Province a few days ahead of Chinese New Year. I was walking with a classmate through a courtyard to his parents' flat in a large housing complex. There were hundreds of people walking to and fro. I kept hearing fireworks go off. To my amazement, two eleven-year-olds were firing bottle rockets, not into the sky, but right into the crowd. One of the bottle rockets whistled past my face. I headed over toward the boys, at my civic-minded best, to teach them a lesson with my swift kicks of justice to their behinds.

My friend stopped me. He said they must be the sons of local officials, and that was why no one was stopping them. The repercussions for crossing an official could be grievous. We took cover behind two trees and watched as these boys continued to fire bottle rockets into crowds of people and expressing their disappointment every time one didn't explode right near someone's face. There are a few times in life when you can't believe what you are seeing and this was one of those times for me.

I once saw a not-so-funny commercial when I was in Shenzhen. It was people standing next to a high rise. They were pointing up to a dot in the sky. When it was too late, they finally realized it was a TV that was falling out of the sky that was about to kill one of them. The message of the commercial was "do not throw your TV away by just pushing it out the window of your high-rise apartment." Sadly, this was not an intellectual exercise or some made-up example. Sometimes it seems the Chinese treat their whole country like a giant garbage can and mindlessly dump trash out of their apartment, out of a train window, or anywhere.

Amazingly, an estimated 240,000 manhole covers were stolen in Beijing alone over a ten-year period from 2003 to 2013 as rising scrap prices increased the demand for used steel. To fight this crime, the authorities started adding GPS to new manhole covers to help catch the thieves. When reading local papers, it is not uncommon to read stories of people falling into the sewer at night because a manhole cover had been stolen. Sometimes, these accidents are even fatal.[110]

One of the most dangerous examples of this disregard for strangers can be found in the baby milk and milk-powder scandals. In 2004, at least fifty babies died from drinking fake milk powder, which was mostly starch, powder, and sugar.[111] In 2008, thousands of babies in China became sick, and a few died, from drinking milk with melamine it. Basically, the guilty milk companies wanted to raise their margins a few percentage points by watering down the milk and then adding the toxic melamine so that the protein content of the milk would pass inspection. It is easy to understand why imported milk powder is so popular in China.

The Chinese are also not big into philanthropy or social work. As Lin puts it, "To a Chinese, social work always looks like 'meddling with other people's business.'"[112] Americans give to charity out of principle and for religious and cultural reasons. The Chinese don't because the recipients are outside of their circle and are strangers. Warren Buffet attempted to cleverly circum-

---

110 Flora Drury, "China Forced to Install Manhole Covers with GPS Tracking in Desperate Effort to Stop Thieves from Stealing Them for Scrap," *Daily Mail*, March 20, 2015, http://www.dailymail.co.uk/news/peoplesdaily/article-3004339/China-forced-install-manhole-covers-GPS-tracking-tie-lampposts-desperate-effort-stop-thieves-stealing-scrap.html.

111 Raksha Shetty, "Fake Milk Powder Causes Baby Death," *CBS NEWS*, June 9, 2004, http://www.cbsnews.com/news/fake-milk-powder-causes-baby-death/ and Jonathan Watts, "Chinese Baby Milk Blamed for 50 Deaths," *The Guardian*, April 20, 2004, https://www.theguardian.com/world/2004/apr/21/china.jonathanwatts.

112 Yutang Lin, *My Country and My People*, 166.

vent this bias by trying to make philanthropy a face issue and had some traction in convincing wealthy Chinese to donate money to worthy causes. But since then, I've also heard numerous stories from newly rich Chinese that did give to Chinese charities only to find out later they were scams.

Guanxi (关系), or connections, become particularly important in a society where the rules are very different for those with whom you have a relationship versus those for strangers. *Guanxi* is basically using relationships to call in favors or to gain favorable treatment. China is a "power society" and not a "rule of law society." My litmus test for rule of law or rule of power is crossing the street. If the cars give way to pedestrians and trucks give way to smaller cars, it is more a rule of law (or in Japan's case, rule of politeness) society. In China, the bigger vehicle always wins and pedestrians take their lives into their hands anytime they go against a car crossing the street. In a rule of power society, rules and fairness can't help, you must have *guanxi*.

When an official steals money from the state to help his family in China, he sees himself as being virtuous. Since so much depends on *guanxi* and with the absence of the rule of law, the scale of corruption in China is mind-blowing. As Lin wrote, "In China, though a man may be arrested for stealing a purse, he is not arrested for stealing the national treasury."[113] This creates an environment

---

113 Yutang Lin, *My Country and My People*, 174.

where low-paid officials feel it is their right and responsibility to make as much as they can while in a position of power.

No doubt, corruption greases the skids for economic growth, so officials tell themselves they are also helping the country as they enrich themselves. This created an environment where corruption was out of control in China. When Xi Jinping came to power in 2012, he started his aggressive anti-corruption campaign because he said the level of corruption had become a threat to the very survival of the party and that corruption would doom the party and the state.

Here are some examples of what has been exposed:

- The head of the railway ministry was arrested in 2011 for corruption and the Chinese press accused him of stealing upwards of a quarter of a billion US dollars.[114]
- The former deputy chief engineer of China's railways was accused of stealing an eye-popping $2.8 billion.[115]
- From Xi Jinping's aggressive anti-corruption campaign, we've learned about the former head of public security in China, who was said to have amassed assets worth over $16 billion, and a former general who had over one ton of cash in his basement along

---

114 "Ex China Rail Minister Liu Zhijun Charged with Corruption," *BBC News*, April 10, 2013, https://www.bbc.com/news/world-asia-china-22089011.

115 Malcolm Moore, "Chinese Rail Crash Scandal: 'Official Steals $2.8 Billion'," The Telegraph, August 1, 2011, http://www.telegraph.co.uk/news/worldnews/asia/china/8674824/Chinese-rail-crash-scandal-official-steals-2.8-billion.html.

with countless jewels and artwork that apparently required ten military trucks to haul away.[116]

- With Bo Xilai's very pubic downfall, we learned that this senior official's family had amassed a fortune of well over $100 million.[117]

- Not to be outdone, the *New York Times* broke a story claiming that Premier Wen Jiabao's family controlled assets worth $2.7 billion.[118]

And these are just a few examples of corrupt top officials and does not include the myriad of mid-level and local-level officials and all of their corruption, which prompted Xi to say that corruption was a threat to the survival of the party and that he would go after both tigers (top officials) and flies (lower-level officials).

One key factor in Chinese society is that Communist Party members are like super citizens. Despite being "communist," they have retaken the role of the former noble class. They are above the ordinary laws and can only be tried by the party and not normal courts. They receive special privileges, have an easier time finding

---

116 Harrison Jacobs, "Here's the The Ridiculous Loot That's Been Found with Corrupt Chinese Officials," *Business Insider*, January 22, 2015, http://www.businessinsider.sg/the-ridiculous-loot-thats-been-found-with-corrupt-chinese-officials-2015-1/#jly5tkTofA6V7WXM.97.

117 David Barboza, "As China Official Rose, His Family's Wealth Grew," *The New York Times*, April 23, 2012, http://www.nytimes.com/2012/04/24/world/asia/bo-xilais-relatives-wealth-is-under-scrutiny.html.

118 David Barboza, "Billions in Hidden Riches for Family of Chinese Leader," *The New York Times*, October 25, 2012, https://www.nytimes.com/2012/10/26/business/global/family-of-wen-jiabao-holds-a-hidden-fortune-in-china.html.

jobs, and are held to higher standards. Communist Party officials are easy to spot on the roads because they have special white license plates and do not have to follow normal traffic laws.

Consistent with the traditional Mandarin Examination System, Party membership is a meritocracy and the top students from top schools are generally invited to join. (It is also hereditary.) These students are then expected to pass a test and go to regular meetings to make sure their thinking is proper and updated. New members must be introduced or sponsored by a Communist Party member, so it is something like joining a club. Out of 1.4 billion people in China, only 90 million or so are party members, or less than 7 percent of the total population. Competition in the party is ferocious and unforgiving. Only the toughest, best connected, smartest, and most competent make it to the top.

Sydney Shapiro wrote a great book on the history of China's criminal justice system. In his book, Shapiro describes China from the twenty-second century BCE as a slave society and in that time, "...while the law was strictly enforced against commoners and slaves, as a rule only the moral code, with its lenient penalties, was applied to the ruling nobles and slave owners."[119] Despite the passage of millennia, that system still sounds familiar for China.

---

119 Sidney Shapiro, *The Law and Lore of China's Criminal Justice*, 15.

CHAPTER 18

INDIVIDUALITY, JOY, AND FRIENDSHIP IN CHINA

It is easy to overstate the negative aspects and to understate the positive effects of the Chinese focus on family. As the Chinese say (林子大什么鸟都有), *if the forest is big, it will contain every kind of bird.* So, in a country as large as China, it is possible to find examples of any kind of bad behavior. What gets ignored or underestimated is how caring Chinese are of family members. Chinese old people will continue to live in their own home with their family, usually all the way to the end of their lives and not in some cold and heartless institutional old folks' home. Working couples are also the norm in China, but instead of letting strangers raise their kids in a profit-driven day care center, one of the child's grandmothers will take care of them. The concepts of strangers in a nursing home or day care center looking after a loved one actually boggles the Chinese mind. According to the Chinese, those people are working for money and not for love. The Chinese have their faults, but their country is safe; they have a very humanistic culture; the people are kind and hardworking; the family takes care of the young and the old; and the society is inclusive.

China is a shame-based society. To Westerners, this doesn't sound so good. In China, if one can get away with a crime and not get caught, then there is nothing wrong with it. In the West, we are much more comfortable with our guilt-based culture, where fear of doing something wrong either for religious or moral reasons keeps us in check. But China is a relative society and doesn't believe in absolute right or wrong, so instead it is the fear of getting caught doing something wrong and shaming one's family that prevents bad behavior. This system works. China is an overpopulated country. There are around 1.4 billion people. So almost anywhere you go, there are, as the Chinese say, "mountains and oceans of people." Therefore, there are lots of potential witnesses to any crime. As a result, China is an extremely safe country. I feel far safer walking around any city in China late at night by myself than I would in my home city of Washington, DC. I'm not sure how much of an impact it actually has, but China's strict enforcement of the death penalty for a wide range of crimes also seems to help.

I have traveled through all but one of the thirty-two provinces in China and have never been robbed, though,

I have, from my Western perspective, been cheated in almost every province I visited. Some instances involved taxi drivers that took an extra-long route or sellers that overcharged me. Sometimes I bargained a good price, but they did the old switcheroo and put low-valued goods into the bag for me to take away. But in all my time in China, I was never the victim of any violent crime. I also never heard of it happening to anyone else I knew. Of course, China does have violent crime and, if you leave something unattended, it will likely get stolen. But muggings are very rare. Crime in China usually occurs at the end of a pen not the end of a gun or knife. Farmers or urban dwellers in socialist-era housing will regularly be pushed off of their land or out of their homes for minimal compensation, while local officials will then resell that land to property developers for multiple higher prices. This type of crime is all too common, but personal safety walking the streets is not an issue (except, of course, crossing a busy street).

China has a very tolerant and pragmatic society. It is a bit difficult to describe, but the Chinese enjoy life, they are exceedingly friendly, and they express and share emotions. Life in Japan is severe. People are exceedingly polite, but not friendly at all. I had more friends in my first few weeks living in China than I had in eight years total living in Japan. I still feel the Japanese word for "friendship" falls far short of the meaning of the English or Chinese words for friendship. The concept is different.

The Japanese are reserved to the extreme, even with each other. The Chinese are very open. I would sum it up by saying there is a lot of expressed love in China. Lin notes that the West failed in understanding what is intrinsically familiar to the Chinese: the end purpose of all knowledge is to serve human happiness. The meaning of life, he writes, is to enjoy it.[120]

The Chinese work hard and are diligent, but will never reach the levels of dedication or precision the Japanese attain. The Chinese frequently say (差不多), which means "more or less" and the Chinese are satisfied often with *close enough* or *good enough* or *not so different*. The Japanese would call this (中途半端), which means *going half-way and being incomplete*. It implies something being done unsatisfactorily and is a big pejorative. The Chinese way is less exact, but is so much more forgiving for the foibles inherent in being human. It makes life in China so much more flexible and tolerant. I'm in no position to judge which is better, but I do think we should recognize the benefits of the Chinese focus on people as much as we recognize the Japanese pursuit of perfection.

The Chinese focus their efforts on living long, healthy, and trouble-free lives as much as possible for themselves and for their family and friends. The Chinese focus on life here on Earth and not some afterlife in heaven.[121]

For comparison, Lin describes how other cultures

---

120 Yutang Lin, *My Country and My People*, 96.

121 Yutang Lin, *My Country and My People*, 98.

focus life's purpose outside of a life well lived. For the Chinese, a life of achievement "is too vainglorious," Nirvana is "too metaphysical," Christianity's view of a reward in heaven is "incomprehensible," and progress for progress' sake is "meaningless." The only meaningful focus for life is to live simply, in harmony with family.[122]

Jiang Menglin, an educator who was the head of Peking University from 1931 to 1945, wrote a book in 1947 called *West Tide,* part of which articulated the contrast of China and Japan. I think Professor Jiang did a great job explaining the key differences between the Japanese and Chinese and what the strengths of Chinese society are. Professor Jiang goes even further to say the Japanese understood loyalty, and justice, and virtue, but missed the key ingredients of Chinese society: forgiveness and kindness. (He was a nationalist and the timing of his book was after the Japanese were defeated, but before the communists took over.) This is my rough translation/ summary of part of that chapter:

> With the Meiji restoration, Japan combined a Confucian system of governance with modern Western social science and natural science. This was the first society to combine Eastern and Western cultures. At the time, young Chinese admired Japan's progress and hoped China could learn from Japan's example and that Japan would repay the favor to her cultural mother. Unfortunately, the Japanese knew

122   Yutang Lin, *My Country and My People*, 96.

how to show loyalty (尽忠), but did not know how to grant forgiveness (施恕). They knew justice and virtue (义), but did not know kindness and benevolence (仁). When Japan learned from Chinese culture, they only learned some of it, but left out some other very important parts, namely forgiveness and benevolence. Loyalty was a virtue necessary in a feudalistic or militaristic society, but kindness or benevolence were virtues of intellectuals.

The Japanese persisted in their own views and were not willing to consider the point of view of others. The Japanese were closed-minded and they even realized this themselves. The Japanese had ambition and they had power, but without benevolence and forgiveness, they didn't have the demeanor or leadership to build and maintain an overseas colonial empire. For the Chinese, on the other hand, loyalty and benevolence go hand in hand. The Chinese never felt that "just because I am loyal to my ideas and beliefs that I must automatically exclude someone else's views and beliefs." The Chinese often put themselves in other people's shoes to consider their views, and this is their so-called forgiveness. The Japanese are very weak at this concept of forgiveness, so they couldn't understand China.[123]

This fits my model for Japanese and Chinese think-

123 Jiang Menglin, "China and Japan," in *China's Peril and Promise,* by Chih-p'ing Chou, Xuedong Wang, Joanne Chiang (Princeton, New Jersey: Princeton University Press, 1996), 286–309.

ing. The Japanese are a literal people and so are not good at seeing something from someone else's point of view. They can only see their own point of view. In contrast, the lateral thinking of the Chinese made it easy for them to shift from thinking from their own point of view to the view of others. There is also an abstract angle to seeing things through someone else's eyes that would be difficult for the literal-minded Japanese.

When I first moved to China from Japan, China was far poorer economically, but I was still happy to make the transition. Japan is an amazing country, but I felt that it lacked warmth. The Chinese were different and far more open. They happily would have random conversations with me, sit with me for a meal in a restaurant, go for a walk to show me around, or invite me to their homes for dinner and would be incredible hosts. In Japan, I was always walking on eggshells, worried about some rule or another, but in China I engaged, and laughed, and shared so much and it felt like such a richer and more human life experience.

Multiple generations often live together in a Chinese household. Extended family and friends often visit also. With so many people crowded together there were really no secrets. In fact, *yinsi* or "privacy" is actually a bad word in Chinese. Without much privacy, everyone knows most everything about everyone else in their circle. Family and friends will comment on everything. The intrusive questions and cutting remarks can be jarring to an American at first. But if the Chinese are making fun of you and everyone is laughing, it isn't mean-spirited or malicious. They are just very open and honest about everything and love pointing out and laughing at each other's foibles. If they are pointing out your flaws, it is a sign that you belong to their circle.

My classmates loved to tell their family and friends the story of when I walked into class wearing a green duffle coat. My mother sent me a duffle coat like the boys wore in the movie *Dead Poets Society* because I was complaining to her how cold the unheated Chinese classrooms were in the winter. When I walked into the room wearing that coat, however, the entire class of around one hundred students exploded into laughter. I had no idea what was going on until a few of them called out to me and asked why I was wearing a girl's coat. Even the teacher was laughing.

One story my Chinese friends loved to retell and laugh about was the time our Marxism teacher was going on about how perfect communist society would be. I raised my hand and asked if there would be divorce in a communist society. Rule number one in a Chinese class is don't ask questions. Rule number two is if you do ask a question, don't ask a ridiculous question. My classmates were laughing and laughing. To the teacher's credit, and she was a dyed-in-the-wool communist, she said that yes there would still be divorce because even if communism was a perfect system, people would remain imperfect.

The number one favorite story was the time I was in a shopping mall and a mother told her daughter to quickly look, there is a foreigner here that looks just like a giraffe. The word for giraffe in Chinese is *long-neck-deer* and I have a long neck, so my friends considered this lady calling me a giraffe tremendously funny. My friends' relatives made me retell this story over and over. But again, it was all in good fun and, as an insider to the circle, they could not have been kinder.

Chinese lateral thinking extends to cooking also. Japanese food is great, but given their literal thinking, the same dish tends to be similar throughout the country. Chinese food is different. If you order Kung Pao Chicken in Beijing, or Shanghai, or Guangdong, or Chongqing, or anywhere in between, it will be different every time. Even in different restaurants in the same city, it will be different. The variety is wonderful. Also, the Chinese have been oppressed for large portions of their long history, but food was the one area where they always had freedom of expression. Chinese life revolves around meals. The Chinese say (民以食为天), which means *to the people, food is heaven.*

Another aspect I love about China is that it is an inclusive society whereas Japan is exclusive to the extreme. China borders more countries than any other. China's inclusiveness becomes apparent rather quickly to a foreigner living there. The Chinese expect you to speak Chinese. The Japanese expect you *not* to speak Japanese.

In China, a foreigner is expected to adopt a Chinese name for use in China. In Japan, this is ludicrous. A foreigner is literally and obviously not Japanese, so how could they have a Japanese name? In China, I could, for example, name myself Wang Jun, but in Japan it would be completely out of the question to call myself Tanaka Hiroe. The Japanese would simply refuse to call me by a Japanese name. Chinese lateral thinking easily accepts a foreigner using a Chinese name.

The Chinese consider China the center of the world and the other people around them to be barbarians. In their hearts, they consider it good fortune that they were born Chinese and naturally believe that is a great thing. They feel a sense of pity on foreigners that they weren't born Chinese. Conversely, the Chinese will readily adopt a foreign name for speaking in a foreign language or if they need to go overseas. As they say (见鬼说鬼话), *when meeting a devil, speak in the devil's tongue*. Or as Mao used to say with a slightly different meaning (到那个山头, 唱那支歌), *when in a village, sing that village's songs*. The Japanese, on the other hand, almost always use their own name even when speaking a foreign language or in a foreign country and isolate themselves far more when they have the misfortune of needing to live outside of Japan.

As a Westerner, I also appreciate how supportive China is of individuality. In Japan, the word to be *wrong* (違います) literally means to be *different*. To be different is to be wrong! This reflects the homogenous nature of the Japanese society and the focus on the culture of conformity. In Chinese, wrong is (不对), which simply means "not correct." The famous Japanese idiom is that *the nail that sticks out gets hammered back in* (出る杭は打たれる). English, just as famously, has the opposite phrase, that *the squeaky wheel gets the grease.* Chinese has both, *the bird that sticks out its head gets shot* (枪打出头鸟), but *the child that cries gets milk to drink* (会哭的孩子有奶吃).

In Chinese, the emphasis is not on avoiding disrupting the harmony of the group by being different, thinking differently, or being a nail that sticks out. Rather, in China, it is better to remain anonymous as fame brings trouble. Such as in the phrase *people fear fame as pigs fear getting fat* (人怕出名, 猪怕壮) because Chinese often get "red-eye disease" (红眼病) or "jealousy" and it is better to not court this. But there is nothing that says you must pursue almost military-like conformity in your personality. One funny difference is that if you get into an argument with someone in Japan, that break in harmony could mean the end of your relationship—forever! China is the exact opposite. The Chinese say (不打不相识), which means that you don't really get to know someone until you've had a fight with them.

"This use of verbal attack, which can be seen as quite insulting, is intended not to break the relationship, but oddly to strengthen it. For the Chinese often feel that they can

positively influence others by scolding, shaming, and embarrassing them."[124]

—LUCIAN PYE

The Chinese do not pursue conformity the way the Japanese do. Van Wolferen explains that all the way back to the time of Confucius, the Chinese learned to not go along with bad conventions and even to speak out against them if they judged the practice to be wrong.[125] In traditional feudal Japan, a commoner would get their head cut off for that kind of behavior. The Chinese are much more independently minded, which is an attitude Americans are much more familiar with.

The Japanese are tolerant of other philosophies as long as they can adapt them to the Japanese system. The Japanese are not tolerant of nonconformity to the standards of their system. The Chinese are tolerant of outside philosophies (Marxism, market economics, etc.) and they are also tolerant of individuality. But they are not tolerant of any challenge to central government authority.

---

124 Lucian W. Pye, *Chinese Negotiating Style—Commercial Approaches and Cultural Principles*, 99.

125 Herrlee Glessner Creel, "Confucius and the Struggle for Human Happiness," in *Chinese Thought from Confucius to Mao Tse-Tung*, (Chicago: The University of Chicago Press, 1953), quoted in Karel van Wolferen, *The Enigma of Japanese Power*, 242.

CHAPTER 19

POOR TEAMWORK IN CHINA

One of the key negative aspects of the strong emphasis on face and on the family is that it hurts the ability of Chinese, particularly Chinese men, to work in teams. As an example, look at the 2010 Olympics, the North Korean soccer team, from an impoverished country of only 20 million people, qualified. Yet China, with a population eighty times bigger and the second biggest economy in the world, could not field a team that could qualify.

The Chinese are good athletes. Chinese men often win gold medals in diving, or ping pong, or shooting, or other individual games. In the 2016 summer Olympics, China won twenty-six gold medals; twenty-five for individual or two-person events. Only the women's volleyball team won gold in a team sport. The Chinese women, unlike the men, do have one of the better women's soccer teams in the world. It is my belief that the difference is Chinese men's overemphasis on the importance of face. If I pass the ball and my teammate looks good for scoring a goal, I naturally look worse in comparison. Every man wants to be the star. This makes Chinese men very weak at teamwork.

In 2011, China was knocked out of the World Cup qualifiers by Iraq, a country that had been at war for a decade. In 2013, China reached new lows with their 5–1 loss to soccer pip-squeak Thailand. Though China only qualified for the World Cup once, in 2002, the country still stops to watch the World Cup matches every four years. Even small town and village folks will put out TVs and people will gather at restaurants and outdoor shops to watch.

In a match for the qualifying rounds for the Russia World Cup in 2018, China accomplished the unthinkable. The Chinese men's soccer team—from a country of 1.4 billion with near unlimited resources—lost to Syria. Yes, Syria, a country of about 23 million (with about 25 percent of the population being displaced refugees) in the midst of a brutal five-year-plus civil war. And the match was played in China!

You are probably thinking perhaps China is just not good at men's soccer? But we can look to traditional sayings in China to see that the Chinese are not good at cooperating. There is a common phrase (一个和尚挑水喝, 两个和尚抬水喝，三个和尚没水喝): *One monk can carry two buckets of water with a pole, balancing one on each side, two monks can carry one bucket of water with a pole balanced between them, three monks would have no water to drink because they couldn't find a fair way to cooperate and carry the water.* In other words, the results get worse as you add people. Chinese will also often say (一个中国人是一条龙，三个中国人是一条虫): *One Chinese is a dragon, three Chinese are a worm.* As I've written earlier, the Chinese will cooperate and sacrifice for the greater good of their family and extended circle, but not for those outside of their circle.

The Chinese also sometimes begrudgingly say that one-on-one they always beat a Japanese, but three-on-three the Japanese always win. The Japanese clearly understand the group ethic better than the Chinese, stressing harmony in all situations. The Chinese only look out for themselves and their family, so they are always wary that someone will take advantage of them when working in groups.

I imagine it was for this reason that Japan historically rolled over the Chinese whenever they met on the battle-field despite being the much smaller country. In the 1894 to 1895 war, Japan ended up with Taiwan. In the second Sino-Japanese war, the Japanese army ran roughshod over China before the small country of Japan could no longer maintain its war effort against the US and China. Of course, the Japanese were always more diligent about training, discipline, and preparation as well as being better at teamwork. The willingness for self-sacrifice is much higher in Japan. Lu Xun, the great author, described Chinese society as (人吃人), something like the English expression *dog-eat-dog,* but he said *people-eat-people.*

Japan has developed huge conglomerates like Hitachi or Mitsubishi Corp with hundreds and hundreds of subsidiaries and affiliates. They have also developed the *zaibatsu* and *keiretsu* systems, where group companies cooperate. A unique trait of the Japanese is to believe one's duty is to perform their best in the role fate has placed them in. They are happy to work as a small part of a larger whole. They even have a word for dying at your desk from overworking, a concept that could not exist in China, or really any other country but Japan. This word is called *karoshi* (過労死—over-work-death) and it doesn't refer to blue-collar workers. It is for white-collar workers that do too much overtime and literally drop dead of exhaustion. My experience working in a Chinese environment is that, from the secretary all the way up, every single person has the ambition to be the top boss. But as long as you are not an owner of the company, you try and leave at 5 p.m. to have dinner at home. In a Japanese office, you can't leave as long as anyone your superior remains in the office.

It's sometimes said that in each Chinese man's heart there beats a dragon. And a dragon wants to be on top. The Chinese have a saying: (宁为鸡头, 无为凤尾), *better to be the head of a chicken, than the tail of a phoenix.* In rural

China, I've heard this phrased as *better to be the head of a chicken than the ass of a cow.* They also say (宁可在小庙里当大和尚，也不要在大庙里当小和尚), *better to be a big monk in a small monastery than a small monk in a large monastery.* This is in direct contrast to the common Japanese phrase (大船にのる気持ち), *the comfort and security one finds by riding in a large boat.*

Once again, it is easy to point out China's weaknesses, and lack of teamwork is one of them. But I do want to emphasize the positive aspects also. Chinese are incredible individual talents and apart from great athletes at individual sports, China also produces great artists, teachers, writers, scientists, engineers, and entrepreneurs. China is unlikely to ever create successful giant conglomerates or *keiretsu* groups like the Japanese, but they are far superior to the Japanese in terms of taking risks and creating new companies.

CHAPTER 20

FACE (面子) *MIANZI*

(人要脸, 树要皮)— "People need face like a tree needs bark."

Lin famously said that face cannot be defined, but he did describe it by giving an example of an official driving in a metropolis. Let's say the speed limit is thirty-five miles per hour, but the official asks his chauffeur to drive at a breezy sixty miles per hour—he gains face by demonstrating his ability to flaunt the rules. When the car hits a man and a policeman comes by to resolve the situation, the official gains face again by silently handing the policeman his card and speeding away. Imagine that the policeman is not appeased; the official temporarily loses face only to gain it back stronger when he asks the policeman if he "knows his father," and then signals the chauffer to drive off. (This practice of intimidating by referring to family connections is called "talking Mandarin.") The most face is gained, then, if the policeman still insists on taking the official down to the station: the official calls the police chief to explain that this lowly policeman does not know his father, and the policeman is summarily fired.[126]

If I had to define face, I would sum it up by saying: *I look better than someone else. I am important.* I believe the closest concept we have in the West is what we refer to as the male ego. Face is an entirely relative concept. There is no directly logical reason for face to be so emphasized in Chinese culture; it is purely given importance by lateral association and is an entirely relative concept. This is often difficult for Westerners to understand, but as Lin said, "it [face] is prized above all earthly possessions."[127] The Chinese will go to great lengths to gain face.

It is a funny concept because you can have face or not have face. It can be given or taken away. Face can be gained or face can be lost. Sometimes you need to withhold saying the truth in order to help someone not lose face and sometimes you need to accept something you don't want to in order to give someone face. Westerners can sometimes inadvertently cause someone to lose face by saying "no" too directly, contradicting something someone says, not listening attentively to someone, interrupting them, criticizing someone publicly, not letting another pay for a meal, turning down a toast, or even not walking as far as possible when sending someone off.

One negative aspect of face in China is that women

126 Yutang Lin, *My Country and My People*, 190.

127 Yutang Lin, *My Country and My People*, 191.

often won't marry a man with a lower education or career level or even who is shorter than she is—unless, of course, he is rich: then the face from marrying a rich man far overrides the loss of face of marrying a short, uneducated, or unattractive man. A few years ago on a TV dating show, a young lady said (宁在宝马车里哭，也不要在自行车上笑) "I would rather cry in a BMW than smile on the back of a bicycle." Riding on the back of a bicycle in today's China implies one is poor and unsuccessful, and is a major loss of face. What the young lady said, in essence, was that face (and money) were more important to her than love.

The Chinese love brands. This tendency causes them to either buy the best or the cheapest options. If they have the money, they want the best in order to show off. If they can't afford the best, then there is no face to be gained buying the second best or an average brand, so they buy the cheapest option. Americans, by contrast, generally want to buy the best value.

Even the extreme Chinese focus on education, at its source, is also about *mianzi* or face. Going to a top school provides the best *mianzi* and for a lifetime. Everyone is embarrassed if their kids go to a bad school. Chinese will invest time and money and sacrifice everything in order to help their kids get into a better school.

The Chinese emphasis on education can be seen in the ancient proverb (孟母三迁), *Mother Meng moved three times*. The mother of Confucian philosopher Mencius moved homes three times, a hugely troublesome and disruptive endeavor in ancient China, in order to get her son into the right school and the right academic environment—an admirable and worthy endeavor that persists in modern China.

One interesting case of *mianzi* is that if you go into a Chinese home, the TV is prominent. A Chinese person will spend months or even years of salary in some cases for a top brand, large screen TV. Washing machines, on the other hand, do not get seen by visitors so are usually very cheap brands. I heard one of the biggest challenges for Victoria's Secret in China was that only one's husband would see a woman's lingerie, so it was unpopular as there is no face to be gained by wearing luxury undergarments. This was in sharp contrast to luxury bags, which are visible publicly. China is one of the biggest markets for luxury bags now. One funny example of this going too far was in 2017 when a Taiwanese grandmother used the $1,000 Louis Vuitton bag her son had given her to carry home fish from the market as she was oblivious to the face this luxury bag was supposed to bring her. She was more impressed herself that the bag was good for carrying fish because it was properly waterproof.[128]

Sometimes the lengths someone will go to achieve face are mind-blowing to a Westerner like me. For example, on a per capita basis, Korea is the leader in cosmetic surgery. Korean plastic surgery is considered the best in

---

[128] "Taiwan Grandma Carried Fish in £900 Louis Vuitton Handbag," *BBC News*, April 3, 2017, http://www.bbc.com/news/world-asia-39477966.

the world and this has become a status symbol in China. So Chinese women will go to Korea for cosmetic surgery and then go out shopping the very next day, while the white bandages are still on their face, so others can see their "face"!

Similarly, there is the case of a seventeen-year-old boy from Anhui province who sold a kidney in order to raise money to buy an Apple iPhone and iPad.[129] Even though China has many lower-priced, knock-off versions of smartphones and tablet devices, the face aspect of having Apple-branded products was more important to him than his own health.

When I was a first-year grad student in the world economics department at Fudan University, I became friends with a second-year student who was always very helpful when I had questions about class or about China. His surname was Wang and he was a year ahead of me, so I respectfully referred to him as *Lao*-Wang or old-Wang. One day, I asked him about face. He shook his head and made a sharp tsk-tsk sound and said I could never understand, that as a foreigner I could never understand face in China. He kept saying "you don't understand" and "you can't understand." In Japan at sushi restaurants, I was often told that as a foreigner, I couldn't understand the subtle flavors of sushi and they would leave it at that.

---

129 Lauren Gambino, "Chinese Boy 'Sells Kidney to Buy iPad'," *The Telegraph*, April 6, 2012, http://www.telegraph.co.uk/news/worldnews/asia/china/9191325/Chinese-boy-sells-kidney-to-buy-iPad.html.

There was no point at explanation. So, I thought Lao Wang was going to let it go. Instead, his mind seemed to drift off and he became very emotional. He told me a story.

Lao Wang's family was from a village in Jiangxi province. A poor part of the country. After the madness of the Cultural Revolution, Mao had finally died and Deng started opening up the country and the economy with his great (改革开放) "Reform and Opening Up" policy. Deng overcame so much of the ideological craziness of the Mao era with simple, yet profound, common sense. One example was his exhortation that (多劳多得) "if you worked more, you would earn more."

Lao Wang's family embraced this new environment and started a small business along-side of farming. China was growing again and they were doing well—so well that his family became the first one in the 1980s in their village to buy a cow. This was intolerable for the other families. The other families all lost face because they didn't have a cow. One of the other families plotted and then killed the Wang's cow late one night. Lao Wang was spitting as he recounted the story, because he was so angry. His family was furious. They didn't get another cow until years later when other families in the village could also afford one. This was Chinese jealousy (红眼病) or "red-eye disease" at its worst. Years later, the family that killed their cow was the first one in the village to have a cell phone. Lao Wang got together with all of his uncles and cousins and they devised and then executed a plan to smash that cell phone while making it look like an accident.

Lao Wang smiled as he described the lengths they went to in order to destroy that cell phone and the big drinking party they had later that night to celebrate. But then he became very wistful. He said America is much better. If your neighbor gets a cow, you don't think of ways to kill that cow. If your neighbor gets a cell phone, you don't think of ways to smash that cell phone. Americans would think of ways to try and be successful themselves, so that they could buy their own cow or get their own cell phone. Not the Chinese. It was a zero-sum society and anyone getting ahead automatically caused those falling behind to lose face and resent deeply the happiness of others. Lao Wang then taught me that unfortunately often useful Chinese phrase (幸灾乐祸), which means "finding happiness in the sufferings and misfortunes of others." In English, we use the German word *schadenfreude*. In Japanese, they say "the sufferings of other people are as sweet as the taste of honey" (他人の不幸は蜜の味).

It took me a while to understand Lao Wang's story. As an American raised to believe in absolute truth, the idea that someone else's suffering should make me look better and feel better about myself was something I couldn't understand at a deeper level. Hearing about someone else's failure may make me feel better for a minute. But the feeling would pass and my thinking would remain on how to improve myself or my life in an absolute sense. With relative truth, the situation is different. The failure of others improves my life in a measurable and permanent way. The failures of others truly are as sweet as honey, because they represent triumphs for me, while the successes of others significantly and permanently diminish me. Therefore, the Chinese (and Japanese) are hypersensitive to the success of others around them. As a result of this contrast, I learned to carefully watch out for feelings of jealousy in China (or Japan) because they can be felt at a much deeper level than I would naturally experience or comprehend.

A terrible example of the cost of face on the national level was during the devastating man-made famine of the Great Leap Forward. While the Communist Party denied that there was a problem in the food supply chain, the death toll from the Great Leap Forward climbed higher than any other famine in modern history. No accurate data exists for the mortality rate during that short window from 1959 to 1961, but Western analysts place the death toll as high as 30 million people. In order to preserve face, China actually exported rice during this time despite tens of millions of Chinese dying from starvation! In his book *Hungry Ghosts: Mao's Secret Famine,* Jasper Becker reports that in addition to increasing exports to the Soviet Union by 50 percent, China "delivered grain gratis to her friends in North Korea, North Vietnam, and Albania."[130]

130 Jasper Becker, *Hungry Ghosts: Mao's Secret Famine* (New York: The Free Press, 1998).

In the mindset of Chinese authorities, millions of people dying wasn't good, but saving face internationally so other countries wouldn't know of Mao's failure was even more important.

Face is more important to the Chinese than even money. As Lin wrote, "it is the goad of ambition and [face] that can overcome the Chinese love of money."[131] So, if you find something Chinese people will spend money on, face is surely involved. For example, they will readily spend money on education. A child going to a top school is the pinnacle of face. They will spend money on luxury that others can see. To brag that one owns five apartments gives big face. To win at the gambling table or to brag about gambling winnings, big face. This also makes the Chinese very generous hosts. Chinese people will literally fight for the right to pay the dinner or lunch bill. Even when they don't have much money, they are happy to use it to treat friends and family to a big meal, as they want to be seen as the munificent "big dragon." Quite differently, the Japanese will split the bill so senior people will pay one amount, juniors another amount and guests for free. Americans usually tend to split the bill evenly.

The first time my "face" as an issue came up, I failed miserably. I was walking through a crowded marketplace in Shanghai with my girlfriend at the time. She bumped into a migrant worker. I didn't think anything of it. I watched the whole thing and neither of them was watch-

---

131 Yutang Lin, *My Country and My People*, 192.

ing where they were going. It was no one's fault. To my great surprise, she told me to hit him. I couldn't believe it. I thought she was joking. He stopped walking and glared at me. She said that if I was a real man, I would stand up for her and hit this clearly very poor, overworked, and far-from-home man that was no more at fault than she was. Being China, a crowd started to gather. She kept telling me to "give his face-color a good look" (给他的脸色瞧一瞧), which oddly means to beat someone up. I said that it was not his fault they bumped into each other. She said that didn't matter. I thought the whole thing was ridiculous, so I said, "I apologize, my girlfriend was talking too much and bumped into you." Everybody laughed and we walked home without incident other than her berating me for the next few days.

Far worse was when I told the story to my Chinese classmates. They said I truly didn't understand things (不懂事), which is something like a combination of naïve, clueless, and stupid. I completely lost face. To my classmates, Americans didn't make any sense as we acted as the world's policeman, interfering and making sacrifices for issues that had nothing to do with us. But in this incident where my face and my girlfriend's face was at stake, I did nothing, and I lost further face by apologizing in order to avoid a fight. They gave me an earful for about a month. Initially they called me an egg, white on the outside and yellow on the inside, but after this incident, they said I would never be a Chinese. I said I had to agree.

To my absolute truth-believing eyes, no one was at fault because neither one was watching where they were going. I was raised with the strict rule not to hit girls. If the migrant worker had bumped into my girlfriend on purpose, make no mistake, I would have cracked him across the jaw. But he was not at fault, so again using my belief in absolute right and wrong, my girlfriend wanting to promote violence without cause was wrong in my eyes. I believed that she was wrong for wanting me to hit him without just cause. With her relative view of truth, it was completely different. Regardless of who was right or wrong, I should have taken her side. In fact, she expected me to take her side no matter what.

CHAPTER 21

CHINESE FACE VERSUS JAPANESE HONOR

I discovered there is an enormous difference in the ever-important concept of "face" in China and "honor" in Japan. As I've discussed, in China, it is all about face. Japan does have the concept of face also, but honor is far more important. The difference became very clear to me in a train station in a small town in China.

After living in China for three years, I felt I was starting to understand the culture. My classmates recommended I read Lu Xun, a great writer from around a hundred years ago. His books helped explain China. Lu Xun was a patriot and wanted to make China great again. Originally, he planned to become a doctor. But when studying medicine in Japan, he saw an image of Japanese soldiers in Manchuria cutting off the head of a Chinese person who had allegedly spied for the Russians against the Japanese. He was shocked by the scene of the other Chinese people who had gathered round to watch and were not only not helping their fellow Chinese citizen, but were there to enjoy the spectacle. Lu Xun immediately gave up studying modern medicine, deciding that the Chinese didn't need their health fixed, but instead needed their minds and spirits fixed. So, he decided to become an author.

To pay homage to Lu Xun, I took a train to visit his hometown of Shaoxing in Zhejiang Province. At the station, waiting for the train back to Shanghai, I witnessed an incident that deeply explained one of the key differences between Japan and China: face versus honor. Normally, in a train station in the smaller towns in China, as a six-foot-four redhead, I would be the center of everyone's attention. Folks would come up and ask all sorts of questions or call out *laowai* (foreigner) having fun pointing me out. But this day, no one seemed to notice me. It was an odd feeling. I saw a group gathering on the other side of the station. I walked over to see what was going on.

A Chinese man around forty years old was arguing with a Chinese woman about fifty years old. The man was a farmer and wore simple clothes and had his belongings in a cloth sack as well as a few kitchen appliances in their boxes. He was part of the rising rural class. Although he was poor, he had enough money to travel and buy a few gifts to bring back to relatives. The woman wore a uniform and worked for the station. She was yelling and screaming at him, while he stood motionless trying his best to ignore her. They spoke with a Zhejiang accent, but finally I figured out that he had spit on the floor of the station and she was fining him 10 RMB for this transgression. He was using the Chinese thick-face strategy of just taking the verbal abuse and hoping she would tire and walk away. She kept saying that he was not allowed to spit in the station and would have to pay a fine of 10 RMB. The gathering crowd grew larger and larger.

Getting frustrated, the station agent dropped the hammer. She said that if he didn't pay the fine, she wouldn't let him on his train. This immediately broke his silence. He first tried denying that he had spit in the station. The station agent pointed to the evidence right at his feet. The crowd made an "ohhhhh" sound in unison, seeing the damning evidence. The man tried a different tack, saying the rule wasn't posted so he couldn't have known and that it wasn't his fault and he shouldn't pay any fine because he wouldn't do it again. The station agent pointed to a large sign on the wall that clearly said, "No spitting in the station." The crowd let out another loud "ohhhhh." The man tried to wait it out some more. The station agent wouldn't budge. He looked at his watch. He was running out of time. The crowd was growing excited.

The man finally took out his billfold and counted out not ten, but 20 RMB. The lady said in a quite annoyed voice that the fine was only 10 RMB for spitting. Then, to everyone's surprise, the man looked skyward. I wondered what he was looking at. We all looked up. Then he made a loud guttural sound. He looked the station agent right in the eyes and then spit right in front of her feet. He then held up the two 10 RMB notes and handed them to the agent. The crowd roared. The station agent was humiliated. The man lost 20 RMB instead of the original 10 RMB he was initially so reluctant to give up, but he walked away a hero. He had lost the argument and lost even more money, but he won face. Amazing! He strutted to his train like he was the king of the world while the crowd kept repeating to each other what they had just seen.

The station agent took a broom and dustpan and cleaned up the two "oysters" on the ground. I now understood why she was so insistent that he pay the fine. She was the one who had to clean up. Eventually, the crowd started to disperse. At this point, the attention started to shift toward me, the foreigner in the crowd. The station agent was still fuming and yelled at me, "What are you looking at?" At the time, China still had dual pricing for many tourist sites for foreigners, so I asked her how much it cost for a foreigner to spit in the station. The remaining crowd grew excited again. They kept repeating my question and waited for the answer. The station agent angrily said "Ten RMB, same as for a Chinese." I started to pull out a 10 RMB note—I wanted to gain some face too—but she just walked away.

This spitting story explained the difference between

face and honor. This man broke the rules, was extremely rude to an elder, never apologized, and then dishonored himself by willfully breaking the rules again in order to gain face and to look good in a social situation. The crowd clearly approved of and was impressed by this man's dishonorable efforts to save and even gain face. A Japanese, by contrast, would never dishonor themselves by breaking a rule intentionally for the selfish purpose of flattering one's own appearance.

The Japanese, on the other hand, are far more sensitive to insults to their honor than the Chinese. Honor in Japan reminds me of the great opening line from Edgar Allen Poe's short story *The Casks of Amontillado*. "The thousand injuries of Fortunato I had borne as best I could, but when he ventured upon insult I vowed revenge." The Japanese are willing to die or kill to protect their honor. This is from *Hagakure: The Book of Samurai*: "Victory and defeat are matters of the temporary force of circumstances. *The way of avoiding shame is different. It is simply in death.*"[132] (Emphasis mine.)

To illustrate the point, there is a story in *Hagakure* of a dinner party at a lord's castle. A particular guest at the dinner party, Master Tokuhisa, had an unfortunate-looking face, and when dinner was served—a mudfish salad—the other guests pointed to the mudfish and laughed, saying it looked like Master Tokuhisa. When a rude guest quoted the joke later in the evening, Master

132 Tsunetomo Yamamoto, *Hagakure*, 30.

Tokuhisa pulled out his sword and killed the man. Guests of the party told the lord of the castle, Lord Naoshige, about the incident. It was against the rules to take out a sword inside a lord's castle, and the infraction was punishable by death. The guests recommended that Master Tokuhisa be sentenced to *Seppuku*, or ritual suicide by disembowelment. Lord Naoshige dismissed the punishment, however, saying that it was the rude guest's fault for being killed: a man who silently endures ridicule is a coward, and Master Tokuhisa had no choice but to cut the man down. That he pulled his sword out in the castle to do it made no difference.[133]

It wasn't that Master Tokuhisa was insulted per se. That was incidental in this case. What matters was that as a samurai he should act decisively when insulted. If someone made fun of him for being dumb or serving a bad salad, that doesn't matter. But if he was guilty of cowardice for not responding to the insult, then he was breaking the samurai ethic. To prove he was not a coward, he had to kill the other man. If his lord or his father had made the exact same comment, it would not have mattered. The insult was not the issue. It was the level of the person that insulted him, and therefore, the necessity of defending his honor.

The Chinese, with their emphasis on reasonableness and pragmatism, and the benefits of a long healthy life, take a completely different view. As Benedict highlighted:

133 Tsunetomo Yamamoto, *Hagakure*, 106.

responding with violence to avenge an insult is not honorable behavior in China, like it is in Japan. In fact, the Chinese see it as a sign of a weak or petty personality.[134]

In terms of spirituality, the original religion of China was ancestor worship. Confucianism and Daoism didn't arrive until around the middle of China's existence. Buddhism came much later. Goethe's had a funny quote that "mathematicians are like Frenchmen: whatever you say to them they translate into their own language and forthwith it is something entirely different." This reminds me of the process of Buddhism going into China. The Chinese translated Indian Buddhist texts into Chinese (a very concrete language) and forthwith, Buddhism in China became something new. As Lin pointed out, Buddhism is what Chinese turn to when life isn't working out to plan, similar to the role of religion in other countries.[135] Buddhism is layered onto Chinese culture, but at its core, China is governed by ancestor worship and Confucianism, followed by Daoism. This hierarchy of spiritual influence led Lin to quip that "all Chinese are Confucianists when successful, and Taoists when they are failures."[136]

Japan is very different. At its core is Shintoism. The original Japanese religion is Shinto and it is a nature religion. This is highly unfamiliar to Westerners because we

---

134 Ruth Benedict, *The Chrysanthemum and the Sword*, 147.

135 Yutang Lin, *My Country and My People*, 117.

136 Yutang Lin, *My Country and My People*, 52.

believe in a fall in the garden and a separation between God and nature, while the Japanese see no such separation. This creates an odd belief system where the Japanese deem everything in the world to be sacred. The trees, rocks, wind, and animals all have divine aspects.

In Japan, death is a fact of nature. If one shames oneself, then suicide is an honorable option. If you get fired from your job, fail your college entrance exam, fall too deeply into debt, or feel some other form of great disgrace, then taking your life is a valid option to restore your honor.

To fail at something is dishonorable to the Japanese. The Chinese may consider it a loss of face depending on the circumstances, but losing face is only embarrassing and not fatal. The Chinese do not worry about the dishonor of failure. Such is life and they are able to bounce back. In fact, part of the Chinese genius is finding success in failure. As has been pointed out many times, the Chinese word for "opportunity" (机会) is a combination of the characters *crisis* (机) and *opportunity* (会). (Without the first character, the meaning of the second character by itself would not be clear.)

The Japanese attitude toward failure is completely different. As Campbell noted: the samurai ethic of honor and loyalty apply across all levels of Japanese society.[137] Any Japanese that feels they have dishonored themselves will feel it is no sin and, actually along with the samurai

---

137 Joseph Campbell, *Sake & Satori*, 293.

ethic, that it is a virtue to take their own life to restore their honor. Naturally, the major outcome of this is that the Chinese are great risk takers because failure is no big deal, whereas the Japanese fear risk and fear failure because the consequences of this loss of honor can be fatal.

The differences in honor and face also show up in Japanese and Chinese etiquette around food. It has always been interesting to me that the Japanese will always do their utmost to eat every morsel of food that is served, while at a Chinese meal with a guest and/or host, copious amounts of food will remain uneaten. To the Japanese, not only is the food sacred, but so is all of the effort that went into bringing the food to their table. Before they eat, the Japanese have a ritual of saying (いただきます)—*itadakimasu*, which means "I receive." It is an expression of gratitude to the animals or vegetables that have given their life for this meal, to the farmers who toiled to produce this food, and to the cook who prepared this food. The Japanese hate waste. They call it *mottainai* and that is the worst of all transgressions. It shows a lack of proper seriousness and a lack of gratitude and sincerity. So, the Japanese will often use their chopsticks to pick out even the last grain of rice sticking to their bowl.

The attitude in China is quite different because of face. When the Chinese eat, there is no prayer beforehand. They just say *kai-fan*, "let's eat." If there is a guest for dinner or if they are eating out and someone is the host, the Chinese will always order too much food, to create leftovers. The reason is that if everyone ate all the food, it would indicate people were still hungry, and that the host was not generous enough. This would be a major loss of face for the host.

Therefore, in Japan it is bad manners to not eat all the food served, while in China it is bad manners to finish all of the food served. (Of course, if the Chinese were eating at home with just family, face would not be an issue, so they would not intentionally prepare extra food and would finish everything served.)

The major insult and easiest way to lose face in China is to be seen as (小气), *xiaoqi*, or having little *qi*. It means cheap, but not just with money. It also implies not having a generous personality and lacking in grace. In Japan, the main insult would be to say someone is *hen* or "strange" and next would be to say someone is not *majime* or "serious." For better or for worse, I am very *xiaoqi* (小气). My girlfriend in China would often get embarrassed at my cheapness. She hated the loss of face from telling her friends that I took her out to dinner, but it was only to McDonalds or having to show me off in the shabby clothes I always wore. So she always called me (铁公鸡)— *tiegongji*. It means "the iron rooster." The word for *penny* in Chinese is the same as for a *feather*, so it implies it is as difficult to get a penny out of me as it would be to pluck a feather off of an iron rooster.

I did have a girlfriend in China, but I was not at all

popular with the Chinese girls. I didn't realize until many years later that it was because I was a face-losing boy-friend. One time, I was standing in the lobby of a hotel in Beijing with my Austrian friend Hans. There were three attractive young Chinese ladies from the same industry chatting with us. I noticed that whenever I talked, they would make a face like something smelled bad, but when Hans spoke they would get all googly-eyed and tilt their heads and sigh. It struck me because the week before, Hans and I were in Japan and the exact opposite situation occurred. The Japanese young ladies we were talking to would frown when Hans spoke and smile and giggle whenever I was talking. I finally realized the difference. The preference in China is for men to be big and strong, with an outgoing personality, well dressed, and generous. Hans is a manly man—gregarious and always stylishly attired. The Chinese ladies loved him. Having a *xiaoqi/cheapskate* boyfriend (like me) in China would cause one to constantly lose face.

Japan is the opposite. They like skinny guys (because they seem more gentle), introverts (because Japan is a nonconfrontational society), and someone thrifty (because an economical man is more reliable). Funnily enough, American woman don't generally like skinny, introverted, cheap guys either. Therefore, it is probably no surprise that I ended up marrying a Japanese woman.

SECTION 3

AMERICAN THINKING

CHAPTER 22

THE US AND THE BELIEF IN ABSOLUTE TRUTH

The quintessential aspect of Western culture is the belief in absolute truths. Westerners look to fixed stars to guide their way through life. The Judeo-Christian belief system is based upon the idea of a single moment of creation. *God said let there be light. On the seventh day he rested.* Time has flowed forward linearly to today from that point and will flow forward linearly until the end of days. Western science says that time started with the big bang 13.8 billion years ago and that the sun at the center of our solar system came into existence 4.5 billion years ago. Time has flowed forward in a linear fashion from those events until today.

In both cases, there is a fixed starting point from which everything can be measured. Everything is absolute. Right and wrong, good and bad, truth and falsehoods are all determinable factors. In a linear-time universe, every person, every animal, every plant is unique. I find this orientation to time to be the biggest difference between the East and West.

The Eastern view of time is that it is circular. Universes are created from big bangs and big compressions or from Brahma opening and closing his eyes. Worlds are infinite. Everything has already occurred before and will occur again. With time moving in a circle, there are no fixed points from which to measure absolute truths. Everything is dynamic. In Japan, the year number resets to one every time they get a new emperor.

I want to delve into this subject because I feel many Westerners are unfamiliar with the philosophy of circular time. This difference in belief in linear versus circular time leads to two major cultural differences between the East and West.

The first is centered on the role of the individual. The second involves the conception of truth.

In an infinitely repeating world, there is nothing unique about me. My ego only clouds my perception of the eternal. I am here to play a role. This is completely at odds with the Western conception that we are all unique snowflakes and individuality is our defining characteristic. The attitude toward truth is also quite different in the East and in the West. With absolute truths in a linear-time framework, if my belief is correct, then your belief, by definition, must be wrong. In a circular-time framework, everything is relative, which means we may both be right. Truth would be dependent upon our perspectives.

THE ROLE OF THE INDIVIDUAL

In a circular-time universe where everything is relative, even god became an impersonal concept. As Campbell highlighted, when people in the Bronze Age discovered that the planets move in set patterns through the fixed stars, it completely changed their view of the universe. Instead of a personal tribal god, the movement of the sun, moon, and planets were all mathematically determined and controlled by an impersonal god. In an impersonal cosmic order, the role of the gods is reduced to mere functionaries.[138]

Westerners believe in a personal relationship with a personal God. This is completely different in the East, where the individual is not unique and god is impersonal. As Campbell explains, Westerners pray to their God and develop a personal relationship. In the East, the universe is seen as divine and we are part of that universe, so people look for that divinity within themselves and others. In the Western tradition, one would get burned at the stake as a heretic for making such claims.[139] [140]

In the West, we believe that God and man are sepa-

---

138 Joseph Campbell, *Myths of Light: Eastern Metaphors of the Eternal*, 4.

139 Joseph Campbell, *Myths of Light: Eastern Metaphors of the Eternal*, 7.

140 Joseph Campbell, *Myths of Light: Eastern Metaphors of the Eternal*, 71.

rate. I grew up believing that God was an older, bearded gentleman sitting in the clouds watching over us with strict rules. The Asian belief is vastly different. In the East, god is seen as being beyond the comprehension of our mortal minds. We can have symbols, but those are just simplifications our minds can understand and that god is not those symbols, but the energy behind those symbols. I was raised to believe God created the universe. In the East, god *is* the universe, and we are part of that universe. Divinity is within us. It can be seen when Indians put their hands together in greeting and say *"Namaste"* or when Japanese bow to each other. These actions are recognition of the divinity in the other. We are all part of a greater whole. This belief system forms the basis of the group orientation in the East.

Campbell describes it this way: "The you that you think you are is not it and the you that you can't even think about *is* it. This paradox, this absurdity, is the essential mystery of the East."[141] This conception of self is completely at odds with the Western belief in our individuality, the belief in a personal God and our relationship. The Eastern belief is that I need to get past my ego and forget myself, and by doing so, I can recognize god in myself, in others, and in everything.

There is a popular story in India of a man saying to Buddha, "I want happiness." Buddha's response was to get rid of "I" that was ego, then get rid of "want" that was

141 Joseph Campbell, *Myths of Light: Eastern Metaphors of the Eternal*, 7.

desire, and then there will only remain happiness. "'All is impermanent. All is without a self.' This is the basic meditation of Buddhism."[142]

Birthdays are an example that always stood out for me. In the West, a birthday is the ultimate celebration of the individual. The birthday girl or boy invites their friends over for a party, they receive gifts and sit at the head of the table with a cake in their honor and everyone sings for them. This is their special day. In traditional Japan or China, however, there is no birthday party or celebration. In the US, when asked our age, we say how old we are right now. If my birthday is in June, but it is still March and I am forty-nine turning fifty that year, I would say I was forty-nine years old. In Japan, *everybody* is a year older on January 1. In China, *everyone* is a year older with the Chinese New Year. If you asked my age, and I were Japanese or Chinese, I would say my age is fifty because I turn fifty sometime that year. (In fact, I would say fifty-one, because they add the almost full year in the womb.) Therefore, New Year's takes on a much deeper meaning in the East. The flip side is that, traditionally, individuals' birthdays were basically non-events.

Wedding anniversaries are equally de-emphasized relative to the West. This difference struck me most in Japan. Couples in Japan would barely recognize, much less celebrate, milestones such as a thirtieth, or fortieth, or even fiftieth wedding anniversary. Companies, on

142 Joseph Campbell, *Myths of Light: Eastern Metaphors of the Eternal*, 129.

the other hand, which represent the group and not the individual, will make a big deal out of their fortieth or fiftieth year of existence and will pay special dividends those years in commemoration.

There is the philosophy of the *Tao* or "the way" in China and Japan. The Tao represents the proper motion of nature and the universe. The goal, therefore, is to live one's life in accordance with "the way." To act with the universe and not against it is the goal. Selfish desires go against "the way" and this philosophy has a noble focus on the group, but at the same time, does not allow for the development of the individual.[143] The concept of "ego" in this philosophy is seen in a negative light, and in fact, there is no native Japanese word for ego. It is pronounced "eh-go" and is a foreign-borrowed word.

The de-emphasis on the individual can be seen in the difference in names. In China and Japan, the last name comes first. In the West, we tend to call each other by our first names. That rarely happens in the East. In Japan, someone is usually called by their title or position. At home, the "mother" is called "mother" by everyone, and not just the children. The husband or grandparents would also call her mother. It is the same for the father. At work, the group head would be called "Group Head" and the president would be called "President." Names would only be used if two people had similar titles. Japanese names are usually made up of four characters, but

---

143 Joseph Campbell, *Myths of Light: Eastern Metaphors of the Eternal*, 63.

sometimes more or less. The first two characters normally represent the last name. If not addressing someone by their title, the next most common choice would be to call them by their last name, followed by *san*. So, Mr. Tanaka would be Tanaka-san. Ms. Watanabe would be Watanabe-san. First names would be used rarely and in only very familiar cases.

In China, I rarely heard anyone called by their first name. Chinese names are usually made up of three characters. The first character is the family name. The next two characters are the given name. For example, Xi Jinping's family name is Xi (to study) and his given name is Jinping (moving toward peace). For my Chinese friends, I would almost always call them by their full names. If they had a title, it would usually be their last name followed by their title. So, professor Hong would be "Hong Teacher." Another simplification is to put the honorific "old" in front of their last name. I would call my friend Cheng Jun, "*Lao* Cheng" or "old Cheng." If there was a younger Cheng, I would call them "little Cheng." The key point is that in the West, where the individual is emphasized, we call each other by our first names, which are unique to us. In Japan and China, you call people by their last names, which represent their families, and the individual name is greatly de-emphasized.

There is a great Zen story about a student who works for many years at meditation and feels he has finally found enlightenment. He has extinguished his ego. He writes a poem about it describing how the four winds (east, west, north, and south) cannot move him. His teacher sees the poem and writes one word on the bottom. "Fart." The student sees this and is furious. He rides across the river to confront his teacher about this disrespectful remark. When the student knocks at the teacher's door, he is angry, but the teacher just calmly replies, "The four winds couldn't move you, but one little word brought you all the way across the river." The student immediately bowed to his teacher and forthwith found enlightenment. The lesson is that while you may have overcome your prime ego, the spiritual ego also needs overcoming.

In circular time, this spring is the same as next spring, this summer the same as last or next summer. They are all springs or summers. This applies to individuals also. I have existed infinite times before and will do so again in the future. So, my role in the East is not to be a unique individual. My responsibility is to play my role in society, however that has been determined, and to do so in a decent way. Campbell points out that "in Sanskrit there is no word that means individual."[144] As an American, raised to believe I am as unique as a snowflake and that a personal God has placed me here to fulfill a specific purpose, I found it almost inconceivable that this ancient Indian language would so ignore the concept of individuality as to not even have a word for it.

144 Joseph Campbell, *Myths of Light: Eastern Metaphors of the Eternal*, 103.

Joseph Campbell describes fulfilling one's life duties well as the Buddhist path. All of life then becomes sacred and one's church and sanctuary. One does not then need to be anxious or worried about their salvation. It is found in living their life well and fulfilling their duties in a self-less and nonegotistical way.[145]

As Campbell further explains, in the East, you do not think about who you are as an individual, but rather what your role is in society. The goal of education then is to teach you what your role is and how best to act while in that role. Westerners naturally get surprised by the level of submissiveness of Eastern students, while Easterners get equally surprised by independent-minded Western students and their lack of respect for the authority of the teacher.[146]

In the East, a teacher garners the absolute respect of their students simply by being in the role of teacher. Students never ask questions and never ever question the teacher's authority. Whatever the teacher says is gospel truth, even if the students disagree with what the teacher is saying. In the West, we respect a teacher's knowledge and abilities, but we do not respect them if we think they don't understand their subject, or if what they are teaching is incorrect. This is not the case in the East.

I learned this lesson the hard way. As an economics student in China, we learned modern Western macro and

---

145 Joseph Campbell, *Myths of Light: Eastern Metaphors of the Eternal*, 130.

146 Joseph Campbell, *Myths of Light: Eastern Metaphors of the Eternal*, 60–61.

micro economics. (Incidentally, from bootlegged copies of MIT textbooks.) At the same time, we also took courses on socialist-planned economics. The Chinese felt there was no problem with the contradiction of studying both at the same time.

The problem with the planned economics class was that much of it didn't make sense because it was often logically incorrect and a total disaster in practice. It ignored the laws of economics as well as of human nature. The teacher was over eighty years old and a fervent communist, who fully believed in planned economics. He would talk about the weakness of Western economics in their profit maximizing principle, whereas planned economics was much better because their principle was maximizing profits while simultaneously minimizing costs. This didn't make any logical sense, so I had to raise my hand and ask, "What about the case where your marginal profits rise from an increase in costs? We raise costs, but profits rise more."

The teacher never answered my question because planned economics doesn't account for the concept of spending a little more money to make your product better, or improve distribution, or advertising, etc., which leads to an even bigger rise in profits. He was furious, not only because I had made him look unknowledgeable, but even worse, I had questioned his authority.

This sense of duty or role that must be played in the East is not negotiable. The student does not need to develop their own opinions. In traditional Eastern thinking, one must submit to their role. This is very different from our Western concept of pursuing what we are passionate about. Yoga of action is to do your duty impersonally with no involvement of your ego or thought of personal gain. This is a severe discipline for a Westerner to follow. Joseph Campbell notes that *"in the Orient a person's duty is dictated to him by his society, that is to say, the society imprints on the individual a system of duties that he is expected to render without criticism, whatever they may be."*[147] (Emphasis mine)

The *tanshinfunin* (単身赴任—single-person-post-assignment) phenomena in Japan shocked me when I first learned about it. Japanese men are often sent on overseas posts for three to five years while their wife and kids stay back in Japan. This worker is called tanshinfunin. This is common in Japanese companies with international operations (there are domestic assignments also). Of course, the man's individual desire is to be with his family. But group responsibility comes first, so the company takes first priority and he is sent overseas alone. The wife would equally like to be with her husband, but her first responsibility is to her neighborhood. She is equally as invested in her neighbors and local school as her husband would be to his job. Her top priorities are her debts and obligations to her neighborhood and not to her husband. Consequently, they live separately while

---

147 Joseph Campbell, *Myths of Light: Eastern Metaphors of the Eternal*, 38-39.

he is overseas. In the East, group responsibilities trump individual wishes.

Lin explains how this concept manifests in China, with the individual subjugated to their role in society as defined by the five key relationships of Confucianism. In China, the family system trumps the importance of the individual and the individual can only be understood through their relationships with those around them. In such an environment, patience is a key virtue when one must always juggle the concerns of a large number of people.[148]

A person's last name or official title tells them their place in society, what their responsibilities are, and how they are expected to behave. When everyone properly knows their place and plays their role, social order is achieved in a Confucian society.[149]

"In short," Lin writes, "the family system is the negation of individualism itself, and it holds a man back, as the reins of the jockey hold back the dashing Arabian horse."[150]

This is all very different from our Western ideals. In Maslow's hierarchy of needs, after safety and shelter, etc., have been satisfied, the top need is self-actualization. Joseph Campbell illustrates the difference: In the West, we believe in the uniqueness of the individual. The

148 Yutang Lin, *My Country and My People*, 45.

149 Yutang Lin, *My Country and My People*, 170.

150 Yutang Lin, *My Country and My People*, 169.

hero we worship in the West is one specific person at one specific point in time. In the East, the hero reincarnates and with reincarnation, any single individual gets de-emphasized to the point of unimportance.[151]

The lesson here is that interacting with Westerners is fundamentally different from interacting with those from the East. With someone from the West, the key is to learn about the individual; their background, interests, motivations, limitations, etc., that define their identity. When interacting with a Chinese or Japanese person, the key is to find out which group they belong to, their role in the group, what the group wants from them, and their place in the group's hierarchy.

In the West, we are expected to take responsibility for our decisions. You decide what you want and live with the consequences. The tradition in the East was what you ate, or wore, or even married was decided for you. There was no development of the individual ego in this environment. Tradition guided you through life.[152]

Richard Nesbitt, in his book *The Geography of Thought*, articulated the difference well: "Westerners are the protagonists of their autobiographical novels; Asians are merely cast members in movies touching on their experience."[153]

As Nakamura pointed out, paradoxically, one must

151 Joseph Campbell, *Myths of Light: Eastern Metaphors of the Eternal*, 61.

152 Joseph Campbell, *Myths of Light: Eastern Metaphors of the Eternal*, 110.

153 Richard E. Nisbett, *The Geography of Thought* (New York: The Free Press, 2003), 87.

not take their life personally. "Presumably, according to the worldview of the Indian people, the universe of world and the social order remain eternal; on the other side, personal life is nothing but one of a succession of lives existing repeatedly in limitless time, and, therefore, finally becomes meaningless."[154] "While the Japanese are keenly conscious of their membership in their small, closed nexus, *they are hardly fully aware of themselves as individuals, or as social beings, to the extent the Western peoples are.*"[155] (Emphasis mine)

Campbell retells a great Japanese story that illustrates this point in a way I found helpful: A samurai hunted down the man that killed his master. The samurai pulled out his sword, but just before he killed the man to earn his revenge, the man spit in the samurai's face. The samurai had no choice but to sheath his sword and walk away.[156]

If the samurai killed the man as an act of duty, that is not a crime. But if he killed him for personal anger for spitting in his face, then it would have been murder. It would have gone against the way of the universe. Similarly, in the Eastern conception, we must go through life doing our duty for society without letting our personal emotions and individual desires interfere with our fulfilling those duties properly.

Benedict explains a similar logic, but with regard to

---

154 Hajime Nakamura, *Ways of Thinking of Eastern Peoples*, 81.

155 Hajime Nakamura, *Ways of Thinking of Eastern Peoples*, 415.

156 Joseph Campbell, *Myths of Light: Eastern Metaphors of the Eternal*, 136.

avenging one's name in Japan as opposed to avenging one's lord. In Japan, a proper duty-driven act of revenge is not a crime. In fact, it is seen as good because it undoes the bad from the original misdeed.[157]

---

157 Ruth Benedict, *The Chrysanthemum and the Sword*, 146.

CHAPTER 23

———

ALL OR NOTHING IN TRUTH, TRADE, HEALTH, AND LAW

嘘も方便—*uso mo hoben*: This is a Japanese phrase that means "lies are just another dialect of language." It is a justification. When it is convenient, you would use a lie. The implication is that it is not a matter of right and wrong, but rather of social necessity.

One aspect of the belief in absolute truth is that once truth has been discovered, other views are shut out. The belief in a Judeo-Christian God implies that the belief in any other God is sacrilegious. Other people that do not believe in the Judeo-Christian God would be lost or in exile.

What is not generally understood about the East is that it is possible to believe in their God or gods, but also have room for other belief systems too. As van Wolferen highlighted: "The occidental intellectual and moral traditions are so deeply rooted in assumptions of the universal validity of certain beliefs that the possibility of a culture without such assumptions is hardly ever contemplated."[158] In other words, the Eastern lack of belief in universal truth is generally not well understood in the West.

The Eastern belief is that the absolute truth underlying the universe is beyond the capability of a mortal human mind to comprehend. All that we can understand is the world that we perceive through our limited human senses. Truth is simply unknowable to humans. As Campbell explains: "The fundamental thought in the Oriental philosophical world is that the mysterious, ultimate truth, that which you seek to know, is absolutely beyond all definition." In the East, all human descriptions or thoughts or symbols will be limited, by definition, to the level of human understanding. Infinite truth will be beyond the scope of this human thought. It transcends the mortal sphere.[159]

Van Wolferen does an excellent job describing this different view of truth in Japan. Modern Asian societies may be less accustomed to the concept of contradictions or flexible truths versus traditional Asian societies, but even still, relative to other Asian societies, Japan today displays

---

158 Karel van Wolferen, *The Enigma of Japanese Power*, 10.

159 Joseph Campbell, *Myths of Light: Eastern Metaphors of the Eternal*, 6.

the most flexibility with regards to the truth. In the West, reality is seen as fixed and absolute and not malleable to manipulation. It is objective and not subjective. Western thinking often reminds us not to deceive ourselves and to deal in reality and not fantasy. Westerners seek truth and not contradictions and this is the foundation of our logic, mathematics, and sciences.[160]

Van Wolferen explains that this flexible view of truth combines with another factor in determining the Japanese view of the world, and that factor is "the near absence of any idea that there can be truths, rules, principles, or morals that always apply, no matter what the circumstances."[161]

Anyone who lives in Japan for a while learns the words *tatemae* and *honne*. *Tatemae* is what you say to maintain harmony and not offend anyone or make anyone look bad. It is the public truth. *Honne* is the real truth. Let me give an example. Say you're in Japan and you are invited to a dinner party where the host has a diametrically-opposed view from your own. If the host asked about a specific issue, you would respond with *tatemae* that you supported their view or even that you strongly supported that view. When you go home, however, you would go back to the *honne* view that represents how you really feel. Someone that sticks to *tatemae* publicly is not considered a liar or someone who has done something bad; the contradiction

---

160 Karel van Wolferen, *The Enigma of Japanese Power*, 8.

161 Karel van Wolferen, *The Enigma of Japanese Power*, 9.

is acceptable. Similarly if a Japanese person gets drunk, then it is fair game (under the right circumstances) to spit out the truth or "vomit out the *honne*" (本音を吐く). This is not at all held against you. But the next day in the office, you would need to go back to the *tatemae* view.

As van Wolferen explains, the Japanese accept these seemingly contradictory experiences as equally necessary, and it allows them to navigate between emotional honesty and public persona easily, without fear of seeming dishonest. Westerners, with their view of absolute truth, require consistency in all interactions, where the Japanese are content being flexible with the specific conditions at hand. The Japanese have a word for people who stubbornly stick to this kind of consistent, narrow logic: they are *rikutsupoi* (理屈ぽい), "reason-freaks."[162][163]

Americans believe in absolute truths; in China and Japan it is always contextual. In the West, we would consider someone that said one thing publicly and the opposite privately as a two-faced liar. We believe in the West that something is true or false and that debates end with someone being right and someone being wrong. In the East, there is a much larger grey area.

The disadvantage for the US belief in absolutes is that if someone disagrees with a Westerner, then as a matter of principle, that person must be wrong. Westerners have

162 Karel van Wolferen, *The Enigma of Japanese Power*, 235.

163 Christie W. Kiefer, "The *danchi zoku* and the Evolution of Metropolitan Mind," in *Japan: The Paradox of Progress*, Ed. Lewis Austin (New Haven, Conn.: Yale University Press, 1976), 281.

fixed beliefs that democracy, capitalism, even God are absolutes and are always and everywhere correct. Since our system is the best, it is good to impose it on other cultures even if they have different histories and circumstances. The US invasion of Iraq was a disastrous example of this logic.

One of the big advantages of believing in absolute truths is that this is consistent with finding win-win outcomes. In the West, we can happily pursue win-win solutions, because we believe they are possible.

In contrast, the Chinese have relative winners and relative losers, as Lucian Pye explains in *Chinese Negotiating Style*.[164] Face plays a role in Chinese negotiations, and this makes each deal a zero-sum game. Even if the outcome of a deal benefits both parties, the Chinese measure their success on the relative benefits they will receive versus the other party, and this comparison determines who has won and who has lost. The deal, then, is not just an exchange between two parties, but a matter of prestige and face. While an American may feel they've "won" when they arrive at terms that benefit them, a Chinese negotiator only feels they've "won" if their terms are better than what the other party gets.

The US had free trade agreements such as NAFTA because it benefited both sides absolutely although not equally. This does not work in a relative thinking framework. If you benefit and I benefit, but you benefit more,

---

164 Lucian W. Pye, *Chinese Negotiating Style—Commercial Approaches and Cultural Principles*, 81.

then I lose relatively. A free trade agreement between China and Japan is almost unthinkable because even if it helped China, there is no way China would want to help Japan more and vice versa.

When negotiations are only between relative truth believing East Asian countries, no agreement can be reached because one country will always be benefiting less than the other and losing in relative terms. But when China entered the World Trade Organization, they were able to take huge advantage of the US desire for a win-win deal. They benefit massively from the WTO deal, while the US benefits much less. Due to the belief in absolute truth, America agreed to these unfair terms because the US was still better off even though China benefited much more.

In a free trade negotiation, even though the overall pie would be larger, the Chinese would only view the gain relative to Japan or Korea as positive and not their own absolute benefit. This relative mindset makes them all extremely mercantilist. They all have very large trade surpluses with the world and this will not change. They wouldn't enter into foreign trade if they were the trade deficit countries. The history behind the awful Opium Wars was that Europe had a large trade deficit with China and large quantities of European silver flowed into China in exchange for China's trade goods. China was unwilling to address this problem because all they cared about was maintaining their large trade surplus. So, the British East

India Company started selling large quantities of opium in China to reverse this flow of silver and redress this large trade deficit.

ABSOLUTE TRUTH AND US SOCIETY

"Freedom consists not in doing what we like, but in having the right to do what we ought."

—POPE JOHN PAUL II

I find the concept of freedom to be one of the defining traits of American society. This emphasis on freedom is a major difference between absolute truth-believing Americans and the relative truth-believing East. Many of the original immigrants to America were pursuing freedom of religion or freedom from oppressive government. Love of freedom is in the American DNA. As Patrick Henry said, "Give me liberty, or give me death!" Americans prize, above all else, their freedom of speech, freedom of religion, freedom of assembly, and freedom of the press. The Japanese and Chinese take very different views toward freedom.

Traditionally, Japanese people had very few freedoms. Their concept of personal freedom really came with the constitution imposed by McArthur after WWII. Japanese society is full of written and tacit rules, and the basic understanding is that you can do what you want as long as it conforms within this narrow set of guidelines. People are basically subjects of the state and their purpose is to fulfill their role within the smaller and larger groups to which they belong. There was no concept of freedom of speech or freedom of religion. The state, through the school system and the media, tells you what to think and what to believe. As literal thinkers, the Japanese quite obediently and quite literally follow the laws of the land. Americans want freedom from arbitrary or despotic government or control. Since the Japanese imperial family was divinely descended, arbitrary or despotic rule was inconceivable, so they fundamentally never even thought to question the rules.

The Chinese are different. China is an overpopulated country with a belief in relative truth and the family as the only reliable institution. Every family or clan needs to look out for themselves, so unlike the literal-minded, rule-following Japanese, the Chinese are constantly looking for a way around rules to gain an advantage. Therefore, China requires strict rules and strict enforcement. For example, Chinese people do not even have freedom of choosing where they live. They have a Hukou system, which is a household registration system that strictly defines which city or village you are allowed to live in. Even the super citizen Chinese Communist Party members have no freedom to choose where they live.

For 5,000 years, the ruling class in China determined that freedom was not an absolute good. In fact, freedom for individuals would lead to a bad outcome for society more broadly. So, they saw lack of freedom as important for maintaining the stability and cohesion of the country. There is no tradition of freedom of religion, or freedom of speech, or freedom of assembly in China. When I ask Chinese about this, they often say that as kids their parents were so focused on their education and that they had to study from 7 a.m. to midnight every day. Freedom was never a consideration and not something they ever even conceived of. Obedience was the defining characteristic of their childhood.

What is interesting is that when China was finally opened to the West in the late nineteenth century and early twentieth century, the first freedom they fought for was freedom of marriage. Up until that point, all marriages were decided by the parents, with some couples being engaged while they were still both in the womb! The modern Chinese wanted the freedom to choose their own marriage partners.

In today's China, I would say the most important freedom people want is the freedom to make money and the freedom to deposit that money in the bank or invest it without fear of the government taking it. People want the freedom of ownership so that they have proper property rights when they put their life savings into buying an apartment. As long as they have freedom of money, Chinese are (for the most part) fine without freedom of religion, freedom of speech, or freedom of assembly. Security and order are far more important values given

China's chaotic history and freedom as a concept is deemed as far less important.

Along with freedom, another important ideal in the US is that all people are created equal. This is the basis for our democracy. One person, one vote. Relative truth societies do not see it this way and, by contrast, are extremely hierarchical. In China, every city is tiered and everyone knows if they are from a tier one city like Beijing or Shanghai, or a tier two city (mostly provincial capitals), or a tier three city, or even tier four, five, or six. People are also tiered by their position, occupation, wealth, education level, and age. In Japan, the exchange of business cards is a must, because without seeing the other person's title, it's simply not possible to know which level of polite language one must use.

This extreme emphasis on hierarchy is the reason that democracy is not a natural fit in Asia and is one reason why Chinese democracy is no more likely than American communism.

The American belief in absolute truth also leads to a tendency toward absolutism in American thinking. Americans tend to believe that something is right or wrong. It is or it isn't. Issues are black or white, without any grey area in between.

American linear logic can be too absolutist, making our punishment of criminals sometimes too legalistic. On the one hand, we have a large number of rules in place to protect the rights of criminals. This can allow criminals to sometimes get away with crimes because they are able to game the system. Asian countries are far more worried about society as a whole and not the rights of criminals. On the other hand, sometimes the US can follow the rules too strictly and overly penalize criminals. With the three strikes law in California, there were cases of people going to jail for life for stealing a few pieces of bread or other similar minor and nonviolent offenses.[165] To a believer in relative truth, sending someone to jail for life for stealing some food when they were hungry would ignore context and simply lack common sense.

Another example is that for many decades, the US government told us, with a blanket statement, that fat was bad. Despite millions of years of eating fat as a species, government nutrition recommendations determined that fat was bad for us. Cholesterol does tend to be high in people with heart disease; therefore, using linear logic, cholesterol must be bad for us. They recommended we eat margarine instead of butter because it has no cholesterol. Never mind that natural fat is a crucial part of the human diet, while trans fat is about the worst thing in the world for us.

Americans went low-fat in their diet at the government's recommendation and subsequently got fatter and fatter. The solution was very simple, but still con-

---

165 Associated Press, "LA Judge Orders Release of Man Sentenced to 25 Years-to-Life for Stealing Food from Church," *Fox News*, August 16, 2010, https://www.foxnews.com/us/la-judge-orders-release-of-man-sentenced-to-25-years-to-life-for-stealing-food-from-church/.

fuses linear-thinking Americans. Good fat is good for you and bad fat is bad for you. Tell that to a Chinese or Japanese and their common-sense thinking would immediately understand. They would even wonder why you bothered to say something so obvious. Tell an absolute truth-believing and linear-thinking American that good fat is good for you and bad fat is bad for you and they will get immediately confused. Their general response is "I thought fat was bad for you." This mistaken simple linear logic has done untold damage to US citizens.

Chinese thinking is different. The essence of Chinese thinking is *zhongyong* (中庸) or "the middle way". The Chinese focus is on moderation and no matter what you are talking about, the dosage makes the poison. Even water in excess can kill a person. The Chinese would never view fat as good or bad. It would depend on the type of fat and the amount. Their philosophy is all things in moderation and even something bad for you could be OK if the dosage were small enough.

Gluten sensitivity is another example. Western medicine recognizes that 1 percent to 2 percent of the population suffers from Celiac disease and is allergic to gluten, the protein found in wheat. It is seen as an either/or situation. One is extremely allergic to wheat or not at all. Common sense would indicate that we've been eating cultivated wheat for less than 1 percent of our existence as a species; therefore, some people are better adapted to eating wheat and some less. There are many shades of grey between perfectly gluten-tolerant people and those with full-blown Celiac disease. Some people are allergic to wheat, some have an intolerance, and some only a sensitivity. But common sense is not given a fair hearing by absolute-truth-believing American thinking, which tends to be all or nothing.

Another current belief in America is that that the sun is bad for you. If you go in the sun, you must have sunscreen on to prevent skin cancer. In fact, we evolved over millions of years with direct sun exposure. Our bodies need sunlight to produce vitamin D, among hundreds of other functions. The best method is the middle path. Too much sun exposure can lead to skin cancer, which is certainly bad. Too little sun exposure is also unnatural and not healthy. Moderate sun exposure is ideal, but Americans struggle with that concept given our all-or-nothing outlook.

Another medical example is that Americans can't find any direct use for tonsils, so the all-or-nothing conclusion is to remove them if there are any issues. The Chinese view tonsils as part of the whole. We may not know their specific function, but they help provide balance to the entire body. The Chinese can't explain scientifically why acupuncture works, they just know that it works from experience and trial and error. The goal of acupuncture is rebalancing the whole and allowing the body's own healing mechanisms to function optimally. Even if we can't understand scientifically, there may be functions served by the tonsils beyond our current understanding.

Americans tend to also have an all or nothing approach to laws. Something is legal or it is illegal. This is in stark contrast to the incremental approach of the relative-truth-believing Chinese. The Chinese pursue new policies incrementally because common sense says that there will be unexpected consequences from any change. Linear thinkers don't account for unexpected consequences. We look at the causes and effects that we can understand. Chinese officials know that any new rule will bring about many new creative ways to get around that rule. Therefore, they start off small and try the new rule out in a few select cities, see how people attempt to get around the rule or take advantage of it, and then course correct. Americans tend to change laws in an all-or-nothing manner.

The case of decriminalizing marijuana in the US is interesting because it is one instance where the US is following the incremental Chinese model and not the all-or-nothing US model. The states can legalize marijuana even if it remains illegal under federal law. Therefore, states like Colorado and Oregon were early in decriminalizing marijuana, and other states and the federal government were able to study the impact on those states. With this incremental rollout, Americans were able to assess how much revenue these states could raise, if the crime rates went up or down, what unexpected impacts there were, etc. This is the way relative-truth-believing and lateral-thinking China rolls out almost all of their new policies. They will start with one or two cities and then expand and adjust according to what they learn along the way.

A BALANCE BETWEEN ABSTRACT AND LITERAL THINKING

My conclusion is that American thinking, in general, is neither dominated by literal nor abstract reasoning, but is instead rather balanced somewhere in the middle. It might seem misinformed to say that Westerners do not think literally given that Western culture is rooted in the belief that Jesus was born of a virgin, died and was resurrected, and physically ascended into heaven.

Many Westerners continue to believe God literally created the universe about 4,000 years ago. Even though these are mythological motifs that occur repeatedly throughout various cultures, the Western tradition is to believe these as facts. This shows that Westerners do sometimes engage in literal thinking. Conversely, in the Indian tradition, Buddha was born from his mother's side and was able to walk and talk right after birth, but Buddhists generally understand these amazing occurrences symbolically and not factually.

On the other hand, Americans are certainly capable of abstract thought. Most of the inventions that make up modern life came out of the US or Europe. The light bulb, the telephone, the airplane, air-conditioning, refrigerators, the radio, television, cars, computers, the internet, etc., were mostly from America (and some from Europe). New inventions require creativity, which requires abstract thinking.

CHAPTER 24

———

AMERICAN LINEAR THINKING

I like these definitions of linear and lateral thinking:

- **Linear thinking:** A way of thinking that moves from subject to object, where ideas are developed building upon each other sequentially.
- **Lateral thinking:** A way of thinking that moves from subject to subject and across subjects establishing context to find solutions considering various points of view.

Linear logic works. It underlies scientific thinking. It is a straight progression from observation to hypothesis to experimentation to conclusions. This thinking underlies the fantastic progress Western society made relative to the rest of the world from the industrial revolution onward. This linear style of logic has been proven to foster the kind of development the West is noted for generating. We are rightly proud of our scientific achievements and the social, political, and economic systems we have developed.

A few examples contrasting linear, lateral, and intuitive reasoning should be helpful in understanding American linear logic.

If a linear thinker was asked to make a car go faster, their straightforward solution would be to make the engine bigger. The outcome of this thinking can be seen in American muscle cars. Japanese intuitive thinking would lead to a different outcome. The Japanese would (and did) focus on the minute details of the engine and power train, and would increase the car's speed by building a smaller, lighter, and more efficient engine. Chinese lateral thinking would focus on using lighter and cheaper parts and materials. The lighter car would go faster with the same drive train, but more importantly, their gross profit margins would also go up.

I find the different ways each country responded to an uncompetitive domestic steel industry to be instructive in this context. When faced with low-cost, high-quality competition from the Japanese steel industry in the 1970s and 1980s, the US basically withdrew from steel production, particularly blast furnace steel production. The linear logic was that our steel plants were not cost-competitive and earned low returns on invested capital;

therefore, it was better to close the plants and invest the money in other areas where US companies were more competitive and could earn higher returns. This made business sense, but, as is typical with linear-logic-derived conclusions, it did lack an element of common sense. Steel is a strategic industry and, in case of war, it would be a weak position to have to rely on steel imports from other countries to supply our military.

The Japanese reacted differently. Facing low-cost competition from Korean and Chinese steel makers, the intuitive Japanese decided not to close their steel plants. They aggressively consolidated steel companies to achieve scale economies and, more importantly, they intensely studied the steel-making process so they could consistently and reliably produce the highest-quality, strongest, and lowest-defect steel in the world. The Japanese didn't mind their steel companies destroying value because this saved jobs and kept strategically-important steel production in Japan.

China is not a naturally low-cost steel producer. Indian and Russian steel producers are structurally lower cost. After China's massive growth phase from around 2001 to 2014, China was left with hundreds of millions of tons of noneconomical excess capacity. Instead of closing down that capacity, using good Chinese lateral thinking, China decided to take their excess steel (and cement) capacity and export it to regional countries using their One-Belt-One-Road policy to help build infrastructure in the region. This helps neighboring countries to develop, making them better future markets for Chinese exports. At the same time, it indebts those countries, increasing Chinese influence and access across the region. Of course, this also supports employment and keeps strategically-important steel production in China.

The problem of excess bad debts provides another interesting contrast between linear, lateral, and intuitive thinkers. During the Global Financial Crisis of 2008, the US accumulated a large amount of bad debts. With typical linear thinking and a belief in absolute truth, Americans naturally wanted to reflect reality and marked the bad debts to their market values. US banks took huge write-downs. This led to a short-term economic crisis and many firms went bankrupt, but clearing the decks of bad debts allowed the economy to recover and grow solidly over the following decade.

Japan, with intuitive thinking and a belief in relative truth, faced a huge bad debt problem after their stock and real estate bubbles burst in the early 1990s. The literal Japanese couldn't understand the financial implications of banks burdened with large amounts of bad loans and zombie companies continuing to use up capital and ruin profit margins for healthier competitors. Relative truth indicated no need to reflect reality, so Japan never wrote-down the bad loans and avoided a short-term crisis, but financial inefficiency led them to slowly deflate over the following two "lost" decades.

China also faced large bad debt burdens. In the late 1990s, up to 30 percent of Chinese bank loans were of dubious quality. With their lateral thinking and no belief in absolute truth, the Chinese felt no need to mark the loans to market value. Instead they aggressively swapped debt for equity and state banks continued to roll the remaining bad loans. Admission into the WTO in 2001 and the subsequent period of incredible growth helped China to successfully outgrow their bad debt problem while avoiding any short-term crises. Today, China is again facing an enormous bad debt problem and is again choosing not to mark loans to market. The banks can avoid taking any big write-downs. Unfortunately for China, instead of joining a new WTO and enjoying another golden expansion period where they can outgrow their existing mountain of bad debts, trade tensions with the US are leading to an opposite outcome. China is now facing the prospect of losing many of their prior trade advantages and are facing a much slower growth era going forward. Not reflecting reality can help China avoid a short-term financial crisis, but a Japanese-style "lost decade" looks increasingly likely.

Here is a case of nonlinear thinking that I suspect will surprise many Americans and help better explain linear thinking. Linear thinking clearly indicates that if you get into a car accident, wearing a seat belt dramatically improves your chances of survival. It is a case of simple cause and effect. In China, surprisingly, people regularly do not put on their seat belt. And it is not just adults. I have countless times seen infants standing up or being held in the back seat with no child seat and no seat belt! It is as though they cannot conceive of what happens to a small child in a car accident.

In an odd example of Chinese creative thinking, ride service cars like Uber or Didi will even have a special card they buy that is inserted into the seat belt buckle so that the car warning light won't go on if the passenger hasn't put on their seat belt! This way, the rider isn't inconvenienced with the need to buckle up. When I ask Chinese people why they don't wear seat belts, even the most intelligent of Chinese will tell me that it's not comfortable and not necessary. Less-educated Chinese generally tell me that it's up to fate when they die and a seat belt won't change that. For a linear thinking American, this sounds like nonsense.

Here is a case of how American linear thinking differs from Japanese intuitive thinking. Linear thinking is sequential; therefore, it is always looking at progression and rarely focuses on the present. Intuitive thinkers are very different in relating an experience. For example, if you ask a linear or lateral thinker how their dinner was at the restaurant last night, they will fairly superficially tell you whether the meal was good, or they may comment on a certain course, the atmosphere, the service or the conversation, etc. The lateral thinker may even start talking about your friendship or some other tangential subject. The intuitive thinker will answer this question differently. They will pause and then go into deep reflection to remember the meal. Intuitive thinkers are far more present when they eat a meal or answer a question. So, if you don't interrupt them, they will go into stunning detail on the order the food was served, how the meal fit together like a symphony or if it clashed, the texture of certain dishes, the seasonality of ingredients, the color combinations, the temperatures at which the food reached the table, the smells, and, of course, the flavors. To Japanese intuitive thinkers, linear American thinkers often appear to them to not be fully present and simply not paying attention.

LINEAR THINKING IN A NONLINEAR WORLD

Although it has served the West well, there are some drawbacks to linear logic. The world does not develop linearly. Change can happen in a nonlinear fashion. Bad subprime lending in the US led to a major financial crisis and dramatic economic slowdown in 2008. This economic crisis was a nonlinear outcome and most observers in the US completely missed forecasting the recession. Even Federal Reserve Chairman Ben Bernanke had to admit: "I and others were mistaken early on in saying that the subprime crisis would be contained. The casual relationship between the housing problem and the broad financial system was very complex and difficult to predict."[166]

This was a clear example where America was hurt by its reliance on linear logic. Our top companies, top economic minds, and top relevant government officials misread the devastating nonlinear outcomes of excessive bad lending.

Here is an example of linear thinking going too far: in the West, we believe that cleanliness is good. There is no doubting the benefits from improved hygiene. There is a downside, however. If cleanliness is good, using linear logic, *more* clean is even better, right? As the Chinese say (物极必反) *take something to the extreme and it becomes the opposite.* Excess cleanliness in the US is now possibly being linked to allergies and diseases such as diabetes and autoimmune issues.[167] We were designed over millions of years of evolution to live in unhygienic environments. Apparently, to develop properly, our immune system requires some dirt and germs to fight. The Chinese have a phrase that I didn't understand at all when I first moved there, but makes more sense now. (不干不净, 吃了没病)—it means *even though the food is not exactly clean, if you eat it, you won't get sick.* The linear logic that cleaner is better is now backfiring on us.

---

166 John Cassidy, "Anatomy of a Meltdown," *The New Yorker*, December 1, 2008, https://www. newyorker.com/magazine/2008/12/01/anatomy-of-a-meltdown.

167 Andrew Curry, "A Hygiene Hypothesis," *Diabetes Forecast*, February 2009, http://www. diabetesforecast.org/2009/feb/a-hygiene-hypothesis.html.

Another negative implementation of linear logic is from the belief that democracy is an absolute good. For example, the US thought it was a good idea to replace the dictatorship in Iraq with democracy, assuming the result would be good because democracy is good. This was a huge error. The thinking was that if we could make Iraq a democracy, this would help bring peace and prosperity to the Middle East. The problem, however, was that Iraq has religious and cultural backgrounds very different from the European world where democracy developed. So, the US embarked on a deadly, destructive, and expensive war to promote a form of government that didn't fit the historical or cultural circumstances of Iraq. Unsurprisingly, it was not successful.

Iraq was an inhomogeneous society comprising three distinct groups locked in a power struggle with each other. By disbanding the existing government and army, without first maintaining stability, the mission to bring democracy to Iraq was doomed to fail despite the expected benefits of representative government. This is a case where common sense would have been much more effective than linear logic.

Another problem from the invasion of Iraq seems to be that the US never thought of the lateral impact of destabilizing countries in the Middle East—which would lead to the creation of ISIS—despite our experience with Al Qaeda. At the end of the movie *Rambo III* it originally said, "This film was dedicated to the brave Mujahedeen fighters of Afghanistan," as this was supportive of the US foreign policy at the time. The US saw the very linear advantage of supporting the Mujahedeen against the Soviets in Afghanistan, but didn't consider the nonlinear outcome that in the process we could be creating a new future enemy for the US.

Here is another example of American linear thinking gone awry. In believing that forest fires were unilaterally bad, the US went to great lengths to prevent them. Eventually, Americans realized that the lack of forest fires led to an overgrowth of trees, which created too much fuel for the inevitable fires that did occur. The excess of trees led to crown fires that burned much hotter and bigger than regular forest fires and were far more destructive. What the Americans really missed was the nonlinear outcome of preventing forest fires: the devastation brought about by the overgrowth of the mountain pine beetle. Forest fires help keep the mountain pine beetle population in check. Without regular forest fires, the beetle population exploded and is now devastating pine forests across the Western part of the US.

From a 2015 *National Geographic* article: "The scale of the current epidemic is unprecedented. Since the 1990s more than 60 million acres of forest, from northern New Mexico through British Columbia, have suffered die-offs. By the time the outbreak in British Columbia peters out, some 60 percent of the mature pines in the province may be dead. That's a billion cubic meters of wood."[168] It is too late now for many of these forests, which are the unfortunate victims of American lack of common sense and linear logic that missed non-linear outcomes.

Although there are multiple advantages to linear thinking, we are also not nearly as logical as we would like to believe.

"Although many of us may think of ourselves as thinking creatures that feel, biologically we are feeling creatures that think."[169]

—JILL BOLTE TAYLOR

Due to our leading position in the world and tendency toward absolutes, Americans feel that their logic is right and other types of reasoning are wrong. But it would be wise to remember Alexander Hamilton's counsel that, "Men are rather reasoning than reasonable animals, for the most part governed by the impulse of passion."

By contrast, the Chinese value reasonableness over reason. Lin describes the difference: while reason is analytical and governed by unchangeable logic, reasonableness is adaptable and understanding. The Chinese are not swayed simply by a logically sound argument as

168 Hillary Rosner, "The Bug That's Eating the Woods," *National Geographic*, April 2015, https://www.nationalgeographic.com/magazine/2015/04/pine-beetles-forest-destruction-canada-rockies/.

169 Jill Bolte Taylor, *My Stroke of Insight: A Brain Scientist's Personal Journey* (New York: Penguin Books, 2009).

Westerners are; they also require that reasoning accounts for human nature. By this measure, reasonableness is far more in touch with reality than reason.[170]

I can think of two examples where Chinese common sense would be better than American linear logic. In the US, a guilty criminal could get off scot-free on a technicality. This would not happen in China. In the US legal system, if someone is found guilty of a crime, but the police wrote the wrong date or missed some procedural detail, it is very possible the guilty party could go free. Chinese common sense would never cave to this logical, but misguided conclusion. The policeman would be reprimanded, but the guilt of the accused would remain.

Similarly, the kind of frivolous lawsuits that can happen in the US would be unthinkable in China. Take the recent cases of a teenager suing a fast-food restaurant for making them fat. The Chinese would see it as common sense that eating too much fast food could make you fat and would never consider a lawsuit against a restaurant for their menu.

Kahneman also gives us a great reminder from his book *Thinking Fast and Slow*, that even if linear logic was the force behind the great development in the West, we are still not nearly always as logical as we would like to believe. As Kahneman states: "The definition of rationality as coherence is impossibly restrictive; it demands adherence to rules of logic that a finite mind is not able to

170 Yutang Lin, *My Country and My People*, 86.

implement. Reasonable people cannot be rational by that definition, but they should not be branded irrational for that reason."[171] In other words, we are not as computer-like rational as we would like to believe. He also writes, "... System 2 (concentrated thinking) is not a paragon of rationality. Its abilities are limited and so is the knowledge to which it has access. We do not always think straight when we reason, and the errors are not always due to intrusive and incorrect intuitions. Often we make mistakes because we (our System 2) do not know any better."[172]

I think we Americans need to recognize that our linear logic is not perfect. Other forms of reasoning have their own advantages, and we are not always as logical as we would like to believe. This awareness could help Americans to be a little more tolerant of, and open-minded toward the different ways of thinking by different peoples. Each type of thinking has its own strengths. Ultimately, we can all learn from each other.

---

171 Daniel Kahneman, *Thinking Fast and Slow*, 411.

172 Daniel Kahneman, *Thinking Fast and Slow*, 415.

CHAPTER 25

HOW THE US IS PERCEIVED FROM ASIA

I've spent most of the past twenty-five years living in Asia and some of my fellow Americans may be surprised at how we are perceived from the Asian perspective. If I had to sum it up: Easterners don't recognize our belief in absolute truth and doubt that we even believe our own truths, while Americans don't recognize the Eastern belief in relative truth and don't understand that they don't believe in our truths.

When Americans advocate human rights, we feel fully justified in our efforts to improve the world. We believe we are doing the right thing and for the right reasons. But it does not get perceived that way. The rest of the world sees 250 years of slavery of Africans and the systematic genocide of the Native American people and cultures. Americans see progress and explain away or ignore the past because it doesn't fit with their current beliefs using absolute truth thinking. Unfortunately, other countries see zero moral authority. From the Chinese point of view, it is the ultimate hypocrisy to have Americans lecture them on human rights. Our lecturing them only pushes the two sides further apart. The US certainly doesn't help its case. Unfortunate events, such as Abu Ghraib, only reconfirmed the belief that America has no moral high ground on which to stand.

As Kissinger highlighted in his book *On China*: "Explanations of America's historic commitment to human rights were dismissed, either as a form of Western 'bullying' or as a sign of the unwarranted righteousness of a country that had its own human rights problems."[173] He went on to highlight that the American belief in the absolute truth of democracy and human rights leaves little room for other points of view and makes compromise-based solutions difficult in the normal give-and-take of foreign policy. "Throughout its history, the United States has often been motivated by visions of the universal relevance of its ideals and of a proclaimed duty to spread them. China has acted on the basis of its singularity; it expanded by cultural osmosis, not missionary zeal."[174]

When we lecture on human rights or the importance of adopting democracy, the Chinese and Japanese people simply do not understand that we actually believe in our

173 Henry Kissinger, *On China*, 422.

174 Henry Kissinger, *On China*, 529.

hearts what we are saying. They feel this argument is used to apply geopolitical pressure, and they question the loopholes in our arguments. For example, how can the US press China on human rights, but not Saudi Arabia? China and Japan do not recognize any moral authority from the US, but they do acknowledge significant geopolitical and military authority. From the East Asian perspective, with their lack of beliefs in absolute truths, they simply cannot understand American idealism. They only see the US as hypocritical given the blight of racism, slavery, and genocide in US history.

Pye highlights this differing view with an example of American idealism being completely ineffective in communicating human rights concerns with China. "The American political style is often to sugarcoat criticisms of others by confessing to one's own faults," he writes, and illustrates this kind of blunder with the example of former President Jimmy Carter's visit to Beijing in 1991. Seeking to offer commiseration alongside his suggestions for improving China's human rights performance, he stated that the US had its own issues with homelessness and health care. Rather than humanizing Carter to the Chinese press, this made him appear a hypocrite who was ill-suited to give advice: the Chinese press reported not on Carter's suggestions, but on America's "human rights" problems.[175]

In China, it is not about right and wrong. It is about

175 Lucian W. Pye, *Chinese Negotiating Style—Commercial Approaches and Cultural Principles*, 21.

who has the authority to decide. It is pure power politics. President Carter's mistake with China was to try and help on principle, but he thereby weakened America's position by being self-critical. President Carter had the idealistic goal of improving human rights in China, but he took the wrong approach. He tried to build rapport by confessing to America's faults first. This was a mistake because in a pure power politics environment, one has authority or one does not. President Carter gave away authority by admitting to human rights problems in America, which meant the Chinese did not need to listen to him.

If the US still had the big stick hanging over the Chinese head of The Most Favored Nation trading status, China would understand our beating them up on human rights. They would consider it bullying, but at least they would understand it. The Chinese would not see it as a moral issue at all. They would only recognize that the US had the bigger economy and had the power to force this on China. Without the force of power politics, moral suasion loses all influence over the Chinese.

If Jimmy Carter really wanted to help human rights in China, he should have argued that with better human rights and protection from the rule of law in America, the most talented minds in China and Chinese wealth would continue to move to the US to the benefit of the US economy and the detriment of China. The Chinese could understand those terms and would reconsider improving human rights and the rule of law in China for their own interests. They were far less persuaded by the appeals of an outsider who was using their own foreign, morally superior, cultural standards to judge them, attempting to make the Chinese lose face publicly.

The Chinese are acutely aware that democracy is one of the main factors holding back growth in the Indian economy and that China's *lack* of democracy has played a huge role in China's economic success. Americans, with their absolutist belief in the superiority of democracy, still struggle to recognize this.

One key aspect of the Chinese economic miracle is their lack of absolute standards and the unequal treatment of property rights. Any outdated housing in China basically has no property rights. Owners can be kicked out and usually with minimal compensation. The old properties are then torn down and rebuilt as modern housing, with full property rights. This massive upgrade and modernization has led to incredible growth in China. Local governments supported big spending programs with revenue garnered from selling this reclaimed land at a huge markup to developers. The local governments used that money to build out the sewage, road, electrical, and other civic infrastructure required for more modern housing. The absence of property rights on older housing also meant developers could literally redraw the city maps and build new roads of any width wherever they wanted. Indian democracy prevents this kind of renewal and it is obvious to anyone that has visited China and India. In China, the skyline of cities small and large are covered with cranes. The absence of cranes in Indian cities is equally stunning.

As a good Westerner, I believe, along with Winston Churchill, that "Democracy is the worst form of government, except for all the others." Japan, South Korea, and Taiwan have all benefited greatly from democracy. But I can also see the Eastern perspective. It is a process. Democracy works best for an educated population. For a poor country, the primary focus is on providing shelter and adequate food and pulling its people out of poverty. The next focus is on educating the population and providing employment opportunities and raising their standard of living. Representative government is very much a later consideration. The circumstances must fit.

Kissinger contrasts the American belief in absolute truths with the Chinese belief in relative truths: "Like the United States, China thought of itself as playing a special role. But it never espoused the American notion of universalism to spread its values around the world. It confined itself to controlling the barbarians immediately at its doorsteps. It strove for tributary states like Korea to recognize China's special status, and in return, it conferred benefits such as trading rights. As for the remote barbarians such as Europeans, about whom they knew little, the Chinese maintained a friendly, if condescending, aloofness. They had little interest in converting them to Chinese ways."[176]

The Japanese *did* try to spread their life philosophy militarily. The goal was to fit other countries into Japan's perceived hierarchy of the world with Japan at the top. They were not spreading abstract ideals such as democracy, human rights, free markets, and open societies. They forced Koreans and Taiwanese to speak Japanese when they colonized them. They were spreading Japanese imperialism. Unfortunately for the Japanese, their imperialism failed, so today they are back to figuring out Japan's place in their perceived global hierarchy of countries.

---

176 Henry Kissinger, *On China*, 17.

CHAPTER 26

WHO IS AN AMERICAN?

Finding an answer to what makes someone an American is difficult. Defining it by passport would be insufficient. My understanding of who is an American comes from my experiences overseas.

I once had a debate with a group of Americans studying in China what constituted being an American. They came to one conclusion that agreed with my experience. If the person had moved to America after they were fourteen years old, they basically retained their original culture. If they moved before five years old, they were basically fully American. Between ages five to fourteen, they were hybrids to one degree or another.

The group started debating tests of American-ness. One of the affable boys stated that if you could sing the song "You're a Grand Old Flag," then you were an American. I shook my head, so the blond girl from California that was the leader of this discussion asked me what I thought. I said being able to sing "You're a Grand Old Flag" to prove you are an American was about the dumbest thing I'd ever heard. Her reaction was to say, "Well, tell us what you think, Mr. Know it All." I thought for a second and said, "If the hair stood up on your neck the first time you watched *Die Hard* when John McClain said 'Yippee Kai Yay Mother*#$%&#', then you're an American." With a beautifully dismissive expression, she smugly smiled and said that was the dumbest thing she'd ever heard in her life.

Even though that is also a silly test of who qualifies as an American, I think I was onto something. A basic definition could be anyone that was born, raised, and educated in the US, or an American household abroad, or who moved to the US before they were five and received an American education. Beyond that definition, I think there is also a deeper meaning to being an American. America is a broad and diverse country with a huge population. It is almost impossible to generalize, but I think there are some basic values we share: freedom and equality of opportunity are crucial; individuality is important; and Americans believe in democracy, free markets, property rights, freedom of speech, freedom of assembly, and the assertion that all people are created equal with the rights to life, liberty, and the pursuit of happiness.

I think there are also tendencies Americans have. We tend to be optimists. We don't overly believe in fate. We tend to be linear thinkers and we generally believe in absolute truth. We are a guilt-driven society and people want to leave society a little bit better than they found it. In the end, however, that distinction rests in the heart of the individual. If you believe you are an American, that is good enough for me (though the US government will certainly have their own view).

The determination of who is Japanese is quite severe. In order to qualify as Japanese to other Japanese people, a person would have to be ethnically Japanese *and* raised in Japan. During Japan's imperial era, people who were 100 percent Japanese by blood were sent to colonize Brazil or China, yet upon their return to Japan, they were not considered Japanese by the Japanese. In fact, there were calls to send these "foreigners" back home. This was an ultra-literal interpretation of who is Japanese, but one that still resonates today.

The Chinese have a much more lateral view on who is Chinese. Anyone who is ethnically Chinese—even if their family has been overseas for generations—is still considered Chinese. When the Chinese proclaim the twenty-first century as the century for the great revival of the Chinese people (21世纪是中华民族伟大复兴的世纪), they are referring to not just the Chinese people in China, but also to all the other ethnically Chinese people around the world.

SECTION 4

COMPARISONS IN AMERICAN AND JAPANESE CULTURE

CHAPTER 27

THE GROUP VERSUS THE INDIVIDUAL

The major difference between Japan and the US is the role of the group versus the individual. The primary concern at all times in Japan is to maintain the harmony of the group. This means suppressing the individuals' goals, desires, wants, and emotions. The great philosopher Thoreau famously said that, "Any man more right than his neighbors constitutes a majority of one." In Japan, where the collective opinion is emphasized, this would be utter nonsense. The group is, by definition, always right. This is a very difficult aspect of Japanese culture for Americans to understand. In the US, one is innocent until proven guilty. The emphasis is on the individuals' rights. In Japan, you are guilty until proven innocent and the emphasis is on the needs of society and not the individual.

Benedict points out that in the Tokugawa era (1579 to

1750), there were at least 1,000 peasant revolts against excessive taxes or unfair treatment. Apparently, the Shogun ruled in the peasants' favor about half of the time. The farmers may have been just in their complaints and their wrongs redressed, but the peasant leaders had to be punished for upsetting the social order with their revolts. "They were therefore condemned to death. The righteousness of their cause had nothing to do with the matter...*the leaders were boiled in oil or beheaded or crucified...*"[177] (Emphasis mine)

In Japan, there is (obviously) intense pressure to conform. The bullying of misfits, and those who don't fit in, is severe. One does not want to stand out for fear of being ostracized. What one may want is far less important than what is wanted of one. This is completely at odds with the American belief in the inalienable right of pursuit of happiness. As Benedict said: "The Japanese...define the supreme task of life as fulfilling one's obligations. They fully accept the fact that repaying *on* [obligations] means sacrificing one's personal desires and pleasures. The idea that the pursuit of happiness is a serious goal of life is to them an amazing and immoral doctrine."[178]

One vast area of difference in interaction is that the desire to maintain harmony motivates the Japanese to be much more indirect in their communication. This makes the Japanese very nonconfrontational. Americans

---

177 Ruth Benedict, *The Chrysanthemum and the Sword*, 66–67.

178 Ruth Benedict, *The Chrysanthemum and the Sword*, 192.

can easily confuse what a Japanese person means. For example, one time my Japanese boss complimented my new coat for looking quite comfortable. I thought what a nice thing to say. Only later did a fellow Japanese colleague point out that our boss didn't like the coat and he was trying to tell me it wasn't professional enough. This marks another distinction. When the Japanese need to communicate something, if they do it directly, it will be very subtle. But more often than not, they will find a go-between to pass the tough message. Americans would just confront the person directly and look down on someone who was not willing to be up front with them. Americans and Japanese people communicate based on a completely different value system.

Another funny situation I've seen countless times with Americans is that they will say something and the Japanese person will respond with "yes." The American will conclude they have agreement. This is almost always a misunderstanding. The Japanese are loath to use the word "no" as it disrupts harmony. When a Japanese person says "yes," the meaning is usually "yes, I understand you" or "I understand your point." It does not mean they are conceding a point of agreement. This is probably the most consistent source of misunderstanding I've seen between Americans and the Japanese. Also, when an American says "maybe," it means they will consider it. But when the Japanese say "maybe" or "I will research it," this means no. The only time a Japanese person will ever directly say "no" is when you compliment them. Say something good about a Japanese friend or colleague, and they will respond modestly with a stream of *noes* and many explanations of how they are not good. Trying to look better than others is bad for group harmony.

Japan operates on the rules and customs of an almost 2,000-year-old society that has experienced comparatively little interaction historically with other people, causing the formation of a homogenous society. Through this long and mostly unbroken stretch of history, Japan has developed a large number of social rules that are understood by all Japanese people. Behavior is strictly demarcated through known custom. For example, one always takes off one's shoes before entering a home and there are strict rules on how shoes should be lined up near the entrance. One does not hold eye contact with a superior. If a superior makes a slight noise, one immediately stops talking and allows the superior to speak. If you are bowed to, you bow back and the timing and degree of the bow is determined by the circumstances and your position relative to the person you are bowing to. There are hundreds, if not thousands of such etiquette rules in Japan.

The challenge for Americans is that the rules in Japan are mostly unspoken and the two societies are so different. In the US, everything is spelled out in detail. We are an immigrant country, so specific rules were necessary to resolve disputes, but are also ever-evolving in our heterogeneous culture. As a foreigner in Japan, you have to figure out the rules through observation or find a Japanese person to teach you and point out mistakes when you make them.

In my very first meeting in Japan, I introduced myself as "Richard-san." This was a major faux-pas. One never uses the honorific -*san* for anyone in their circle, particularly for themselves. The polite Japanese didn't bat an eye. I never noticed the mistake. I only learned later at a drinking session when an inebriated fellow junior colleague pointed it out and everyone erupted into laughter. It was super embarrassing. I never made the same mistake again, but I have made many others and always walk on eggshells in Japan. The nice part about being a foreigner in Japan is that you are not expected to know the rules. We foreigners are usually given a pass.

For Japanese people, however, infractions are unforgivable. For this reason, Japanese people who have lived overseas and then return often feel intense stress when they move back into Japanese society. It is said that the experience of moving back to Japan is like taking a bonsai plant out of its small pot, allowing it to grow freely, and then trying to force it back into its original mini container.

Another area ripe for misinterpretation is the Japanese emphasis on hierarchy. Americans share a fundamental belief that all people are created equal. Japanese society is built on an entirely different foundation. Japan traditionally had a caste system. One was born into their station in life and changing caste was not possible. This is the opposite of the "American Dream" where anyone can succeed with hard work. Japanese culture stresses hierarchy as much as we stress equality (of opportunity) and freedom. Benedict states of the Japanese, "Their reliance upon order and hierarchy and our faith in freedom and equality are poles apart and it is hard for us to give hierarchy its just due as possible social mechanism."[179]

In *Japanese Culture*, Paul Varley points out that Japanese and American concepts of individualism are equally polarized:

> "Whereas modern Western humanism became absorbed with people as individuals, with all their personal peculiarities, feelings, and ways, Japanese humanism of the Tokugawa period scarcely conceived of the existence of true individuals at all; rather, it focused on 'the people' and regarded them as comprising essentially types, such as samurai, farmer, and courtesans...For the most part, characters in Tokugawa literature do what we suppose they will do; there is little in the literature as a whole of that quality—character development—that is probably the single most important feature of the modern Western novel."[180] (Emphasis mine)

179 Ruth Benedict, *The Chrysanthemum and the Sword*, 43.

180 Paul Varley, *Japanese Culture* (Honolulu, Hawaii: University of Hawaii Press, 2000), 186.

The Japanese do not believe in the development of the individual for the individual's own sake because the needs of the group always take precedence. As an American, one bewildering aspect of interacting with Japanese people is their lack of opinions. Japanese education is focused on rote learning. There is no emphasis at all on critical thinking. Van Wolferen has a quote on this major difference in teaching styles: William Griffis, an American missionary, and one of the earliest foreign teachers in Japan, noted that in Japan the "chief duty was to stuff and cram the minds...of pupils. To expand or develop the mental powers of a boy, to enlarge his mental visions, to teach him to think for himself, would have been precisely what it was the teacher's business to prevent."[181] [182] While Japanese people *will* discuss issues, the process will be very slow, and they will not move forward until the entire group reaches consensus. When Americans debate, the leaders judge which argument is correct and move in that direction, with some people still possibly in disagreement. It shocks the Japanese to see how much Americans argue and interrupt each other on their TV news shows.

"Japanese thought processes, in contrast with those of the West, are said to be nonrational, nonlogical, situational, emotional

181 Karel van Wolferen, *The Enigma of Japanese Power*, 88–89.

182 "Education in Japan," as cited in *Griffis in Japan: The Fukui Interlude, 1871*, Ed. Edward R. Beauchamp (Connecticut: Linnet Books, 1978), 58.

and socially dependent; and this is presented not as a deficiency, but as a sign of superiority."[183]

—KAREL VAN WOLFEREN

My daughter studied for a year in a Japanese school. It is something I've never done. I asked her the difference between a Japanese school and an American school. She said that in the Japanese school everything is strictly on point. The lesson is decided ahead of time and they spend the class learning that lesson. There is no discussion. Students rarely asked questions and only for clarification. Her only role was to memorize the lesson and regurgitate it during exams, and the teacher never asked for her view or opinion. Conformity to the group was also extreme. Not only did every student wear the same uniform, they also had the same shoes, socks, hats, and school bags. If their hair was curly or not jet black, they needed a note proving this was natural.

A side note: when our daughter was five, we read her a Japanese kids' book that stressed the importance of the group. There was one boy in the story that always wanted to go first. In the playground, he wanted to go first down the slide. At break time, he wanted to be the first in line to get his snack. He wanted to be first to go to the bathroom. The teacher kindly explained that it was important to take turns and let others go first also. The boy learned his lesson and started waiting his turn. Reading this story

---

183 Karel van Wolferen, *The Enigma of Japanese Power*, 248.

turned out to be a big fail on our part as parents. Apparently, our daughter was more American than we realized. Before she read the book, she didn't have the concept of going first. But the next time at the playground, she kept pushing ahead of the others because she now always wanted to be first! The other Japanese parents looked on with disapproving frowns.

Japan traditionally had four distinct social classes. The top class were the nobles and the samurai. This was followed by the commoners, which were grouped in order as farmers, craftsmen, and merchants. Farmers were not actually well respected, but were classified as the top commoners as they provided food, which was critical for everyone. Merchants were at the bottom as Japan traditionally looked down on selfish greed and money making.

In the pre-Meiji Restoration feudal era, Japan had very strict sumptuary laws that restricted consumption and had very precise rules as to which social class could wear which clothing to make one's caste clear. There was also actually a fifth social class, the *burakumin* or untouchables. But they were so low, they were beyond consideration. They did the so-called "unclean jobs" such as butcher, undertaker, or tanner. *Burakumin* still exist even today. When a Japanese person plans to get married, their parents will often investigate the partner's family history to make sure they aren't *burakumin* or Koreans that came over during the colonial period.

This is to prevent their child from accidentally marrying someone from the wrong social class.

Of course, I'm not saying the US is without prejudice. That would certainly not be true. But the significant difference is that in America, nothing succeeds like success, and anyone from any background can succeed and move up in society. In Japan, one's position is far more fixed. The example that comes to mind for me is Muhammad Ali. He started off as a poor minority. He later became famous as a boxer, but was vilified for his stance as a draft dodger and for joining the controversial Nation of Islam. Yet, when he died, he may have been one of the most popular and beloved Americans of all time precisely because he stood up for his own beliefs. That dramatic movement up the social ladder simply could not happen in Japan.

Where Westerners look to an individual's passions and ambitions as a sign of strength, the Japanese see it as a sign of weakness. As Benedict points out, these feelings distract the Japanese hero from his *gimu* or his *giri*. "The strong, according to Japanese verdict, are those who disregard personal happiness and fulfill their obligations."[184]

The Japanese emphasis of modesty is another major difference between Japanese and American culture. Japanese people will always put themselves down and downplay their abilities in order to not make anyone else look bad and to maintain the harmony of the group. To Americans, this humility will come across as a lack of

---

184 Ruth Benedict, *The Chrysanthemum and the Sword*, 207.

confidence. For the Japanese, the way Americans boast about their own skills and accomplishments feels insincere and selfish.

The Japanese sense of obligation is heavy. Therefore, when they give a gift, it will be prefaced with: "This is just nothing" or "a not interesting thing" to reduce the burden the receiver will feel. The receiver of gifts will also protest repeatedly before receiving a gift to show that they don't feel worthy. In the past, the Japanese would not even open a present in front of the giver. The fear was that their reaction would not be positive enough and this would embarrass the giver. Today, customs have changed, and the receiver will ask permission to open the present and will open it on the spot. If you give an American a present that they already have, they will more often than not, in my experience, gladly point out that they already have the item. A Japanese person would never do anything that might hurt the giver's feelings in such a manner and would express how thankful they were even if they were not.

I once saw a Japanese person give an American a gift and preface it with, "I apologize, this isn't a very good gift, but please accept it." The American replied, "If this isn't a very good gift, why are you giving it to me?" Big mutual confusion ensued.

In the West we also have the concept that it is better to give than to receive. Given the Japanese literal view on any debts, monetary or otherwise, this is an alien concept in Japan. From the Japanese view, Americans happily will receive any gift and say thank you without protesting or feeling uncomfortable. Americans will never display any big sense of obligation because they see themselves as entitled and deserving of any good thing that comes their way. From the American point of view, giving is good, intrinsically, and if we don't happily receive gifts then others never have the opportunity to give and to share. We help each other reciprocally. The obligation to return a gift or a kindness is there, but that obligation is far lighter than the Japanese would feel.

As Benedict highlighted: Japanese even take social debts literally. The Japanese view the obligation to pay back a favor with the strictness an American would view the responsibility to pay back borrowed money. Japanese track these with favors carefully and the failure to pay back a favor would be as bad as not repaying a financial debt. Therefore, one must not be careless in any social interaction in Japan lest you unintentionally incur a debt and then forget to ever repay.[185] Not responding to a gift, favor, or kind word with a return gift, favor, or kind word of similar perceived value is a big no-no in Japan.

One of the funniest examples of the difference between Americans and Japanese is the concept of "simple." One often observes a Japanese person that received a gift saying, "I love it, it is very simple." Given the Zen focus on simplicity in aesthetics, simple has a

---

185 Ruth Benedict, *The Chrysanthemum and the Sword*, 141.

good meaning in Japan. In the US, if you tell someone their haircut looks simple, they will feel you are saying they look dumb. In Japan, a haircut being called simple would be a high compliment. If an American were told their dress, or their purse, or their home was very simple, they would get offended. In Japan, this would be praise.

One more fundamental difference between the Japanese and Americans is the concept of competition. In the West, we believe competition leads to superior results, as it brings out the best in people. In Japan, however, competition goes against the group dynamic and is viewed in a negative light. Benedict explained why: In social experiments in Japan, competition actually caused people's results to be notably worse relative to when they worked in isolation. The reason was that the fear of failure forced their concentration onto their competition as opposed to on the task they were working on.[186] The Japanese are very uncomfortable with any type of confrontation.

Other areas of difference between the Japanese and Americans that stand out for me are that Americans are optimists by nature, while Japanese society is very pessimistic. Americans are comfortable with risk, whereas Japanese are very risk adverse. Americans are also very friendly. To the Japanese, an American can seem superficial when they say hello energetically or with a big smile, or ask someone they barely know—or don't even know at all—how they are doing. The Japanese are also

186 Ruth Benedict, *The Chrysanthemum and the Sword*, 153-154.

shocked at how lightly and frequently Americans will use the phrase *I love you*. It strikes them as lacking sincerity. Conversely, Americans would generally be surprised to learn that many Japanese husbands may have never once have said *I love you* to their wives.

CHAPTER 28

BUSINESS IN JAPAN

In Japan, the CEO/president is usually one of the longest-tenured at the company and has risen through the ranks. Often, they start as engineers and then progress to head increasingly larger business units. If a promising executive can manage their businesses and the consensus political environment, they have a shot at the top position. The strength of this model is that managers are 100 percent loyal to the company, employees, and customers, plus they understand the technology. The weakness of this model is often those that ascend to the top aren't particularly skilled in running a company and certainly not in the financial aspects required of the job.

This is very different from the US, where running a company is considered a skill in itself. Lateral hires for a top leadership position, which are very rare in Japan, are common in America. Often, a new American boss is good at sales and is outgoing and good at speaking and presenting. Japanese managers are often from an engineering background, so are generally more introverted, less well-spoken, and not skilled marketers.

Lateral hires are rare in Japan, but they do happen. For example, Carlos Ghosn, as an outsider taking over Nissan, was a shocking case to the Japanese. Nissan was in trouble, so they took a chance and Ghosn was a success. Ghosn used his Le Cost Killer reputation from Renault and made changes a Japanese manager could never make, such as closing a large number of domestic factories, slashing workers, and cutting many long-standing supplier relationships. Ghosn's background was actually in tire manufacturing. It was very unusual for a non-company person and someone with a different background (tires versus cars) to run a company in Japan. Despite the success, few Japanese companies have tried anything similar. Foreign CEOs are now even less likely in Japan after the recent arrest of Carlos Ghosn.[187]

From the Japanese perspective, the replacement of Steve Jobs at Apple was incomprehensible. The board decision to replace the product genius Steve Jobs with a soda pop salesperson from Pepsi to become the head of a computer company made absolutely no sense to them. The Japanese ideal is lifetime employment. Loyalty is one of their top values. To them, promoting someone

---

187 Daniel Shane, "After Carlos Ghosn, Japan May Never Hire Another Foreign CEO," *CNN Business*, November 30, 2018, https://www.cnn.com/2018/11/30/business/japan-foreign-ceos-carlos-ghosn/index.html.

from outside of the company with different experience is discouraging and disconcerting. They view political positions in a similar light. The Japanese see the selections of Barack Obama and Donald Trump as presidents as odd choices given their backgrounds. Both are very well-spoken and market themselves well, but did not have long political careers and, in both cases, had no executive political experience. Japanese prime ministers tend not to last very long or have much of an impact, but they do all come with a long history of political experience.

Business strategy is one of the key areas where the difference between Japanese literal-intuitive thinking and American linear thinking shows itself. I would describe the American business process as **ready-aim-fire**. This very linear, step-by-step process begins with developing a business plan, raising funds, developing a marketing plan, and then executing the business plan. The Japanese follow no such linear formula, which can seem incomprehensible to an American. The Japanese appear to follow something more like **aim-fire-aim-fire**. The Japanese develop a product and make it the best they possibly can without regard to customer desires. Then they start selling this product. If it doesn't sell well, they go back and try and make the product even better and try selling the new version.

Japanese companies are not good at incorporating market feedback in product development. There is very little of what I would call "ready." They are also very poor at forecasting what the consumer is going to want, and it seems up to chance whether they are in an industry where demand happens to be high for what they produce. Car demand is strong globally and the world is willing to pay more for higher-quality automobiles. So, the Japanese auto companies are successful. I think Sony and Sharp, and the other big Japanese electronics companies, are good counter examples. They continued to make better and better electronic products, but it just led them to over-spec and to lack innovation. So, companies like Samsung or LG undercut them on price while Apple killed them by creating new product categories.

The literal thinking aspect is that these Japanese companies see themselves as makers of a specific product. This impedes creative thinking that could lead Japanese business leaders to see how the market could change or develop (linear), or how they could change how or what they do (lateral). On the other hand, in markets where demand is naturally good for what the Japanese produce, and precision and durability requirements are high, their method works.

The Japanese are quite conservative and very slow to change. During their economic heyday, the Japanese looked at the US business logic of cutting swathes of workers as completely heartless and inhumane. They could not follow the logic that a company would become more profitable following this strategy and in time could invest those profits into new and better businesses, ultimately hiring more workers in the long run. They believed the Japanese model worked best. Instead of firing workers, everyone would take a pay cut, share the pain, and thereby create a corporate spirit that foreign companies couldn't match.

Looking back after lost decades of growth, the Japanese are slowly, but finally starting to realize that this lack of faith in creative destruction has caused them to focus on too many dead-end and value-destroying businesses. Furthermore, the lack of profits and cash flows has ultimately hurt their overall economy and ability to create new jobs. The young workforce has been the main victim of this strategy. Japanese companies always struggled with abstract concepts such as return on invested capital or return on equity. But with their economy being eclipsed by the rise of China, they are starting to make the effort to understand and implement these ideas. Results are mixed so far, but at least they have finally recognized there is a problem and are moving in the right direction.

The Japanese also take a very different view toward recruiting. The goal of a Japanese hiring manager is to find good team members as opposed to talented people. As van Wolferen highlights: The Japanese elite's "ranks have been selected mainly for stamina and dedication. Todai (Tokyo University) graduates tend to be 'bright,' but many Japanese with very capable minds of a different cast are discarded and doomed permanently to operate on the fringes. Much capacity for original thinking is wasted.

The Japanese ruling class is far more thoroughly schooled than it is educated..." and represents "membership in a class of people that has managed the art of passing the most abstruse entrance examinations."[188]

When hiring in Japan, attitude counts far more than ability. The government and the business world value persistence, dedication, and memory much more highly than initiative and inventiveness. Van Wolferen describes how new employees are indoctrinated into a company similarly to recruits in the military: companies understand they need to create discipline and obedience in the new workers they bring on.[189]

Could you imagine if a candidate for the US Marines bragged to them how much he knew about shooting a gun or physical fitness? As though he could teach the Marines about these things or impress them? The Marines would reject that candidate out of hand as he would have the wrong attitude for military service and could not hack it. This philosophy manifests itself in Japanese job interviews as well. A Japanese job candidate will literally say that they don't know anything, and their goal is to learn, earning points for humility. On the other hand, this interviewing style would never work with Western companies. If a candidate said they didn't understand anything and they presented themselves so modestly, the Americans

---

188 Karel van Wolferen, *The Enigma of Japanese Power*, 308.

189 Karel van Wolferen, *The Enigma of Japanese Power*, 160-161.

would interpret this as a lack of self-confidence and the candidate would get dismissed outright.

BEST PRACTICES FOR BUSINESS MEETINGS IN JAPAN

The first outstanding characteristic of business in Japan is that everything is very formal. A formal suit and tie is almost always appropriate. Post the Fukushima nuclear disaster, the Japanese began to cut down on air-conditioning use in the summer to save electricity, so short sleeves and no tie are acceptable. They call it "cool biz," but the underlying outfit remains: the suit pants and an ironed button-down shirt. Just no tie. Visiting another office, even on a sweltering day, one may not remove their jacket without first asking permission. Another oddity peculiar to Japan is that, in the winter, one should not enter someone else's office wearing a coat. The coat should be removed before entering their office or even a Japanese home. Otherwise, the implication is that the person's home or office is too cold and that would be impolite to infer their home was somehow unwelcoming. Also, putting your hands in your pockets is considered quite rude. In fact, boy's school uniform pants in Japan have the pockets sewn shut so the boys could never develop the slovenly habit of putting their hands in their pockets. Blowing your nose or chewing gum in front of others are equally offensive.

Arriving a few minutes ahead of a scheduled meeting

is expected and, for the literal-minded Japanese, showing up late is strongly frowned upon. Meticulously dressed receptionists usually will show you to the meeting room. As guests, you are expected to sit farthest away from the door. This is the seat of honor as the most important samurai chose this seat to first see any enemies entering the room. The most important person sits in the middle. The most junior member of the host company sits closest to the door to be the first line of defense in case the room were attacked. If there is a window in the room, the guests should have the window at their back. This way, the pleasant view behind them makes them look better.

In a Japanese business meeting, the most important person goes in first and the others follow by rank. The first step is to exchange business cards starting with the most senior person in each group. Japanese employees are expected to have a nice business card holder and cards are taken out one at a time and offered and received using two hands. Business cards should clearly show one's title or position. This way, the Japanese know which level of politeness to use when interacting. When exchanging cards, always say the name of your company first and then your own name second. The group is more important than the individual in Japan. Never write on someone's business card in front of them and try not to let them see you put it away. During the meeting, any business card you receive should be placed on the table, ideally in order according to where everyone is seated.

One should not sit down until the top-ranked person sits down first. Additionally, the Japanese dislike eye contact. So, best not to stare. Japanese new employees are taught to look at the other person's tie to avoid eye contact.[190] Also, the big boss may sometimes close his eyes during a meeting. He's not sleeping. Just listening. Meetings should start with you apologizing for taking their precious time and should finish at the scheduled time thanking them again for their precious time.

How far one walks with a guest that is leaving is an important sign of respect. If you say goodbye at the meeting room, that is a faux pas. If Japanese guests visit you and you are on the ground floor for the meeting, you should walk them to their car. If the meeting is in a tall building, it is customary to walk them all the way to the elevator. As the elevator door closes, you should face them squarely and bow, while they bow back to you. Don't worry about how well you bow. Although the Japanese are trained quite specifically in bowing, as a foreigner, you are not expected to know the proper etiquette.

I learned the etiquette of bowing from Muramatsu-san, my first boss in Japan: 15 degrees with a quick bow for someone at an equal level, 30 degrees with heels together and a longer hold for a superior, and 45 degrees for an apology with heels together and eyes fixed on the ground below for a count of five to ten seconds. Extreme

---

190 In Feudal Japan, if a commoner made eye contact with a samurai, the samurai had every right to chop off that person's head.

apologies would require a 90-degree or even 120-degree bow. In the most extreme cases, one would prostrate themselves on the ground in the Japanese *seiza* seated position. (In pre-WWII, the Japanese people had never seen Emperor Hirohito, because if they were in his presence, their faces would've been pressed to the ground.)

After the formalities are finished and you sit down for a meeting with a Japanese company, it is worthwhile to keep a few basic guidelines in mind. The Japanese hate unpredictability, maintaining a harmonious atmosphere is critical, and avoidance of sarcasm or abstract questions is important. Furthermore, I strongly recommend sticking to one idea at a time.

One big difference between Americans and the Japanese is their approach to small talk. Americans will often engage in small talk at the beginning of a meeting. It helps everyone get to know each other, usually doesn't have a point, but helps break the ice and get the momentum of the meeting started. The Japanese are the exact opposite. They will not engage in any small talk at the start of a meeting or the start of a project, etc. Specifically, this means that in Japan, I would never ask personal questions at the start of a meeting such as about family or holiday plans. When the meeting is over or the project complete and their responsibilities fulfilled, only then will the Japanese engage in small talk. I think the reason is that small talk is personal. And personal issues should always be subordinate to one's work responsibilities. It is notable that Japanese will not have pictures of their spouse or kids at their desks. This would be improperly mixing their professional and private lives.

Another interesting aspect is that in the US it is polite to remain silent when someone else is speaking to show one is attentively listening. This is different in Japan. The Japanese will deliver a stream of subtle grunts and noises to acknowledge the speaker's points and show they are listening intently. Japanese cannot show their attention through eye contact the way Westerners do, so *aizuchi*, or various noises in response, are necessary. Silence would be considered rude. Slightly different subtle noises and gestures are used to indicate when one wants to interrupt, disagree, or ask a question.

If you are meeting with a Japanese company, they will often request information ahead of time. They will have reams of questions for your side, prepared for negotiations. If you are meeting to learn more about them, they will ask for a list of your questions, in detail, ahead of time. If you meet with the president/CEO, oftentimes he will spend the first ten to fifteen minutes of the meeting reading out a speech line by line. Unlike meetings with Chinese companies where their ramblings early in a meeting can be surprisingly informative and useful, these speeches by Japanese presidents/CEOs are usually quite bland and a waste of time. Westerners will be very tempted to cut the president/CEO off, but in my experience, this isn't a good idea. He (I've met very few female heads of Japanese companies) will have planned for hours for this meticulously prepared little speech. And if he presents in English, this ten to fifteen minutes has been no small source of consternation. Cutting him off will be a big disappointment for him and incredibly disrespectful, and will negatively impact the quality of the remainder of the meeting. My advice is to patiently wait it out and then comment on how good his English is.

To maintain a harmonious meeting atmosphere, my strategy when meeting with Japanese companies is something like serving a three-course meal. I start off with the appetizer—easy and positive points. Then move on to the main course—the bulk of the meeting. This is where I cover all of the main points and build up rapport at the same time. Dessert comes last. These are the difficult or uncomfortable issues. If I cover these too early, it can ruin the mood and the Japanese may shut off, so the entire meeting ends up less helpful. The Japanese react very poorly to confrontation. With some rapport built up, however, the final part of the meeting is the best chance to dive into areas of criticism or philosophical differences.

To get the most out of the meeting, it is important not to confuse the Japanese. With their literal mindset, sarcasm will be completely misunderstood. Abstract questions or ideas will also go over their heads. My recommendation is to avoid long streams of conscious thoughts or any broad discussion of communication styles. Asking questions one subject at a time works best and the Japanese very much prefer data. As believers in relative truth, establishing context is always important and if you can establish context numerically that is generally a big help. It is a challenge for Westerners, but try to remain as literal as possible when asking questions. For example, take a project that has lost a lot of money: if you ask, "Why wasn't such and such project a success?", the Japanese may still have considered it a success if the project worked technically. You would be much better off asking why it was behind schedule for however many months or why it lost however much money.

Translators can also be a problem. Unlike in Korea or China, even younger Japanese executives are often not comfortable conducting meetings in English. Unfortunately, the translator in Japan that is skilled going both from English to Japanese and then back from Japanese to English is quite rare. This makes it doubly imperative to simplify questions. What often happens is that after the Westerner asks a question, the Japanese executive has a conversation with the translator trying to understand the context of the question. After a lengthy discussion, the translator comes back with an answer of only "yes" and the Western party feels they have missed a lot. Abstract questions also often get misinterpreted, so by the time the answer comes back, it appears the Japanese person is answering a completely different question. There aren't any good solutions to this problem, but the best practice is to keep questions simple and have a Japanese person on your side that can help supplement the translations or give you a good rundown after the meeting.

After all of that, if you can establish context, build a nonconfrontational rapport, and keep questions literal, the Japanese are intuitive thinkers and can come up with some pretty interesting ideas and answers. The big challenge for Westerners here is that Japanese are very comfortable with silence, they are very deliberate thinkers, and they are perfectionists. So, while the Japanese person is thinking and pondering, and taking up to a minute to answer a question, the impatient Westerner is already well on their way to asking the next question or raising the next topic. If the Japanese person's eyes are looking around side to side or they are subtly nodding their head up and down, my advice is to wait and see what they end up saying. They will let you know if they are ready to move on to the next topic. They will also appreciate your patience.

To highlight the challenge of communicating with the Japanese, here is an example of the different ways linear, lateral, and intuitive thinkers would answer the question, "What are your expectations for steel prices over the next twelve months?"

The linear thinker, for example, would answer, "We expect steel prices to fall. The reason is that prices are currently high, supply is starting to increase, inventories are building up, and demand is moderating, so we expect steel prices to fall."

The lateral thinker may start talking about their profit margins and the sensitivity of their margins to changes in steel prices because they think this is what you are most interested in. If you asked again, they may start talking about trends in property construction, or auto demand, or supply/demand factors impacting iron ore and coking coal markets. In my experience, you often need to ask these types of questions three times before they directly answer what they expect steel prices to do over the next twelve months.

The intuitive thinker will get caught up on details and context. They will ask whether you mean long or flat steel prices. Do you mean hot-rolled coil or cold-rolled coil, or galvanized steel? Do you mean for the domestic market or for export? You mean domestic hot-rolled coil, OK, do you mean the contract price or the spot price? After a lot of back and forth, you can eventually get to a standardized average price. Instead of asking such an open-ended question, I would usually give them their average selling price for the prior year or prior quarter, then ask whether the price is going higher or lower. After getting that answer, I would then ask their expectations for how much higher or lower, and only after getting that answer I would ask why.

I have a friend that sometimes asks Japanese managers "How do you think about pricing?" That question is very confusing for the literal-minded Japanese. How they think about pricing is that it is literally how much the customer needs to pay them for their product. What my friend means to ask is "You have very high market share for your product; why don't you charge a higher price?" The key is to be as specific as possible.

As a general rule in Japan (or China), Americans should also resist the urge to talk too much. East Asians tend to be deferential and their education system didn't teach them to debate or argue. My recommendation is to try to speak less and put more effort into listening and asking follow-up questions to try to draw out their views. I can't tell you the number of times I've seen Westerners talk over Japanese or Chinese and cut them off right before they were going to get to their point.

At the end of the day, all that will come out in a formal meeting will be the *tatemae* truth. Unless you've known your business associates for a long time and they've given you some body language clues as to the *honne* truth, formal meetings will stick to the surface-level truth. To uncover the *honne* truth, you'll need to build up the relationship. Ways to build a relationship with Japanese business associates include: playing a few rounds of golf, smoking some cigarettes together, eating some meals together, and going out for *karaoke* or other drinking *nijikai* or after-party parties.

FILTERS FOR UNDERSTANDING JAPANESE BEHAVIOR

- Maintain harmony always. Avoid any and all confrontation.
- Do not directly contradict, disagree with, or argue with others. Do not lose control of your emotions, ever.
- In Japan, society takes top priority.
- Place the company or group you belong to as your next top priority. Remember to act with the best interests of the group in mind.
- Acting with personal considerations as a top priority is seen as selfish and severely frowned upon. Avoid any actions that would shame the group.
- Family takes the third priority. Avoid any actions that would shame the family.
- No surprises. Try not to say or do anything unexpected or not fitting the circumstances.
- Try and impress upon others that you are reliable, trustworthy, loyal, and predictable.
- Never cause a superior to lose face.
- Always try and present oneself in a modest manner. Showing off or bragging is viewed negatively.
- Try not to seem too happy. If you are hardworking and serious, and have serious thoughts and considerations on your mind, excess happiness would reflect an irresponsible and insincere attitude.
- To gain the esteem of others, show yourself as one who can endure difficulties and is willing to readily sacrifice personal desires for the good of your group.

- Strive to do the best job possible in your position and give others the impression that you understand your position in the hierarchy.
- Corporate hierarchy is not determined by age, but rather by time working at the company. The *senpai* (senior)/*kohai* (junior) relationship is important.
- Avoid criticism as best as possible. Better to make no decision than a bad decision that could be criticized later.
- When given a clear task to accomplish, do the best job possible. Not the best job adjusted for time or money or effort. Just the best job possible.
- Interpret everything literally.
- Find related third parties or go-betweens to communicate criticisms or resolve disputes.
- Never discuss politics.
- Try not to have strong opinions (or keep them to yourself).

COMPARISONS IN AMERICAN AND CHINESE CULTURE

CHAPTER 29

SIMILARITIES AND DIFFERENCES BETWEEN AMERICAN AND CHINESE CULTURE

Despite the extremely different histories, there are many cultural similarities between Americans and the Chinese. Both countries believe they are great powers destined to have leading roles in the world and both naturally assume that they are always right. Personally, I've found the Chinese easier to understand and relate to than the Japanese. The value systems of Americans and Chinese are closer. Unlike the Japanese, Americans and Chinese people both look upon money and getting rich as good things. We also both consider a long life as a good thing and do not share the culture of death that developed in Japan.

Furthermore, both countries lack the caste mentality. Americans believe in the American Dream; anyone can become a success through hard work, grit, determination, having good ideas, and some luck. The Chinese dream of the same things and believe in the potential for success despite one's station at birth. Chinese and English also share roughly similar grammar and we both tend to be direct in our communication styles versus the indirect and always inscrutable Japanese.

One of the great difficulties in learning Japanese is that Japanese people do not expect a foreigner to speak their language, so are reluctant to converse with them. The Chinese are more like Americans in that we both expect overseas visitors to speak, or at least try to speak, our native languages. With China's large population and friendly populace, a foreign visitor has nearly unlimited potential language partners. The Chinese also express themselves quite similarly to Americans, and direct translation generally works well. The Chinese are very direct communicators, and, in fact, foreigners tend to be surprised at the blunt honesty of the Chinese.

This direct approach infiltrates every aspect of Chinese culture. For example, when I studied Aikido in Japan, I watched closely for the subtle clues from the sensei to see if I was moving correctly. My experience in China could not have been more different. After learning *Yang*-style Tai Chi, I moved on to a Chinese style of kung fu called *Meihuazhuang*, or *Plum Blossom Style*.

Experts could execute the moves on top of a grid of plum blossom stakes. Our *Shifu,* or teacher, taught in a very different style from what I observed in Japan. Class was disorganized, and there seemed to be no rhyme or reason as to which techniques he would focus on that day. Chinese martial arts developed set sequences of moves to help the practitioner to learn and remember the various techniques—something like a set dance with devastating kung fu moves hidden within. We would always spend the first twenty to thirty minutes of practice doing these routines. This was followed by instruction on specific moves.

A core tenet in martial arts is to never let your knee get over your toes. This is a weak position. One day in class, I accidentally ended up in a pose with my knee over my toes. I knew my position was weak. I didn't dare move my head, but shifted my eyes around looking for instruction from my *Shifu.* With all the subtlety of a jackhammer, the *Shifu* came from behind and leveled me with a forearm shiver. This whiplashed my neck, knocked the wind out of me, and put a shock through my entire nervous system. I sprawled to the ground. My first thought was *I'm not in Kansas anymore.* I was also aggrieved with my typical sense of American entitlement. How dare he hit me like that! When I got up, *Shifu*'s face was deadly serious. I never made that mistake again. Chinese feedback was hyper-direct. Oddly, the other Chinese students were jealous because they felt the *Shifu* was knocking me on my butt more often than them. That was special attention I would have gladly shared.

Another similarity between Chinese and American culture is that both are strongly motivated by money. Despite having a nominally communist government, the Chinese are naturally just as capitalistic as Americans. Successful Chinese entrepreneurs, usually from coastal southern China, can be found all over the world. Chinese history has not supported the rule of law, property rights, or political freedom, so a constant stream of immigrants left China to try their luck elsewhere. Many were successful.

This flow of emigrants increased after the communists took power. Mao was a brilliant military strategist, but did not understand economics. Anyone accused of being a capitalist roader or capitalist running dog during his rule was persecuted without mercy.

This all changed when Deng Xiaoping came to power. After the madness of the Cultural Revolution, there were too many crimes to be redressed. Deng said everyone needed to forget the past and look only to the future. In Chinese it is (向前看) face-future-look, but with the exact same pronunciation, it would also sound like (向钱看) face-money-look. I don't believe this was a coincidence. Deng understood economics and he understood the Chinese. Ever since his Reform and Opening Up policy, the Chinese have pursued wealth, driving incredible economic growth. The Chinese show the same strong work ethic and entrepreneurial spirit as Americans and they now have the second biggest economy in the world.

Like America, Chinese society does not have a caste system. The Confucian ideal dictates that the imperial examination system will find and reward the top students. Since this is based on exam scores, it is quite meritocratic.

This system remains even with the communist government. The Chinese Communist Party is actually a brutal meritocracy where the smartest, hardest working, and the most politically skilled advance. New blood must be found every generation and the Communist Party in China brings in the best and the brightest by offering invitations to join the party to the top students in the top schools across China. The stress is on bringing in the best students as opposed to those with the best party spirit. Successful capitalists are also invited to join the party. This way the privileged class absorbs those who would most effectively oppose the system.[191]

The Chinese, like Americans, also resist the urge to conform and this is present in diverse ways. In China, the family is the top consideration, but after that, the individual matters. When I learned Tai Chi for the first time, I was stunned at how virtually every single one of the thirty to forty or so Chinese people I was practicing with had their own unique flourishes and their moves were anything but mimicking the teacher. Hanging out

---

191 Richard McGregor's book *The Party* deeply influenced my views of the Chinese Communist Party and remains the best book I've read on how the party is structured and operates.

with my Chinese friends was interesting in a similar way as they all had unique views. Unlike the Japanese, the Chinese are very opinionated. Discussions are rich and varied and I always learned something new. With their lateral thought process, they consistently surprised me with their unique insights. The Chinese are also tolerant of others being different. This made life much easier as a foreigner than it was in Japan.

The Japanese have a dreadfully pessimistic view on life, they do not like to laugh much and what humor they do have is awfully dark. As an American, interaction with the Japanese tends to be quite serious. China is different. Given their history, the Chinese are cynical, but similar to Americans, the Chinese like to laugh. Their jokes are often more contextually driven and they love puns. Most of their linguistically-related jokes would not translate. A Western joke that reminds me of Chinese humor is the one about the frog that says, "Time is fun when you are having flies." The Chinese do also have jokes that end in punch lines and they like to make political jokes. Here are a few examples of Chinese jokes:

At the Chinese border, Jackie Chan was going through customs, but forgot his passport. The inspector asked him to prove he was Jackie Chan. He did some kung fu moves so the inspector waved him through. Yao Ming was next, but he also forgot his passport. He did some slam dunk moves so the inspector waved him through. Li Peng was next. (Li Peng is a famous politician in China that earned a bad reputation for taking sides against the students at Tiananmen.) He also forgot his passport. The inspector asked him to prove who he was. Li Peng apologized and said, "I'm sorry I can't do anything." The inspector waved him through.

A big brown bear asks a white rabbit if he is afraid of getting dirty. The rabbit says no. The bear asks if he fears bad smells. The rabbit says no. The bear asks if the rabbit is scared of the dark. The rabbit says no. So, the bear picks up the white rabbit and uses him to wipe his butt.

In 2013, thousands of dead pigs started to appear in rivers near Shanghai.[192] Unfortunately, this seemed to be the consequence of improving standards in China. Diseased pigs were supposed to be disposed of, but often ended up butchered and sold for meat in the black market. The clamp down on this black market led to many dead pigs ending up in the rivers. At the time, when thousands of dead pigs started to appear in rivers near Shanghai, a common joke in Shanghai was how lucky they all were. Breathing the polluted air was like free cigarettes and all they had to do was turn on their water taps to get free pork soup. Very cynical.

The major difference between China and the US is that China has a 5,000-year history as a continuous civilization, whereas the United States of America isn't even 250 years old.

---

192 Nicola Davison, "Rivers of Blood: The Dead Pigs Rotting in China's Water Supply," *The Guardian*, March 29, 2013, https://www.theguardian.com/world/2013/mar/29/dead-pigs-china-water-supply.

The Chinese are more fatalistic than Americans and are willing to accept unsatisfactory circumstances better. The Chinese have what they call the ability to "eat bitter" (吃苦) which means to deal with hardships. When I was a student in China, the Chinese undergrads were six to a room and only had hot water two hours per day. Their rooms had no heat and no air-conditioning, and they had to study at night by twenty-watt bulbs. Imagine studying in that dim light with all of the noise of five other people crowded into a room, usually with at least a couple of them talking. Yet, I rarely heard my Chinese classmates complain. According to Lin, the Chinese put up with far worse political and social environments than any country in the West and the Chinese just accepted this as the natural course of events.[193]

One of the first words foreigners learn in Chinese is *meibanfa* (没办法). It means *there is no way,* or *it can't be done,* or *it must be so.* For an American, it is frustrating how readily the Chinese will revert to the excuse of *meibanfa.*

Why is the pollution so bad? *Meibanfa.*

Can we get hot water in the dorms in the morning? *Meibanfa.*

Could we get fresh vegetables in the cafeteria? *Meibanfa.*

Can I install my own air-conditioner in my dorm? *Meibanfa.*

After a while, foreigners realize it is a convenient

---

193 Yutang Lin, *My Country and My People*, 44.

word. When you get invited to a lunch you don't want to attend, tell them your professor is scheduled to meet with you, so it is *meibanfa*. Get a question you don't want to answer, like "Why does America have to act as the world's policeman?" and it is sufficient to just answer: *meibanfa*.

Coincidentally, I flew back to Shanghai from Tibet the day after the US bombed the Chinese embassy in Belgrade in 1997. I had no idea it had happened. It was May and I needed to submit my final thesis to my professor. As I rode my bike across campus, I was surprised by the crowds of students and the artistic posters they put up. Some were drawings such as Bill Clinton cutting up the world like a piece of cake with blood dripping from his knife or the Statue of Liberty spitting on a large dragon.

As I was riding along looking at the signs, someone suddenly reached out and grabbed the handlebars of my bicycle. About twenty to thirty Chinese students menacingly circled me. They were mad, but I didn't have time to find out why. One screamed at me that America was an imperialist hegemon. I asked what that had to do with me. It didn't seem like a good time for a debate, so I claimed I was Canadian. The guy's fury subsided, and he let go of my bike. I thought I was free and clear. But then a girl in the back screamed out that Canada was an imperialist hegemon also. He grabbed my handlebars again. I started to panic, but then said something I'd read in a newspaper: the US is the big brother and Canada is just the little brother and must do what the US says. It is *meibanfa*. I was also *meibanfa* for what the US does. *Meibanfa* saved the day and they let me go. I decided to abandon my errand and seek out my professor a few days later.

Another striking difference for Westerners in China is the limited influence of religion. China has largely been a pragmatic society with little thought toward the supernatural.

Western morality comes out of a belief in God, but Chinese morality is different: it is based upon the best ways for people to treat other people with commandments that didn't come down from above, but from ethics that were written by scholars. Whereas Westerners find it surprising that morality could be non-religiously based, the Chinese find it equally odd that the supernatural needs to be invoked in order for people to behave decently with each other.[194]

It was interesting to have religious discussions with my Chinese friends. Communism doesn't allow for religion and this was brutally enforced in the Cultural Revolution. If you go to Taiwan, there are strong and visible Buddhist and Christian influences, but this is almost completely lacking in mainland China. The religious faith that is so important to Americans is replaced by a lukewarm to nonexistent faith in the Chinese Communist Party and a strong faith in the power of money. The irony is that despite being a so-called socialist economy, China has a wicked wealth gap problem. And now, many

194 Yutang Lin, *My Country and My People*, 101.

of those left behind are looking for something else. Many are turning to religion. China continues to crack down hard on religious expression, and most practitioners are underground, but there are a surprisingly large number of downtrodden believers in China that have turned to Christianity.

The impact of lack of religion can pop up in unexpected places. When I was living in Shanghai in the '90s, Chinese pedestrians would often wantonly jaywalk across big multilane streets late at night. Therefore, drivers rarely got in legal trouble for hitting a pedestrian at night. Drivers couldn't see them, and it was almost always the pedestrian's fault. The authorities, however, started noticing an odd trend. An unusually large number of cases were happening where drivers hit someone and then went back and ran them over again before driving off. The reason was that funeral expenses were far cheaper than hospital bills, so the drivers went back to finish the job. As a few taxi drivers explained to me, the authorities raised the cost of funerals for car accident victims and the problem was solved, at least in Shanghai. One would wish, at least from this Westerner's perspective, that religion or some other form of morality would have prevented those drivers from so callously taking life. I don't mean to pick on Shanghai. I've heard of many similar cases in many other parts of China over the years.

The Chinese education system also differs from the West. Chinese teaching is focused on rote learning. They call it "stuffed duck" (填鸭式) style education as teachers cram knowledge down their students throats like force-fed ducks. American education, alternatively, is focused on developing critical thinking. One outstanding difference I noticed right away in China was that the Chinese have extremely strong memories and powers of concentration due to the years and years of memorizing thousands of Chinese characters. US students do very little memorizing. For this reason, the Chinese do very well on standardized tests such as TOEFL, the GRE, the GMAT, etc. The flip side is that American students develop much better problem-solving abilities.

Despite not being linear thinkers, it's both a stereotype and a bit of a truism that Asians tend to be good at linear math. This is because their education emphasizes memorization and repetition. Schools in Asia drill math far more intensely than Americans, and practice makes perfect. This is something about Americans I've never understood. Math is one area where our "can-do" attitude wilts away. For some reason, we believe that kids are either born good at math or not good at math. It is one case where Americans say *meibanfa* and give up without a fight.

The Chinese (and Japanese) believe anyone can be good at math if they work at it. Their test scores speak for themselves. With exposure to both systems, it is clear that Americans are weak at math because the schools teach at a low level and don't drill. Oddly, Americans think drilling math problems will harm their kids somehow. After seeing the benefits of the Asian system, it looks like one team training to play football, but never doing running or weight training because it would be considered mindless repetition, while the other team gets to build up their strength and endurance with physical training. Naturally, the stronger and faster team wins.

China was an oppressed society for much of their history, but food was the one area where people were allowed to be creative and find enjoyment. This makes food a critical part of Chinese culture. Americans happily eat fast food or microwaved dinners and eat what has been called S.A.D. or the Standard American Diet. The Chinese are quite different. Home-cooked meals are the norm. When evaluating a Chinese company, I like to visit the cafeteria because you can tell from the food the company serves how it values its workers. (Fun fact: in the US, the stock market is open from 9:30 a.m. straight to 4 p.m. In China and Japan, the stock market closes for lunch, highlighting the importance of meals.)

Another striking difference is the attitude toward family. A Chinese friend that lived in the US explained it well to me. He said that in America you think of it as my family, whereas in China we think of it as our family. Being from southern China with the extreme emphasis on the clan, he could trace his roots back over 1,000 years.

With America's focus on individuality, we often give family a lower priority. In both societies, working couples are normal, but the Chinese would be baffled by the US proclivity to let strangers raise their children in day care centers while grandparents were left to live alone. Probably it is a reflection of the Chinese view that relationships are the only basis for trust, so grandparents would be the natural choice for watching their children. The US, on the other hand, focuses on convenience and capability. American parents probably feel that twenty-three-year-old day care workers have more energy to watch the kids. Obviously, Confucian emphasis on respect and appreciation for elders is in stark contrast to US materialism, a system that perpetuates the belief that old people are less productive, troublesome, expendable, and best sent off to old folks' homes.

If you are Chinese and are reading this, it might be helpful to know that humility is an Asian virtue, but not an American one. Something that always hurts me when I deal with Americans now is that they take my humble attitude for weakness, whereas in Japan or China one wins points for not bragging or for downplaying one's abilities. It's a great skill to turn down compliments in China and absolutely necessary to build relationships. Chinese people bristle when a foreigner accepts compliments or adopts what Chinese people consider to be an arrogant attitude. In the West, people tend to take humility and a humble attitude at face value and think you have low self-esteem and/or are truly incompetent. This also works against Asians when they interview with American companies.

Privacy is also viewed differently in China versus the West. China is an overpopulated country, so it is difficult to get any privacy. Plus, the Chinese love to (好管闲事) or *meddle in other people's personal affairs.* I always joked with my classmates that Americans leave other people alone, but we love to meddle in other countries' business, while China leaves other countries alone, but Chinese people love to meddle in other people's private lives. The word for privacy in Chinese is (隐私), which literally means *hiding myself* and the implication is that you are doing something wrong and want to hide it. In China, it takes a little while to get used to everyone asking you how much you earn at work, how much your shoes or jacket cost, how old you are, whether you have a girlfriend or are married, etc. In China this actually is a form of friendliness, but it is very different and very intrusive compared to our conventions in the West.

My worst privacy experience in China was as a grad student. I was in class when my stomach started to hurt. There were thirty minutes left in class. The pain was unbearable. I had no choice but to get up and run out to the bathroom.

The toilet was a trench with no doors and not even partitions. Just an open trench. I squatted down. Another student came in. I was embarrassed, but had bigger problems. The trench was about twenty feet long, but, inexplicably, he squatted right next to me. He lit up a cigarette. I hate cigarettes and was going to complain, but

I'd never shared a public toilet in China before so kept my mouth shut. He then went about his business. The smell was horrific. I asked him for a cigarette which he happily obliged. I never ever smoke, but I made an exception that day. A third student came into the bathroom. I was wondering how many more. He started chatting with me. I couldn't believe it. He asked where I was from, which department I was in, what my name was. I hadn't brought toilet paper with me, and I was cursing my luck. When he pulled a roll of toilet paper out of his bag, I sang hallelujah! Bizarrely, he examined the state of my bowel movement and told me I had diarrhea and should go home and eat an apple. Why an apple? No idea! Anyway, no privacy there!

In my experience, the Chinese and Americans also have a totally different sense of beauty. When I started as a local student, my male classmates asked me who I thought was the prettiest girl in the grad school. When I gave my answer, they laughed and laughed and said she was the ugliest. When I asked who they thought was the prettiest, I could only shake my head and agree with Kipling that "East is East and West is West and never the twain shall meet." They then repeated a phrase I have heard a number of times, "Thank goodness for the *laowai* (foreigners), otherwise the ugly girls in China would never have boyfriends." They then kicked themselves laughing.

CHAPTER 30

RULE OF LAW VERSUS RULE OF POWER

As I've mentioned in previous chapters, my litmus test for the level of rule of power in a society is crossing the street. If cars give way to pedestrians, there is something at work beyond the rule of power. In the US, cars generally give way, and this is mainly due to our emphasis on the rule of law. Other countries may criticize us for being excessively litigious, but that is a fair price for protecting the rights of people and property that we value so highly. In Japan, cars give way to pedestrians out of courtesy and respect. They don't need rules to tell them proper behavior. Tradition is enough. The Japanese also bow to each other for similar reasons. In China, cars will not give way to pedestrians and won't even stop at a red light if they are turning right. Even in broad daylight, pedestrians need to be very careful. Often, you'll see pedestrians cross the street in

China in large groups. This is the safest way. Otherwise, the rule on the road in China is that the bigger guy has right of way. (If the car has the white license plate of an official or the military, then you need to doubly get out of the way!)

One time, I was in a taxi on the way to the airport in Shanghai. I'd been in China for fifteen months straight and wanted to get home to see my family (and eat some decent desserts). It wasn't rush hour, but the streets were still busy. As we accelerated through a yellow light, an old man on a bicycle swerved right in front of us. We smashed into him. I'd never seen a car hit a person and assumed he was dead. I was overcome with horrific guilt. How come this man had to die just because I wanted to go home? It seemed so wrong. Then to my amazement, rising like Lazarus, the old man got to his feet and started scream-ing at the taxi driver. I was in shock. I couldn't close my mouth. The taxi driver then started screaming insults at the old man, telling him to watch where he was going.

I was sure I would miss my flight as we'd have to wait for the police. To my further surprise, we were soon back on our way to the airport. I looked through the rear window as the old man dusted himself off and walked away with his bicycle and a noticeable limp. I asked the driver what happened. He said that if he had been liable, he would have offered the man money. If it were enough, they would leave it at that. If it were not enough, they would have to wait for the police. But since it was the fault of the old man on the bike, there was no reason to pay any money. He told me it happened every day. I thought about how different it would be in the far more legalistic and litigious US.

China has a different philosophy toward law than we do in the West. As Shapiro highlighted, in China, historically, laws were meant to suppress unwanted behavior. "One of the main bulwarks of feudalism was its judicial system, embracing laws and a legal philosophy whose primary function was to suppress activities designated as crimes. Despite occasional slight modifications, the laws and philosophies remained essentially the same for over two millennia—something of a record in world judicial history."[195] The law was not there for the common people. Shapiro also explained that laws were not made public until 536 BC in the state of Zheng.[196] Before that, for at least 1,500 years of recorded history, citizens didn't know the laws or their consequences until they were punished for breaking them.

Chinese law always focused on rule of power and not justice for or the rights of the people. Speaking of a Chinese philosopher from over 2,000 years ago, Lin noted the lack of legal protection was a big source of official corruption and the helplessness of the people. Even 2,000 years ago, this philosopher had remarked that the lack of the rule of law was the main problem with the Chinese

---

195 Sidney Shapiro, *The Law and Lore of China's Criminal Justice*, 9.

196 Sidney Shapiro, *The Law and Lore of China's Criminal Justice*, 17.

system, and Lin saw this was still an influence in modern times.[197]

Lin faults the lack of faith in linear logic as one of the reasons China did not embrace the rule of law. Rule of law, after all is a system applied universally to all conditions, and to the Chinese this lack of adaptability is inhuman. Because they value reasonableness over reason, the Chinese detest inflexible rules, and rule of law is culturally impossible.[198] Without the rule of law in place, officials were free to abuse their power and that trickled down into society, with the result that "the great officials break the great laws, the small officials break the small laws."[199] Universal discipline simply does not exist.

This led to *rule of people* instead of *rule by abstract laws*. Mao said that laws are dead, but people are living, so people should decide right and wrong. Chinese morality and ethics focused on relationships, primarily the Five Cardinal Relationships as laid out by Confucius. This caused the Chinese to de-emphasize universal laws that would apply for any person at any time in any society.[200] Rule of law implies blind or impartial justice and that just doesn't work in hierarchical societies where all people are decidedly not created equal.

Westerners have a difficult time understanding the

197 Yutang Lin, *My Country and My People*, 199.

198 Yutang Lin, *My Country and My People*, 107.

199 Yutang Lin, *My Country and My People*, 176.

200 Hajime Nakamura, *Ways of Thinking of Eastern Peoples*, 248.

concept of *rule of power* as opposed to *rule of law*. But for people in the East, order is the top priority and disorder is the top fear. East Asians are willing to sacrifice rule of law, personal liberties, and property rights in exchange for the security that a strong central leader can provide. To wit, van Wolferen states:

> "Westerners take it for granted that society is regulated automatically by laws and universal principles that they almost never fully appreciate the acute Japanese sense of the need for constant vigilance. In so far as the order as represented by the system has ultimate meaning, unchallenged by any religious or secular belief system, maintenance of order must be an ultimate aim."[201]

It is the same in China, where an iron fist is the only solution for maintaining order. This is a major point of misunderstanding for Americans looking for justification of China's draconian laws, such as their one-child policy.

Without rule of law or a strong role for abstract religion, behavior became regulated by shame. Benedict explained the differences between shame and guilt cultures: Shame cultures are driven by punishments from those in authority, while guilt cultures are driven by personal feeling of having sinned against a rule of God, who is always watching. A person in a shame culture does not have to worry if their bad behavior is undiscovered. There

---

201 Karel van Wolferen, *The Enigma of Japanese Power*, 363.

would be no reason ever for any voluntary confession like we could find in Western religions.[202]

China and Japan are shame cultures, which is to say personal behavior is motivated by the avoidance of shame. Chinese people will do anything not to bring shame to their clan. Japanese people will do anything not to bring shame to their country or immediate family. This creates a very orderly and fairly safe environment. The flaw in this system is that no behavior is considered wrong as long as the perpetrator doesn't get caught. Also, when order breaks down, such as during the Cultural Revolution or the Nanjing massacre, this lack of guilt-based restraint can lead to extreme behavior.

Western society is guilt-based. It is far less strict, but God is always watching, so something can be wrong even if one does not get caught.

As a Westerner, I've always struggled with where a society without God finds its moral compass. In Japan and China, the view of not shaming the family or not getting caught and punished are the big restraints on behavior. But what about when no one is watching? Adultery seems (to me) to be much more common in the East. For example, my Chinese friends have a saying: "MBA" meaning "married-but-available." Many of my Chinese friends don't see anything wrong with this. Their rationalization is that Westerners often fool around before marriage, but this option isn't available to the Chinese as they are much

202 Ruth Benedict, *The Chrysanthemum and the Sword*, 223.

more serious in their student days. So, their turn to fool around is after they are married. In Japan, it is not uncommon for the wife to stop sleeping in the same room as her husband once the children are all born. If everything is kept hush-hush, outside relationships don't seem to be a problem.

Another major difference in a shame/rule of power culture versus a guilt/rule of law culture is what to do after you've broken a rule. My experience is that if you break a rule in America, the best course of action is to come clean as quickly as possible with full cooperation. This usually wins goodwill for presenting the infraction before being discovered and minimizes punishment. On the other hand, in China, it is best to immediately stop doing the action/behavior in question and, if the relevant Chinese regulators find out about your infraction, but you've already stopped, then the issue will disappear. At worst, you will just be warned in private to not do it again. If you preemptively admit you've been breaking the rules, the relevant authorities will lose face and have no choice but to punish you severely.

Benedict describes this situation from the perspective of Americans in Japanese prisoner of war camps. Even in Japanese POW camps, the American prisoners were told by their guards to hide any rule breaking. The guards tolerated rule breaking as long as it was kept well hidden.[203]

Once you've been caught breaking a rule in Asia, the

203 Ruth Benedict, *The Chrysanthemum and the Sword*, 39.

only choice is to apologize profusely. If you have been accused of a crime in Asia, you are guilty until proven innocent and a confession is expected even if you aren't guilty. Not confessing could get you into even more trouble. Just to be accused means you must have done something wrong.

Van Wolferen writes that in Japan, "police and prosecutors love apologies," and this seems applicable across East Asia. One of the primary factors in a judgment in the East is the defendant's display of remorse. Whether guilty or innocent, a suspect is expected to unleash innumerable apologies. The more apologies offered, the more "sincere" their remorse.[204]

What an absolute truth-believing Westerner would miss in this scenario is that even if you are not guilty, a stream of apologies is required. (One corollary for China is that if you are being accused by a fellow commoner in a social situation, never apologize; thus you can avoid admitting guilt and therefore liability.)

Without the rule of law to support regulation, China's fundamental complication is in figuring out how to restrain the behavior of those in power. This conundrum jumped into the public spotlight with the Li Gang incident. In 2010, in Hebei Province, a son of an official hit two people on a college campus while he was driving drunk. The accident killed one of them. He drove away from the scene, but security guards finally tracked him

204 Karel van Wolferen, *The Enigma of Japanese Power*, 188.

down. When arrested, he infamously shouted out, "Go ahead, sue me if you dare. My Dad is Li Gang." His father was a local official in the public security bureau. The story spread on the internet and now the phrase "My Dad is Li Gang" is used online to mean someone who does not want to take responsibility.[205]

There was plenty of outrage at this incident, but this special privilege for officials and their families has been around for thousands of years. As Lin described, China has really only ever had two distinct social classes. The ruling class was above the law, while the regular people did all of the hard work and received no special privileges or rights. However, one's status in this system was not fixed. Through the meritocratic Imperial Examination System, anyone from any level of society could become a member of the ruling class.[206] Amazingly or not, this system survives to this day with the 90 million or so Communist Party members as the new ruling class with diplomatic immunity inside their own country.

Democracy in China remains a strongly hoped-for Western political goal. There still remains an idea that as China gets wealthier and more exposed to the outside world, the emerging middle class and left-behind lower class will push for democracy and the overthrowing of the Communist Party. Many believe that the extent of

---

205 "My Dad is Li Gang!" *Know Your Meme,* January 15, 2011, https://knowyourmeme.com/memes/events/my-dad-is-li-gang-我爸是李刚.

206 Yutang Lin, *My Country and My People*, 180.

the protests in 1989 at Tiananmen Square indicate a democratic revolution will eventually occur in China. This, of course, couldn't be further from the truth. Order is the top psychological need of the Chinese people and the majority of the Chinese population prefer the order the Communist Party provides. Most protests are against local officials and most people support and believe in the central government. Plus, the institutions and philosophies that have ruled China have been in place for thousands of years. Despite the belief of Americans, that cannot be simply changed by outside pressure and a new constitution.

Even eighty years ago, Lin recognized that the hurdle standing in the way of Chinese democracy was (and still is) face. Chinese officials lose face when they adhere to a rule of law, and until they are willing to give up this class privilege, true democracy cannot be formed.[207]

One of the key reasons (motivated by linear logic) behind allowing China into the WTO was the assumption that China's entrance to the global trading system would accelerate its wealth creation and transition to democracy—similar to what happened in Taiwan and Korea. It is clear looking back, (and was also obvious at the time) that allowing a country without a market-based financial system into the global trading system was a huge mistake. Chinese banks can subsidize Chinese companies with an effectively 0 percent cost of capital. Competing against

---

207 Yutang Lin, *My Country and My People*, 179.

companies with such low funding costs is extremely difficult. Add to that the lack of effective unions; super-lax labor laws; subsidies on land, water, and electricity; and unenforced environmental restrictions, there was no way American workers could compete. The shift of manufacturing jobs to China devastated the manufacturing sector in the US.

Adding insult to injury, this transition was advocated with the reasoning that the ability for Americans to import goods from China at such low prices would benefit consumers. That was terribly misguided and elitist. Which American cares if they can buy cheap stuff from Walmart if their job has been outsourced to China? Shifting jobs to China meant we shifted the means for creating wealth to China. So, letting China into the WTO was a terrible mistake for the US from a jobs- and wealth-creation perspective. It also accelerated the transition of technology, by hook or by crook, from American companies to Chinese companies.

For those more cynically minded, there was a benefit to the ruling class in the US. Allowing China into the WTO was very deflationary globally, allowing the US to maintain lower interest rates and more aggressive monetary policy on average. This pushed up asset prices and particularly benefited the so-called 1 percent.

For those that are still waiting for democracy in China, my advice is: don't hold your breath. Xi Jinping recently scrapped his term limits, making him president for life.

Instead of moving toward democracy, Xi just crowned himself the new Emperor of China.

CHAPTER 31

BUSINESS IN CHINA

The Chinese economy is a hybrid model, mixing social-ism and capitalism. China started off as a socialist economy, but that was too inefficient so, thanks to the remarkably flexible lateral thinking of Deng Xiaoping, they adopted market economics. Basically, today China is a socialist economy with high state ownership and control over companies and industries, but this structure has cap-italist features in that they allow for market-based pricing and for private companies to operate. The financial sector, however, remains dominated by the state. In the US, we are familiar with the government owning the post office or the water company, but with the Chinese system, the government also owns big stakes in the equivalents of Citibank and JP Morgan, General Motors and Ford, GE and Exxon Mobile, as well as companies like Disney or the *New York Times* or CNN. Unlike the US, where we try to minimize government involvement, the Chinese government develops detailed five-year plans for the economy and directs companies to achieve the goals set therein. We are currently in the thirteenth five-year plan (2016 to 2020). Given the awesome development of China over the past thirty years, the merits of this socialist-capitalist model are increasingly being discussed.

When doing business in China, the first step is to determine what kind of company you are dealing with. Is it a central-government-owned state-owned enterprise (SOE), a provincial- or city-government-owned SOE, or a private non-government-related company? The lower the level of government ownership, generally the higher the focus on profits. In China, a "private" company would mean it is run by a non-government management whose leadership was not appointed by the government, and in which the government would not have a stake. A company's public or private status does not reflect its presence on the stock exchange. The Chinese would simply refer to a company as "listed" or "non-listed." A listed SOE is publicly traded on a stock market and owned by the government. A listed private company would be similarly publicly traded on a stock market, but privately owned.

The most influential companies in China are SOEs. That moniker is a bit of a misnomer, however, as they are in reality POEs or party-owned enterprises. We are used to thinking of countries being run by their government, but in China's case, it is the Chinese Communist Party and not the government that runs China.

In Chinese communist political philosophy, economics is just one branch of politics. The key point here is that in China the Communist Party runs the government and the economy, and views the two as closely interrelated. Mao famously said, "Political power comes from the barrel of a gun (枪杆子里面出政权)." Everything is a function of politics, so politics and business go hand in hand. For example, the party may promote a promising official from running a town to running an SOE. And after that stint is over, the official could seamlessly move back from the business world to a new political position.

Imagine if the mayor of New York were installed as the head of Boeing and, if that went well, was then transferred to become the governor of Texas.

The challenge with the Chinese state-dominated system is that SOE managers rarely have a stake in the company. They don't care if the SOE becomes over-leveraged with debt and they don't really care about profitability (or the environment). They benefit from size. Local officials have traditionally been promoted on delivering employment and GDP growth. Therefore, local officials lean on the banks to lend to the SOEs, who invest for growth without too much consideration for returns.

The government owns the SOEs and also owns the banks, so a bank lending to an SOE is like shifting money from one pocket to another pocket in the same pair of pants. The result is that bank borrowing costs are quite low or effectively zero for SOEs, but are much higher for private companies. There are two reasons for this: The first is that bank lending is restricted by quota and SOEs leverage their relationship with the state-owned banks to use up that quota. Private companies without access to the bank lending quota are forced to borrow from the shadow banking market. The second reason is that private companies have the potential to default, while SOEs, in theory, can always pay back loans as they can always borrow more to repay existing loans. If that sounds troubling, it should. Non-risk-adjusted lending is fine during growth booms, but once the boom ends, bad debts become a colossal burden.

This lack of incentivizing profit is one of the reasons China has such a large industrial over-capacity problem. Even if an SOE is operating at a loss, the government will resist closure or shrinkage. First off, there is no disincentive to management or the local government if the company is not profitable, as they can always get the local state-owned bank to roll their loans. Secondly, closing or downsizing the factory will hurt employment. Finally, local governments collect part of the Value-Added-Tax (VAT) in China, which is assessed on top-line sales. So, if a company keeps producing at a loss at the net profit level, the local government will still receive their VAT share from top-line revenues.

It is difficult for private (non-state) companies in China to compete with SOEs due to much higher capital costs. One advantage held by private companies, however, is that they can be far more nimble and profit focused. Many SOEs have difficulty developing technology. Chinese SOEs had joint ventures with leading global auto companies for almost twenty years in some cases, but these Chinese companies have yet to produce a competitive Chinese car model. Some would say they are too fat and happy in their profitable joint ventures (JVs) and less incentivized to innovate. Others would say it is the SOE mentality to be less market oriented. Either way, the best Chinese locally-developed cars are coming from the smaller, private Chinese auto companies. Private or State Owned, the Chinese government will use soft loans and subsidies to support any company they believe can develop into a successful global brand.

Chinese SOEs are huge value destroyers relative to the private companies in China. Chinese SOEs receive over 80 percent of total bank loans and, for the stock market listed SOEs, their return on assets was 2.2 percent in 2015 versus 5.2 percent for the listed private companies.[208] Despite getting 80 percent of bank loans, only 25 percent of gross industrial output comes from state-owned companies.[209] The majority of job creation also comes from private companies.[210]

---

208 Wu Jiangang, "SOE Reforms Provide Opportunities for Foreign Investment," *The Telegraph*, November 13, 2015, http://www.telegraph.co.uk/sponsored/china-watch/business/11980699/china-soe-reforms-foreign-investment.html.

209 Peter R. Orszag, "Private Companies are Driving China's Growth," *Bloomberg Opinion*, October 14, 2014, https://www.bloomberg.com/view/articles/2014-10-14/private-companies-are-driving-china-s-growth.

210 "Chart: In China, Employment Growth is Led by the Private Sector," *The World Bank*, October 25, 2012, http://blogs.worldbank.org/developmenttalk/chart-in-china-employment-growth-is-led-by-the-private-sector.

SOE REFORM

In the late '90s, Zhu Rongji set the pieces for China's incredible growth over the past fifteen years. He gave all of the public housing units to the people, which was a big shift in wealth and mindset. He also embarked on bold SOE reform. Many smaller SOEs were sold to private managers, some of the worst were shut down, and millions of state workers were laid off. The economy became dramatically more efficient.

The current government's efforts on SOE reform are quite different. Instead of moving toward more private control, they are actually moving toward more state control. The true underlying problem in the Chinese economy is the non-market allocation of capital. Moving in the direction of state control only makes capital allocation worse. The Chinese are making other efforts to reform their SOEs, but mostly the changes have been cosmetic and not addressing the core issues. They are merging some of the bigger SOEs together, but this is amalgamation and not consolidation. Chinese officials also talk about switching to professional management, but aren't ready to take this step. The good news, however, is the country as a whole is finally getting more aggressive at addressing the over-capacity problem and closing down outdated, energy inefficient, and highly polluting capacity, particularly if it is privately owned.

AIM-FIRE-READY

One big difference between American companies and private Chinese companies is the way they develop new businesses. For linear-thinking Americans, the steps to start a business are **ready-aim-fire**: develop a business plan (ready), raise the money required to create the business and develop a marketing plan (aim), then execute the plan (fire). Basically, Americans look at the market and then develop a product. Chinese are lateral thinkers and more of what I would call **aim-fire-ready**. The Chinese will look at how much money they have or can raise (aim) and develop a business to fit their budget and start selling (fire). Then, according to how the business goes, they will adjust their plan (ready). (Some of my Chinese friends disagree and think the Chinese business style is fire-fire-fire.)

Here is an example of a Chinese company following the aim-fire-ready model. One of the biggest flat panel producers in the world decided to acquire hospitals. I asked the company what producing screens for TVs or smartphones had to do with running a hospital. They didn't bat an eye. Here was their lateral logic: since they operate mega-sized factories, they have very good relationships with the governments in the localities where they operate. They said that everyone knows running hospitals in China is a good business, but the difficult part was buying out poorly run, existing state-owned hospitals. With their government connections, they realized their advantage over competitors in securing these deals. So, they "aimed" at hospitals, they "fired" by acquiring some, and now they were getting "ready" to operate them. I asked again what they knew about running hospitals. Their answer was that they would learn as they went along! Aim-fire-ready.

I think BYD is another good example of Chinese entrepreneurial business development. They started off as a small maker of rechargeable batteries. They grew over time and, with the money they had amassed, decided to start making gasoline engine cars. This lateral move from manufacturing cell phone batteries to producing gasoline engine cars seemed inscrutable to stock market investors, who were unable to draw a connection between these two products. BYD's thinking was that they were good at batteries so they could make electric vehicles in the future, therefore normal cars would be a good in-between step. The business started well, which allowed the company to leverage this success to go into solar equipment and electric buses. BYD went into new businesses first with only lateral connections: rechargeable batteries to gasoline engine cars to solar to electric buses to electric cars, and they learned each new business as they went along.

CHINESE COST COMPETITIVENESS

Another big difference between American and Chinese

businesses is the Chinese attitude toward costs. Chinese companies originally started off with huge cost advantages. The perception in the West was that this was primarily due to cheap labor, but there were many other factors. If the Chinese company was state owned, well connected, or focused only on gaining market share, the management wouldn't factor funding, advertising, R&D, management costs, fixed factory costs, depreciation, or anything else at the SG&A line into pricing. Energy and water prices are also artificially low for industrial companies in China. Only the variable costs of materials, manufacturing wages, and distribution are considered. Pension or medical costs for employees are low. There are no real unions, and costs from environmental concerns are minimal. On top of all of that, Chinese companies get export tax rebates of up to 17 percent to help them sell overseas. China also massively weakened their currency in the mid-1990s and rode that tailwind for two decades. Lastly, they are not shy about reverse engineering or patent infringement, which dramatically lowers development costs.

Amazingly, almost twenty years too late, the US is realizing it made a mistake allowing China into the WTO because of these unfair, low-cost aspects of manufacturing in China. It took a long time, but the resultant massive trade deficit the US has with China and the huge loss of manufacturing jobs in the US, as well as the incredible amounts of intellectual property China has infringed upon or stolen have finally caused the US to wake up to the problem and to respond by ratcheting up trade tensions.

On top of the rising threats of a trade war, another challenge for China today is that labor costs have risen more than double digits for most of the past fifteen years. Chinese labor is no longer cheap and automation technology is improving rapidly. The government is also increasing its enforcement of environmental standards. The Chinese response to this situation is pragmatic. They would rather the Chinese companies lay off workers and add robots to the workforce than to allow the factories to move back overseas. Huge supply chains have built up in China over the past decades, so this strategy appears sound. Blue-collar employment remains the open question. But with the one-child policy and shrinking working age population, increased automation is not as big a problem as it seems. Most one-child policy kids don't want to work fifteen hours a day, six days a week in an assembly shop anyway, as they've grown up as the spoiled generation. Amazingly, despite the 1.4 billion person population, one of the most frequent complaints I hear from factory owners in China today is the shrinking labor pool. They simply cannot find enough workers and need to run their plants at below full capacity as they ramp up automation.

CHINESE QUALITY VERSUS JAPANESE QUALITY

The final aspect of doing business in China I would high-light is the surprising trend toward a decline in quality over time of Chinese manufacturing runs. Of course, overall Chinese manufacturing is steadily moving up the quality curve. They are producing increasingly sophisticated goods. The Chinese pace of advancement is dizzyingly fast as they attempt to or are leapfrogging in such areas as telecommunications, ecommerce, mobile payments, artificial intelligence, machine learning, robotics, semi-conductors, new energy, electric vehicles, and genomics.

The issue is that production on existing product models in China tends to decline over time. This is different from Japanese companies. Japanese manufacturing quality on a specific product almost always improves over time. The Japanese have a word for this, *kaizen* or "constant and never-ending improvement." The Japanese have a tendency to become absorbed and obsessed with perfecting what they are working on. Chinese manufac-turers have an opposing goal. They are obsessed with accomplishing something new, but, once accomplished, they start to lose interest. I've heard many times over the years that the best-quality ships, cars, or various man-ufactured goods in China are in the first runs and the quality of later runs actually declines over time.

The other issue is the cost-cutting mentality that impacts quality. In his brilliant book *Poorly Made in China*, Paul Midler describes it as "quality fade," where "the incremental degradation [of Chinese products] was subtle and continuous..."[211] Basically, the Chinese would price new products attractively to gain new business and then over time find ways to cut corners to lower costs and increase their margins. Buyers were often locked into contracts and would have difficulty switching suppliers.

Fundamentally, the Japanese have a strong focus on craftsmanship, whereas the Chinese focus on money and profits. If you ask any Chinese businessman what his margins are, he will almost always tell you in terms of gross margins. (Japanese account for investment and other overhead costs and will tell you their operating margins.) To the Chinese, what matters is the incremental benefit from selling one more item on a cash basis. Gross margins are the key. And the best ways to increase their gross margins are to raise prices or lower costs of goods sold. If a Chinese manufacturer can't push or sneak through a price increase, the only alternative is to reduce costs. Chinese manufacturers will relentlessly look for any angle to use cheaper materials or processes to lower costs, which adds directly to their gross margins, but also hurts quality.

The funny thing from my experience is that if you get deep into one of these discussions and the Chinese business owner has found a way to raise gross margins just 1 percent, they will start laughing and proudly exclaim their cunning in finding this way to raise margins 1 per-

---

211 Paul Midler, "Introduction," in *Poorly Made in China* (Hoboken, New Jersey: John Wiley & Sons, Inc., 2011), xvii.

cent. At 2 percent they go into fits of laughter (behavior that would seem odd for an American and is completely unthinkable for a Japanese business person).

BEST PRACTICES FOR BUSINESS MEETINGS IN CHINA

Compared to Japan, business meetings in China are much more casual. Chit-chat to break the ice is allowed at the start of the meeting. No need to wear the formal attire that would be customary for a meeting in Japan: dark suit with a light shirt and a tie. It is OK to dress formally in Beijing or Shanghai, but business casual is better. Outside of the major cities, business casual works the best. If you are in a smaller town, don't be surprised to see the Chinese businessman dressed in a polo shirt. The exchange of business cards is also less formal. The Japanese treat the business card as sacred, but not the Chinese. Anyway, today it is more important to exchange WeChat QR codes than it is to exchange business cards.

One bit of advice for foreigners visiting companies in China: you may think making an appointment for a meeting is enough, but it is not that easy. You'll need to reconfirm meetings in China one week ahead, one day ahead, and again that morning. Things can always change. The Chinese don't feel it is rude to reconfirm so many times and they don't think it is rude to change their schedule if something more important comes up. So, if you are traveling all the way to China, have some backup meeting ideas just in case you need to make some last-minute changes.

Chinese managers will always keep their cell phone on and even take calls during meetings and think nothing of it. The caller could be a more important person, about a more important event, or from their spouse or significant other. My advice is to smile and wait patiently. (My experience is that if a Chinese wife/girlfriend or husband/boyfriend doesn't have their call answered, they tend to get very suspicious. So, one always keeps their phone charged and answers every time it rings.)

One striking difference from Japan is the number of female managers in Chinese companies. In twenty years, I've met one female CEO of a Japanese company, and I've never met a female CFO in Japan. In China, female CEOs are not unusual and female CFOs are even more common. (This is just a personal observation, but in my experience, female CFOs in China generally have a much better grasp of the numbers than male CFOs.)

When asking questions in a business meeting in China, my advice again is to be patient. Linear-thinking Americans will answer the question that is asked. The Chinese will answer what they think you are asking. When a Westerner asks a question, they expect a logical answer related to their question, but the *Chinese person will put it into context and try and answer what they think you need to know.* In other words, Chinese people think contextually and not logically. This causes huge mischief as the Chinese person will often think they know better what you want and this causes huge frustration, confusion, and anger for the Westerner. My advice to Americans is to not react. Listen and see what they say, particularly earlier in the meeting. You may not learn what you were expecting, but you will learn what they think is important.

To give a flavor for communicating with lateral thinkers (and in contrast to linear or intuitive thinkers), this is an example of different conversations I've had recently regarding the potential impact of autonomous driving.

The linear-thinking American I asked talked about cause and effect. Many truck drivers, bus drivers, and taxi/Uber drivers would lose their jobs. At the same time, the accident rate should decline a lot and it would be much safer. Auto insurance companies would lose a lot of business. Once the linear thinker felt that autonomous driving was better than human drivers, their all or nothing mind-set concluded that most or all cars should become autonomous.

The Chinese lateral thinker I asked immediately went off on a tangent and their answer was that their government would manage the centralized control system and could determine how fast each car goes. So for example, if I have a low social score (perhaps I criticized the Communist Party when I was in high school), then my car would go slower. I'd waste time and lose face as my higher-social-score neighbors' cars would go faster and take the more efficient routes. The shift to autonomous cars would increase government control of society. As a lateral thinker, they also focused more on incremental change and unexpected consequences, such as considering whether the cost benefit of fuel savings and fewer accidents needed to be weighed against lost jobs and other unknown side effects. The shift, they said, needs to happen over a phased transition period. Autonomous cars should be tried out in certain cities first to see how it goes, and then adjust and expand in steps.

The Japanese intuitive thinker I asked first focused on details and context. It seemed like a straightforward question, but they asked if I meant autonomous level I (cruise control), which we've had for decades, or autonomous level II or level III like a Tesla has today, or level IV, or completely autonomous level V. Once I defined the level of autonomous driving as level V, they talked about the details of how the car would change—for example, no steering wheel, no brakes, no gear shift. They described how cars would become standardized and commoditized and the dramatic impact that would have on auto companies. I stayed quiet and allowed them time to contemplate and they then also talked about how driving will be much safer and cars will require less steel, but more plastic and the impact this would have on the steel industry.

When talking with lateral thinkers, if you don't get what you are looking for with their initial answer, my trick is to ask the exact same question three times in a row. Chinese lateral minds will often switch the subject in their answer. By the third time, your Chinese conversation partner will generally realize you mean specifically the subject you are asking about and will answer your question directly. If other Westerners are in your meeting, let them know what you are doing so they don't cut in the middle with a different line of questions or look at you like you are crazy for asking the exact same question three times in a row.

As a reminder from Lin: "We have a natural distrust of arguments that are too perfect and theories that are too logical. Against such logical freaks of theories, common sense is the best and most effective antidote."[212] Chinese people think differently from us. They will jump from 40,000 feet to minute details and back again. It can feel like whiplash. Try to find common ground. When in a disagreement, don't try to explain logically what you want; instead make statements (even if they are irrelevant) that they will agree with. This will create common understanding.

If you feel the meeting is not getting anywhere, try throwing out a word or two and see how they react. With their lateral minds, the meeting can go to some interesting places.

If you need a specific answer, however, try a different technique. First, you need to set the context of the past. Then the context of the present. Numbers are the best if possible, so using concrete examples of units manufac-

212   Yutang Lin, *My Country and My People*, 104.

tured or pricing metrics is a good tactic. Then ask them about the future. With the context established, they will know how to answer what you are looking for.

For example, if you ask the leader of a company what their future expansion plans are, the answer invariably will be that they will grow with the market. If you then ask how much they expect the market to grow, their lateral minds will leap into all of the factors that impact market growth. The answer will never come. Better to ask what their production was last year, then this year. With those numbers in their mind, then ask what number for next year and the target for three years from now. You can understand their expectations for growth from their capacity expansion plans. If you need a specific answer, they'll need a specific context.

If the meeting goes well, Chinese managers will sometimes invite you to lunch or to dinner. They usually are not just being polite and it is a good idea to accept their invitation. On top of a delicious multicourse banquet with lots of different dishes you may have never seen before, this is a great opportunity for exchanging information and building your relationship. This makes future meetings much better. If you are willing to toast with them, an even deeper relationship can be built. All the better if you smoke also. Don't be surprised if your Chinese dinner companions use their chopsticks to put food onto your plate. That is a sign of friendship. In the US, we tend to do business and then build the relationship, whereas in China you build the relationship first and then do business.

My advice to Chinese (or Japanese) people when communicating with linear-thinking Americans is to start with the conclusion. This will feel very unnatural, as East Asian instincts are to set the context first and explain the arguments and counter-arguments. Asians often tell me that repeating the conclusion seems too repetitive to them. The problem is that the American will lose interest very quickly and wonder what the point is. The solution for communicating with Americans is the classic advice to "tell 'em what you're going to tell 'em; tell 'em; then tell 'em what you told 'em." If Americans are interested in anything beyond your conclusions, wait for their questions. And again, give the answer first followed by an explanation.

CHAPTER 32

NEGOTIATING WITH THE CHINESE

The Chinese are extremely tough negotiators. Their mental flexibility and lateral thinking make them skilled at finding compromise solutions that often work in their favor. Their sense of truth is also different from ours in the West, and that can lead to further misunderstandings. On top of that, during the backward era of socialist economics under Mao, they had to learn to negotiate from a position of weakness. Negotiating with the Chinese is never easy. Of everyone I've ever met or talked to or read, Lucian Pye was the best at describing how to negotiate with the Chinese, so I strongly recommend anyone interested in learning more about the ins and outs of negotiating with the Chinese read Pye's books.

Pye lists his key factors: "The most elementary rules for negotiating with the Chinese are: (1) practice patience;

(2) accept as normal prolonged periods of no movement; (3) control against exaggerated expectations; (4) expect that the Chinese will try to influence by shaming; (5) resist the temptation to believe that difficulties may be caused by one's own mistakes; (6) try to understand Chinese cultural traits, but never believe that a foreigner can practice them better than the Chinese."[213]

Patience is a key point. "For Chinese officials, displaying impatience is a major sin, and they are masters of the art of stalling while keeping alive the other party's hopes."[214] Westerners often do not appreciate the incredible powers of patience the Chinese possess. I've seen Chinese students sit in an uncomfortable wooden chair in an unheated classroom in the winter to study for their TOEFL or GMAT exams for seven hours straight. The competition of a country of 1.4 billion people is enormous and forces people to extremes in order to stand out and move ahead. I could never sit in one place with my head in a book for seven straight hours. I need to get up to stretch, get a snack, go to the bathroom, take a break and clear my head, or go have a chat with someone. My Chinese classmates, however, would sit there locked in concentration and (amazingly) seemed not too fussed when they were finished.

Contrast this with the ADHD culture in America where we want instant news and instant gratification. "...

213 Lucian W. Pye, *Chinese Negotiating Style—Commercial Approaches and Cultural Principles*, xvi.

214 Lucian W. Pye, *Chinese Negotiating Style—Commercial Approaches and Cultural Principles*, xiv.

the Chinese consciously use such slowdown techniques as bargaining ploys because they believe they can exploit a natural American tendency for impatience."[215] If you are in negotiations with the Chinese, devise strategies to get rest or share the burden with a partner. Having a deadline where you have to leave is also important. Otherwise, your Chinese counterpart will fill up any available space with the kind of meaningless back and forth that is designed to wear you down. The deadline and your threats to walk away are the best defense you have. If you go in with the attitude that you must get a deal done, they will take advantage of your urgency and use it against you.

Another outstanding feature of negotiating with the Chinese in my observation is that they start off asking for way more than they expect to get and offer far less than they are willing to give. The Chinese consider negotiating a game. They want to see how much they can get for how little offered. Their culture of no absolute truths and finding middle ground makes them masters of compromise.

Anyone negotiating with the Chinese also needs to go into the process asking for more than they expect and with concessions held back that they don't mind giving up in the process. I cry for the Americans when I think about the negotiations that allowed the Chinese into the WTO. In exchange for open economy access to the WTO trading system, China only had to promise opening up measures that they could delay on (or not even follow through with)

215 Lucian W. Pye, *Chinese Negotiating Style—Commercial Approaches and Cultural Principles*, 14.

indefinitely and promise to stop infringing on US intellectual property in the future. They could even keep their closed financial system that subsidizes their companies directly and indirectly. Why American negotiators let a country with a non-market financial system into the same trade bloc remains baffling to me to this day. Even worse, their other concession was the ephemeral promise of future democracy in China, which for them was like getting something for nothing. The Chinese negotiators clearly also took advantage of American optimism.

The only areas China gave in on in WTO negotiations were conditions they wanted in the first place to help their domestic economy. The areas where America had demands beyond what was in China's interest, the Chinese only had to make promises for the future. This agreement was like that of Fred Flintstone negotiating with his paperboy Arnold, where Fred always ended up with a worse deal versus what he started with.

China's entry into the WTO was a disaster for the working class in America, but there were definitely some positive benefits. For example, it was a boon for China as the subsequent economic boom brought hundreds of millions of Chinese out of poverty. The world will now benefit as literally hundreds of millions more Chinese will get proper nutrition and proper education, and will contribute much more meaningfully to the development and advancement of human knowledge. Also, I personally hope that China does not develop into an enemy of the US: we have many shared interests and I believe we are both non-empire-building cultures (though both are bullies) that can successfully coexist as China reemerges as the dominant power in Asia.

Another negotiation example to look at would be the first trade deal with China negotiated by the Trump administration in 2017. Bottom line, that trade deal did nothing to address the massive trade deficit the US has with China. Some specific US financial firms benefited (surprise, surprise). And what have the Chinese given up? They promised to import more US beef—a good win for US farmers. In exchange, the US will open its market to Chinese poultry. This seems like an equitable trade except for the fact that beef requires almost five times as much water to produce pound per pound versus chicken. Importing US beef and exporting Chinese chicken is, in reality, a Chinese lateral strategy to import US water (and soil). Northern China has a huge water shortage problem. It looks like a win for the US, but actually China is getting the more valuable part of the deal. (One random observation—and I have no explanation why—but Chinese chicken is delicious. There is something different about it from US chickens. So, at least we are getting what seems to me to be a different variety of chicken.)

The Chinese have also agreed to buy US liquefied natural gas (LNG). But how much of a concession is this? China is an energy-short country. Burning US hydrocarbon reserves to drive the Chinese economy seems more like a benefit to China than a concession.

The Chinese can't be blamed for the US not under-standing them and not seriously negotiating for better terms along the way. For seventeen years, the Chinese waited for the US to negotiate the opening of the Chi-nese financial markets. The US dithered while China developed their banks, insurance companies, payment companies, etc., as best they could. Finally, almost two decades after the entrance of China to the WTO, the US is negotiating in earnest for changes they thought would just happen naturally and in due course.

I normally don't expect much success for the US nego-tiators vis-à-vis China. I generally doubt we can lower our trade deficit much through negotiations, as any meaning-ful change would require going through a difficult trade war. At the end of the day, Americans believe in win-win solutions and the Chinese don't. With our absolute-truth mindset, we are loath to go into a difficult but necessary lose-lose trade war. The Chinese know this and are very willing to go into a tit-for-tat trade war, knowing the threat of loss will prevent the US from sticking to any truly tough measures.

Trump is the wildcard here because he is a win-lose negotiator and is the rare American with a zero-sum mindset that is willing to take a tough stance against the Chinese. After his unsuccessful first deal, Trump has assembled a stronger trade team and has taken a much tougher stance against China with high and rising tar-iffs on imports from China. The Chinese appear to have misread Trump's win-lose mentality and, under pressure from Trump, it looks like China may finally start to honor some of their commitments from joining the WTO. The key for real progress, however, will be Trump's willingness to go into a full trade war, where the Chinese have much more to lose given their tremendously large trade surplus with the US. Ironically, absolute-truth believing, win-win Americans will have a difficult time supporting this strategy even though it would benefit them hugely.

A typical Chinese tactic is excuses. For example, even if they opened their car market, the US couldn't sell many cars into China. So, if the US has a 2.5 percent tariff on buying Chinese cars and China has 25 percent tariffs on US car imports, it wouldn't matter if they changed it anyway because there wouldn't be a big market for these US imports. Of course, if it wouldn't have any impact, the Chinese would have lowered their tariff a long time ago. That's why they kept the high tariff: to keep US car imports out. The Chinese would never negotiate that away without getting something in return. For some reason, the US historically was always pacified by these types of excuses. (China did recently lower the auto tariff to 15 percent—which was about ten years too late—but then subsequently raised them to 40 percent for the US in retaliation for new US tariffs, but then recently temporarily lowered them back to 15 percent.)

China also uses blame as another negotiating tactic. The problem, in their view, is the US savings rate is too low or the US doesn't invest enough in infrastructure. The idea that Google, or Visa, or Citibank, or Ford don't have fair access to the Chinese market because the US savings rate is too low is nonsense. Under Trump, it appears that the US is no longer falling for these misdirection tactics. The Chinese know they need to reduce the trade gap, so they are looking for relative wins by buying more US resources without having to open their own markets. China says they can lower the trade gap if we sold them more coal, gas, and other commodities, but the US goal of fair and free trade with China is not as a resource supplier like some third-world colony. What China is really after is US energy, water, and soil. This also misdirects the US away from fair access into the Chinese market.

The Chinese have used their other tried-and-true gambit of making promises and pledges. China pledges to better protect US IP and promises to lower tariffs a number of years out. In 2001, all China had to promise was to eventually open up their economy and become more democratic. This was despite zero intentions of ever adopting democracy. Americans—with their belief in absolute truth and, frankly, idealistic and naïve nature—fell for it.

Another Chinese tactic is to make temporary changes when faced with US pressure. When the Obama admin-istration pressed China on their aggressive industrial espionage, the Chinese backed off. They explained to the (naïve) Americans that it was a process and the short-term decline in industrial espionage activity was a sign of improvement. Once the Americans got distracted, like the proverbial frog in the pot, the Chinese slowly re-ramped their systematic IP theft activities. Bizarrely, officials from the Obama administration still talk about that agreement as a success.

When it comes to renegotiating China's terms in the WTO, one more tactic is at play: waiting it out. The Chinese have stalled on negotiations because they know Trump may be gone in a few years. They don't have any pesky elections to worry about. Continuity is on their side. In the end, a deal would need to be more favorable for China than it is for the US, which would not likely result in a meaningful shift in the trade deficit.

Another big challenge I've noticed for Americans negotiating with the Chinese is that Americans often don't realize who they are negotiating with—as in, they don't accurately identify the person in the room with the most power. Pye describes authority in large Chinese negotiation teams as "diffuse and vague," and notes that the Chinese negotiators may not have clearly defined mandates, or know what their superiors will decide. This can lead to a false sense of progress in negotiations.[216]

The Chinese find strength in numbers. Oftentimes two Westerners can be negotiating with a team of ten or more Chinese negotiators. This is also true in Japan. East Asians like numerical superiority. Pye notes that as

216 Lucian W. Pye, *Chinese Negotiating Style—Commercial Approaches and Cultural Principles,* xv.

negotiations progress between these two groups—a large Chinese team and a small American team—the American negotiators tend to narrow their attention to a one-on-one relationship, while the Chinese negotiators broaden their attention to the layers of bureaucracy, committees, and senior officials that will need to be coordinated to manage the deal.[217]

The Chinese team sent in to meet with the Americans will not have any authority to make a decision. This can be extremely frustrating to Americans who may think they have a deal only to find the people they've negotiated with still need to run the deal by the person who is the true decision maker.

Pye does a great job describing the culturally different views on authority and responsibility. Americans, he says, set up clear paths for power and responsibility. When an important activity needs to be done, Americans select the person responsible for executing it. The Chinese, however, divorce power from responsibility, and in their bureaucratic decision-making process, "the critical art is to avoid responsibilities, diffuse decisions, and blunt all commands that might later leave one vulnerable to criticisms." Where a powerful American can cut through problems with decisive command, the Chinese wield power differently. As Pye explains, *"in the ranks of the*

---

217 Lucian W. Pye, *Chinese Negotiating Style—Commercial Approaches and Cultural Principles*, 65-66.

powerful, proof of importance lies precisely in being shielded from accountability (Emphasis mine)."[218]

As believers in fixed truth, Americans tend to deem contracts as agreements and the end to negotiations. "In contrast to American practices, the Chinese do not treat the signing of a contract as a signaling of a completed agreement; rather, they conceive of the relationship in longer and more continuous terms..."[219] Pye goes on to explain that the contract is just the beginning of a growing relationship that will continue to be characterized by unending negotiation. While American negotiators fear that canceling a contract could damage the relationship, Chinese negotiators are comfortable with making increasing demands. This is very different from Japan, where the contract is set once agreement has been reached (but the Japanese will have reams of questions before they will sign a contract). The Chinese will restart the process many times—even after having an agreement—trying to get more concessions. Ultimately, for the Chinese, it is always negotiable.

The Chinese also love to play different parties against each other. For example, Siemens, G.E., or Mitsubishi Heavy would never have agreed to transfer their super technical and very difficult gas turbine technology to the Chinese as a group decision. However, they each wanted access to the huge and fast-growing Chinese market. The

218 Lucian W. Pye, *Chinese Negotiating Style—Commercial Approaches and Cultural Principles*, 18.

219 Lucian W. Pye, *Chinese Negotiating Style—Commercial Approaches and Cultural Principles*, xvi.

Chinese negotiated with each of them individually, and all three ended up in joint ventures with Chinese companies with varying degrees of technology transfer. If all three had teamed up, they could have negotiated much better terms. It is in American interests to beware of the Chinese divide-and-conquer strategy.

My experience is that Americans also often assume that if they've made a good personal contact in China, even a friendship, that they are immune to devious tactics when it comes to money. In my first business-related transaction in China, I got screwed over by one of my best friends. When I asked him why, he just shrugged his shoulders and said *meibanfa* (it couldn't be helped). I considered it a learning experience and the money I lost was my tuition. We remained friends and he never brought it up again. In any negotiation in China, I now always try to do everything possible to make it a multi-game situation, because in single-game situations the Chinese are obligated to get as much as possible for themselves as quickly as possible, consequences be damned. Fairness is not even a consideration. Now I know that it's better to leave them hoping for something more in the future to secure a fair deal in the present.

Remember that with their belief in relative truths, the Chinese don't like to focus too much on details. This is because details can change all the time:

"The Chinese reject the typical American notion that agree-

ment is best sought by focusing on specific details and avoiding discussions of generalities. They prefer instead agreeing on the general principles of the relationship before dealing with troublesome details."[220]

—LUCIAN PYE

Also, remember to protect your "face" as the Chinese will try to use your sense of shame and decency against you. Pye notes that the Chinese expect the other party in a negotiation to be "shattered by the shame of their faults," and will make the most out of mistakes, slip-ups, and misstatements to put the other party on the defensive.[221]

When the negotiations conclude, the Chinese will play down how much they have won and stress mutual benefit. Though the Chinese continually make demands and focus on victory in a win-lose outcome, Pye notes that once a point of settlement has been reached, they will finally recognize that both sides had mutual interests all along.[222]

Further, once a relationship is established in China (business or personal) they will include you in their circle, which means they will do a lot for you, but will also ask a lot of you. Pye points out that Americans and Chinese have contrasting views on how the relationship continues after an agreement. For Americans, an agreement marks

---

220 Lucian W. Pye, *Chinese Negotiating Style—Commercial Approaches and Cultural Principles*, xiv.

221 Lucian W. Pye, *Chinese Negotiating Style—Commercial Approaches and Cultural Principles*, xv.

222 Lucian W. Pye, *Chinese Negotiating Style—Commercial Approaches and Cultural Principles*, 87.

a mutual understanding that ends the stage of negotiations; for the Chinese, establishing a good business relationship allows both parties to strip off inhibitions, and continue to ask for bigger favors.[223]

FILTERS FOR UNDERSTANDING CHINESE BEHAVIOR

- Face is most important. Never lose face.
- Family comes first and the extended clan second.
- The individual traditionally comes third and the country fourth. (The Communist Party has tried with some success to change this with decades of propaganda.)
- Do nothing that will shame or bring difficulty to the family or clan.
- Follow the money. (Love of money is a huge motivation in China.)
- Try to show others that you are important, influential, connected, and generous.
- Competition with non-family members is considered dog-eat-dog (or people-eat-people in Chinese) so fight with no holds barred.
- Strive to increase your position and try to advance up as much as possible, as fast as possible, as efficiently as possible, by any means necessary.
- Take risks if this can help you advance. The family is always there to fall back on.
- No loyalty to companies. No loyalty to brands either.

223 Lucian W. Pye, *Chinese Negotiating Style—Commercial Approaches and Cultural Principles*, 89.

- Truth is flexible.
- Might makes right. Whoever has the gold, makes the rules.
- China goes through massive cycles of good and bad times. We are in a good cycle now. Take advantage as much as possible. Learn and experience as much as possible now that China is open to the world.
- Be direct and sometimes brutally honest.
- When the Chinese are being loud it does not mean they are fighting. They like *renao*, or loud and lively discussion. Usually it is just a very standard conversation.
- Do not take conflicts, arguments, or disagreements personally.

SECTION 6

THE JAPANESE AND CHINESE ECONOMIES AND FUTURE OUTLOOKS

CHAPTER 33

THE JAPANESE ECONOMY

When I was in college in the late '80s, the Japanese economic juggernaut seemed on pace to take over the world. How quaint that view seems now. Japan was the first non-Christian country to enter the special international club of developed economies. Prior to Japan's rise, the prevailing belief was that successful economic development was dependent upon having the Protestant work ethic, Western laws and institutions, and a Judeo-Christian-driven culture. Japan's success shattered that belief with its unique growth model.

The keys to Japan's development were a high domestic savings rate, protected domestic markets, a strong focus on education, and the proliferation of companies with an intense focus on constantly improving quality.

The high domestic savings rate was a critical component of Japan's success. In the inflationary 1970s, high savings meant low consumption, which lowered inflationary pressures and allowed Japan to keep interest rates lower, all else equal. The large pool of savings also provided companies with access to sufficient capital for investment and low borrowing costs that gave them a competitive advantage as exporters. With suppressed domestic demand and relatively low production and borrowing costs, Japan became an export powerhouse.

A major ongoing challenge for most developing countries is their reliance on foreign borrowing to fund domestic investments. Not only does this cause most developing countries to get buried under the burden of debt and interest payments, it also makes them vulnerable to currency risk. The debt is generally dominated in dollars and any weakness in the native currency causes the dollar-dominated debt burden to rise in local currency terms, leading to further flight from that currency and a very negative self-reinforcing loop. With its high domestic savings rate and large trade surplus, Japan was able to fund all its investments internally and avoid the foreign currency debt trap.

In accord with their belief in relative truth, the Japanese tend to see only win-lose outcomes, historically facilitating a culture of dyed-in-the-wool mercantilists. Mercantilism, as Jacob Soll defines it, "is the idea that world's supply of gold and raw materials is finite and that whichever country dominates these supplies will, in turn, dominate the world economy."[224]

224 Jacob Soll, "Colbertism Failed in France. Will It Work in China?" *Boston Globe*, July 14, 2013, https://www.bostonglobe.com/ideas/2013/07/13/colbertism-failed-france-will-work-china/Q9iiZEpieHhcTOhbkYrJSP/story.html.

As Japan is also a very resource-poor country, it wisely made it a mission to become a large trade surplus country. Like a good *weiqi* player, Japan carefully protected its domestic market, primarily through non-tariff trade barriers, while using that strength at home to attack foreign markets. Japanese companies could earn higher profit margins in the lower-competition home market and use that to subsidize their quest to gain market shares overseas.

Another clever move early in Japan's development phase was to invest in domestic ship-building capacity and also in overseas mining projects. This helped lower the costs of obtaining the resources necessary for Japan's development. Japan ended up importing raw materials and exporting high value-added goods. This led to a large trade surplus, which helped fund domestic investment, build up large foreign currency reserves, and ultimately allowed Japan to become a major supplier of credit to the rest of the world. If compound interest is indeed the eighth wonder of the world, Japan made sure they were earning interest and not paying it.

Japanese society has an intense focus on education, providing its industry with a large supply of well-educated, disciplined, loyal, and dedicated workers. As previously stated, Japan's literal view of the world and intuitive reasoning process impeded their use of the scientific method, but supported their efforts at imitation. This orientation was a great advantage in Japan's economic catch-up phase after WWII. Starting with textiles and light industry in the 1950s and 1960s, Japanese companies took advantage of their employees' proclivity toward perfectionism and innovative ability stemming from their intuitive reasoning process to steadily move up the manufacturing value-added and quality curves. During this rapid development phase, investments in domestic infrastructure yielded high returns while Japanese manufacturing companies took advantage of the weak yen, low borrowing costs, a protected domestic market, aggressive pricing, and world-beating quality to become export powerhouses. This growth model was particularly well-suited to the inflationary environment of the 1970s.

One cause of inflation is demand for goods growing faster than supply. Japan's suppression of domestic demand and high investment in production capacity was naturally disinflationary. The marginal return on investment in infrastructure was also high. The return on the first few modern bridges, highways, subway lines, trains, power plants, electricity grids, and sewage treatment plants was tremendous. The marginal return on new upgraded and modern shipyards, auto plants, machinery plants, and electronics factories was equally lucrative. Japan was an economic star through the 1960s, 1970s, and 1980s.

Unfortunately for Japan, their economy ran into five major headwinds: 1) the world transitioning from inflationary to deflationary; 2) a shrinking and aging Japanese population; 3) falling returns on new investment; 4) lack of creativity and inventiveness; and 5) their literal minds' weakness at grasping financial concepts.

Japan's relatively low level of domestic consumption and high investment in productive capacity were virtues in a period of high inflation, but became vices as the world became deflationary. Japan's relative economic strength peaked out with their stock market bubble at the very end of the 1980s. The entrance of China and Eastern Europe as open economies into the global economy in the 1990s led to a large increase in the global labor supply, which was deflationary. Costs came down around the world as manufacturing shifted to these new low-cost markets. With over a billion people and the world's highest savings rate, China's emergence also led to a large increase in the level of global savings relative to the marginal demand they added. This, in turn, generated lower interest rates and inflation rates globally.

In the simplest terms, Japanese domestic supply of savings exceeded their domestic demand for money. Interest rates are used to balance the supply and demand for money. In growing economies, we are used to having positive interest rates as the demand for money is greater than supply of savings. Interest rates are used to define the time value of money and help guide consumers and investors. In Japan, however, with weak consumption and excess capacity in infrastructure and industrialization, demand for money ended up lower than supply, so interest rates fell to zero. With chronic deflation, money gains purchasing power over time, and our concepts of time value of money get flipped on their heads. It was under these conditions that Japan fell into the dreaded liquidity trap. Negative interest rates were required to clear Japan's market for money, but if interest rates become very negative, then people can always take their money out of the bank and hold cash, which always yields 0 percent. In this situation traditional monetary policy became ineffective.

Japan is now also faced with an aging and shrinking population. With Japan's literal interpretation of Japanese nationality, immigration was minimal. As I wrote earlier, even 100 percent racially Japanese returning from Brazil and China were not accepted as citizens. Other non-Japanese were completely out of the question. Possessing one of the lowest birth rates in the world and very limited immigration, Japan's declining workforce became increasingly problematic.

As Japan's working-age population peaked out, economic growth became anemic. Japan had fewer people to work and consume, and this was coupled with the aging population's tendency to reduce consumption and increase saving. With the declining birthrate, the older population couldn't rely on the younger generation to support them in their retirement years, and were incentivized to save even more for fear that Japan's public pension system would be underfunded. This shrinking and aging population led to even weaker domestic consumption, lower demand for money, even more deflation, and an even higher level of savings.

It became a vicious cycle because lower spending led to deflation, and continually falling prices meant the longer people waited to consume, the more purchasing power their money had. The catch-22 was that as people saved more to consume later at lower prices, the fall in current spending hurt the economy and employment. Fewer people taking home paychecks then further worsened the deflation, creating a vicious cycle. Keynes called this the paradox of thrift.

Japan's population peaked in 2010 and has declined ever since. For the economy, the working-age population (fifteen to sixty-four-year-olds) is far more important. In Japan's case, the working-age population peaked out and started falling from around 1996 to 1997. Because the number of workers is a key variable in economic growth, the Japanese economy basically stopped growing from 1997 and is not meaningfully bigger today, twenty years later.

Japan also ran into the wall of declining new returns on investment. The multiplier effect on building the first new roads, bridges, electric grids, power plants, trains, subways, etc., was quite high in the 1950s to 1980s high growth period. But the returns on bridges to nowhere, repaving perfectly good roads, or of building the 158th rail/subway line in metropolitan Tokyo were zero at best or even negative. Similarly, the return on investment in the next steel plant, or shipyard, or auto plant, or chemical plant, in the presence of excess capacity, was very low or even zero. New projects could no longer earn an economic return. In other words, when a Japanese company invested in a new plant, factory, or other infrastructure, they generally lost money.

Japan's growth model was built upon leveraging the large pool of domestic savings and investing those savings into productive infrastructure and manufacturing capacity. But with zero or even negative expected returns, no one rationally wanted to borrow to invest. The telltale sign that Japan ran out of investment opportunities domestically was their late 1980s foray into high-priced foreign assets such as their high-profile purchases of the Rockefeller Center in New York City, Columbia Pictures in Hollywood, and the Pebble Beach Golf Course in California.

Lack of creativity also hurt the Japanese economy. Japan enjoyed strong growth that inevitably slowed as they caught up with the developed world. Ultimately, their inability to innovate led to their economic stagnation and competitors such as Korea, Taiwan, and eventually China started to catch up.

It is funny, in a sense, since the Japanese did not see this problem coming. Japanese arrogance also peaked in the late 1980s and they thought it was the US that was primed for stagnation and decline. Anyone that interacted with the Japanese in the late '80s or early '90s remembers the absolute dismissiveness with which they regarded American manufacturing, products, and society. The Japanese believed that the decline in US morals, breakdown of the family system, widespread drug abuse, lazy students with an excessively high sense of entitlement, short-sighted business cultures, low savings and high borrowing levels that supported excess conspicuous consumption, and large trade and budget deficits all signaled the decline of the US economic empire.

What the Japanese underestimated was what Lee Kwan Yew described as Americans' "can-do attitude" and the ability of US companies and entrepreneurs to create. Look at the average American day today. An American wakes up and turns on their iPhone and checks Facebook, Twitter, Snapchat, and/or Instagram. Maybe they drive a Tesla or call an Uber to take them to work, grabbing a Starbucks along the way, ordering some books from Amazon, searching anything they want to know on Google, then going home and watching a movie on Netflix. America is defining the new economy.[225] The internet was the game changer and Japan's literal mindset worked against Japanese economic growth as they were far more adept at the task of manufacturing and engineering tangible outputs and far less prepared to do well in the abstract online world.

Japan's weakness at finance was the hammer blow to Japan's economic ambitions. Japan never developed

225 This idea came out of a conversation I had with David Scott of CHA-AM Advisors.

globally-competitive banks that could price risk, lend on a risk-adjusted basis, or mark assets to market properly. Japan also failed to develop leading financial technologies. In fact, Japanese financial technology, or what they called *zaiteku*, turned out to be a bad joke. *Zaiteku* was where Japanese companies would try to make money off of the stock market or other financial instruments as opposed to earning profits from their core business.

As the marginal return on new investments declined, the Japanese economy turned to increased leverage and a massive property bubble to drive growth. Companies and local governments borrowed against rising land collateral values, believing that Japan's fast economic growth was due to the superior spirit of the Japanese people. Investment banks guaranteed returns, the stock market skyrocketed, and investment bankers actually flocked to a hostess-turned-restaurant-owner in Osaka that got her stock tips from a giant ceramic frog.[226] The property bubble grew so large that the land under the Imperial Palace in Tokyo was apparently worth more than all of California.

Unfortunately, Japan had not repealed the laws of economics. The stock market and property market bubbles both burst. Since Japan had a relative view of truth, there was no need to mark-to-market to make assets reflect reality the way the (absolute-truth-believing)

---

226 "The Celebrated Ceramic Toad of Osaka," *Museum of Hoaxes*, September 30, 2002, http://hoaxes.org/weblog/comments/the_celebrated_ceramic_toad_of_osaka.

Americans did after the 2008 GFC. As bad loans were only very slowly recognized and accounted for, the Japanese economy deflated slowly over the following decade.

Japan's weakness at finance also generated misguided and unhelpful government policy. For example, in 1997, and in opposition to deflationary pressure, Japan raised their consumption tax from 3 percent to 5 percent. After over a decade of deflation, in 2014, Japan raised their consumption tax from 5 percent to 8 percent. The plan now is to raise it to 10 percent. The corporate tax rate, on the other hand, was cut from 41 percent in 2011 to 31 percent in 2016 with plans to lower it below 30 percent.

Counterproductively, in an environment of deflation with not enough demand and too much supply, Japan is actually raising taxes on consumers while lowering taxes on producers! If that sounds like madness, that understanding is correct; this policy is exactly wrong for solving deflation. Inflation is not a rise in prices, it is a rising price level, and that abstract distinction has proven too difficult for the literal-minded Japanese to understand.

The Japanese economists will argue that taxes on consumers are low in Japan, which is true if you ignore all of the (not insignificant) indirect taxes on consumers. But in economics, change at the margin is key. Raising taxes on consumers *is* at the margin, which weakens consumption on the margin and leads to worsening deflation.

Japan also has a massive budget deficit. Their solution to insufficient domestic demand is huge public works projects. Of course, this government-allocated spending is inefficient and a waste of money. With any understanding of finance and economics, the solution should be obvious: minimize government spending. Cutting taxes on corporations is a good move to help their companies' competitiveness, but this should be funded not by raising taxes on Japan's beleaguered consumers, but rather by cutting their gigantically wasteful and inefficient government spending! Unfortunately, special interests won't let that happen. One has to conclude that Japanese bureaucrats think we are still in the inflationary world of the 1970s, as crazy as that may seem.

Another factor to consider in the Japanese economy are real interest rates, which are impacted by deflation. Deflation pushes up real interest rates and effectively leads to tighter monetary policy. This is the exact opposite of what Japan needs. Admittedly real interest rates are not what most people think about. But for balanced-linear thinkers, the concept is not too difficult to grasp once explained. This is not the case, however, for the literal-minded Japanese.

The longer you hold on to your savings in a financial environment where prices are falling, the greater the purchasing power over time. While this might be good for the individual, in aggregate, this is terrible in an economy where the demand for money falls short of the supply of money and society needs a negative real interest rate to match the supply and demand of money. This creates a negative feedback loop where people are incentivized to save more, creating even more deflation and even more of an incentive to save more. On top of that, the positive real interest rates and high trade surplus lead to a continually strengthening currency. The stronger yen is another headwind for the Japanese economy.

The solution to this conundrum is to create enough inflation through printing money to create negative real interest rates sufficient to incentivize people to consume today and not to save. The good news is that Paul Krugman explained this solution all the way back in 1998.[227] The bad news was that the solution was far too abstract for the literal-minded Japanese to understand. Japan seemed to go out of their way to ignore this solution by actually raising interest rates in August 2000! This was the opposite of what Japan needed. Amazingly, as if to prove they had no idea what they were doing, Japan tried interest rate hikes again in 2006 and 2007 despite the disastrous effects.

Over the past four to five years, Japan did finally embark on an aggressive Quantitative Easing program, but this failed to end deflation because Japan still did not understand (or want to solve) the fundamental problem of weak domestic demand and lack of inflation. The Bank of Japan declared they would buy an unlimited amount of government bonds as well as purchase other assets.

---

227 Paul Krugman, "Japan's Trap," May 1998, https://www.princeton.edu/~pkrugman/japans_trap.pdf.

This did not, however, address the problems of zero or negative return on new investment domestically or falling price levels for consumers. No matter how much money they "print" it does not enter the economy. They are pushing on the proverbial string.

The solution, of course, is to not spend the money buying government bonds and trying to fix an interest rate mechanism that is broken. Rather, Japan needs to take that money and give it, yes *give it,* to the people. If they continually give money to their citizenry, eventually consumption will pick up, inflation will return, and savers will be incentivized to consume more. Additionally, return on new investment, at least for domestic-oriented businesses, will turn positive again. However, it seems highly unlikely Japan will do this, half because they don't truly understand inflation and the time value of money, and half because raising domestic consumption means higher imports which will hurt Japan's all-important trade surplus. Mercantilism and keeping their spot as the world's top creditor nation remain far more important to the Japanese than generating inflation.

Amazingly, the Bank of Japan experimented with negative interest rates, with the hope that Japanese consumers would react to the negative returns and possibly be motivated to consume more and save less. With their Confucian background, Japanese savers, however, are far less incentivized by interest rate levels and care much more about their total level of savings. With negative interest rates, their motivation was to save even more to hit their savings target level. The confusion of negative interest rates also raised uncertainty and caused them to save more. Mind-bogglingly, the Japanese authorities had no idea how Japanese people would respond to negative interest rates.

Government debt is now over 250 percent of GDP. The Bank of Japan's balance sheet is over 500 trillion yen and now almost as big as Japan's nominal GDP. By contrast, the US Fed's balance sheet is only around 25 percent of US GDP. With these policies, Japanese inflation is no more likely than Chinese democracy.

The situation today does not look good, but we should not be too pessimistic about Japan in the long term. They remain leaders at many cutting-edge technologies, and unlike American companies that prioritize share buybacks, Japanese companies continue to invest heavily into research and development. Japan's falling population numbers may turn out to be a blessing in disguise as rapid advances in automation technology may ultimately eliminate the need for large working-age populations. The demographic dividend of a well-shaped population pyramid of the past may turn into a demographic tax in the future.

CHAPTER 34

THE CHINESE ECONOMY

The Chinese economy has some interesting parallels
with the Japanese economy, including their mercantilist attitude, hard-working labor force, and banking
system whose primary function is to channel the large
domestic savings pool and direct capital at low interest
rates to domestic investment. However, China's open-
ness to foreign investment, risk-taking entrepreneurial
spirit, and ability to create and invent distinguish it
from Japan.

The Chinese economy that Deng Xiaoping took over
in 1978 was socialist and completely state owned. The
economy was moribund. Deng's Reform and Opening
Up policy introduced the invisible hand of the market and
Chinese growth started to take off. China's economy was
reformed in the following stages:

- 1980s: liberalization of the rural sector

- Early 1990s: introduction of the coastal free trade zones and the stock market
- Late 1990s: incredible contributions by Zhu Rongji through SOE reform, giving all state-owned housing to the people, introducing property rights, devaluing the RMB 33 percent (overnight in January 1994 like any good mercantilist would recommend), and implementing a VAT that increased tax revenues for the central and local governments
- Early 2000s: China entered the WTO and set the stage for a decade of incredible growth, which helped China to outgrow its legacy bad bank loan problem

Zhu's VAT program was an excellent example of Chinese lateral thinking at work. In general, Chinese firms don't like to pay taxes. Many firms underreport profits to avoid paying taxes. Using this knowledge, Zhu focused on a value-added tax, which taxes sales instead of profits. No matter what financial shenanigans Chinese companies used to manipulate their bottom-line profits, it is much harder to manipulate top-line sales. The initiative was a huge success. One problem, however, was that even though it did increase tax revenues for the central government, conversely, it made the local governments more reliant on land sales to raise funds. This sowed the seeds for some bad future behavior and reckless spending by local governments.

Similar to Japan, China historically also enjoyed a

high domestic savings rate. The banking system pooled this money and lent on a non-risk-adjusted basis. Simple linear thinking and Western economic analysis would say this non-risk-adjusted, relationship-based bank lending would not earn economic returns and would fail. During much of the 2000s, many Western observers even believed that China was over-inflating their economic growth numbers. However, if anything, China was under-reporting growth at the time.

What the Western economists missed were the non-linear and lateral impacts from China's massive growth phase post their entry into the WTO. For example, a company perhaps was losing money on sales or exports as they worked to grow domestic and/or global market share. Maybe they lost money and destroyed value for a couple of years. But eventually, they grew past a certain size, and scale economies kicked in and began to create value. Many early infrastructure projects would never earn an economic return and on a stand-alone basis should never have been built. But in aggregate, the knock-on effects of the improved infrastructure led to huge economic benefits. Synergistic supply chains were also built up. One plus one equaled three. There is an economic principle called Time, Place, and Utility (TPU), and China's investment in development led to huge unquantified gains in TPU.

At the same time, the Chinese property market boomed. As TPU improved across China, the value of the underlying real estate also boomed. For example, a plot on the outskirts of a city would not be worth much on a stand-alone basis, but when a metro station was built nearby and after water, electricity, and road infrastructure were also built up, then, of course, the TPU of that plot and its subsequent market value would rise strongly.

Zhu gave the ownership of homes to the people, but he didn't give them ownership of the land. To fund their budgets, local governments would take some of their large land holdings and sell those to developers. So, the local governments were incentivized to push people out of their old homes for minimal compensation, selling the underlying land for a huge markup to developers, who then demolished the old homes and built modern housing.

The value creation from replacing outdated housing with modern housing was huge and rose even further as the local governments used revenue from their land sales to build up the infrastructure that raised the aforementioned TPU of those areas. The property developers also made a killing. Cities were redesigned virtually at will. People protested being kicked out of their homes, but they had little recourse and were often moved to the outskirts of the cities they used to live in. The joke in Shanghai was that in downtown Shanghai the language of choice was English, in the surrounding areas it was Mandarin Chinese, and in the far outskirts you could hear

Shanghainese spoken as that was where they had all been relocated. (It sounds funnier in Chinese.)

This property boom further supercharged Chinese growth. As developers made large profits selling modern housing units to an eager market, they could leverage those profits to buy increasingly larger stakes of land to build even bigger projects. Local governments were enjoying bigger and bigger spending budgets as they sold more land and at higher prices. Apart from the not-insignificant sums that ended up being gambled in Macau or squirreled away overseas, a large amount of money was spent building up much needed infrastructure across China. As property prices continued to rise, homeowners felt wealthier and many earned large sums investing in property. There were other related benefits as the banking sector enjoyed the growth of a relatively stable and high return mortgage market, the steel and cement sectors saw a massive increase in demand, and the home furnishings sector boomed. Unfortunately, China's large wealth gap was exacerbated by this huge rise in prices. The rich already owned property and could buy more and more apartment units, while the average earner got priced out of the market.

Another one of the secret sauces for China (and major differences with Japan) was that the Chinese were open to foreign investment. This super-duper-charged Chinese growth. China raised GDP per capita from $1,000 to $8,000 in about thirty years versus ninety years for Japan and the 180 years it took the US.[228]

Foreign investment brought China four major benefits. The first was access to foreign technology which leaked into other Chinese companies through JVs or other less scrupulous means such as forced technology transfer or even outright intellectual property theft. Many Chinese companies were also formed by managers and engineers that learned the business while working for a foreign company located in China.

The second benefit of foreign investment was a big increase in employment. Foreign companies took advantage of not only the low labor costs in China, but also the low taxes, subsidized utility prices, weak labor laws, unenforced environmental regulations, and the skilled and hardworking Chinese labor force. I've visited many foreign factories in China that ran three shifts, working twenty-four hours a day. Depreciation costs on equipment could be one-third of developed market factories that only ran eight hours per day. This provided good jobs and incomes for China's massive blue-collar labor force.

The third major benefit was that foreign-invested companies initially were primarily focused on exports, which helped China develop a large trade surplus with the rest of the world and build up huge foreign currency

---

228 "The China Effect on Global Innovation," McKinsey Global Institute, October 2015, http:// china-trade-research.hktdc.com/resources/MI_Portal/Article/obor/2016/03/473784/1458204 781849_TheChinaEffectOnGlobalInnovation.pdf, 20.

reserves. A self-reinforcing cycle kicked in. As exports rose, dollars from overseas increasingly flowed into China. To prevent the RMB from appreciating too much or at all, the People's Bank of China would buy those dollars with new RMB they printed. Those dollars became China's large foreign exchange reserves and the RMB they printed increased domestic money supply. This loose monetary policy further boosted domestic growth.

The domestic economy was heavily investment focused, so faster growth meant higher levels of investment. With the high domestic savings rate and relatively low level of consumption, this meant more goods produced for export. Normally, this type of aggressive monetary policy would be inflationary and become a major problem. But the nonlinear magic at work was that the rising money supply that got turned into increased investment, led to higher production capacity and larger growth in marginal supply relative to marginal demand, which provided a deflationary offset.

China was in a Goldilocks-like magic growth period where the inflationary pressures from aggressive money supply growth was offset by the deflationary pressures of rising output, lower costs from rising scales of economy, and huge productivity gains as China industrialized, mechanized, and even automated. Commodity prices around the world skyrocketed in the 2000s as the world was not ready to meet China's exploding demand for resources. In effect, China was inflationary upstream and deflationary downstream.

The fourth benefit of foreign investment was that with a large number of foreign firms setting up factories in China, foreign and domestic supply chains built up around these factories, initiating a network effect. As more companies moved to China and supply chains were further built up, the more attractive it became for other companies to relocate manufacturing to China. The network and scale benefits brought large cost advantages to companies producing in China for export or for the domestic market.

Like the Japanese in the late 1980s, the Chinese today believe they have solved the economic cycle and are entitled to continuous and well-deserved high growth rates for decades to come. Also, like the Japanese, the Chinese ended up with rapidly falling marginal returns on new investment as their economy matured, massive levels of bad debts as their non-market-based lending caught up with them, a declining working-age population and rapidly aging society (exacerbated by China's one-child policy), and the willfulness to rely on ever-increasing amounts of credit to try to maintain growth and push the bad debt can down the road. China's policy today is accurately described as "extend and pretend."

For anyone who remembers Japan's heyday, it is fun to note the similarities between Japan in the late '80s and early '90s and China today. From the hordes of new overseas tourists to the large and visible investments overseas (as investment opportunities at home dried up), to the trade friction as domestic demand was weak and trade surpluses grew ever larger, to the property bubble, to the Western fears of their rise, to the accusations of unfair competition and technology theft, the economic landscapes of 1980s Japan and present day China are very similar. The arrogance is equally as evident. The Japanese in the late '80s had unconquerable self-confidence that melted away in the 1990s. Today, the arrogance of the Chinese echoes this. (Don't get me wrong: I'm not saying Americans aren't arrogant. We certainly are. But the big difference for me is that Americans don't have the wild swings from inconsolable self-pity to world-conquering self-confidence and back again the way I've witnessed in Asia.)

Another unfortunate similarity with Japan was China's huge debt that accumulated in the financial system. This came about as the underlying economic model had run its course. Industrial overcapacity meant that the marginal return on the next plant or factory in China was zero (or even negative) for most industries. Infrastructure also reached saturation and marginal returns on new train lines to sparsely populated areas (or little used bridges, or useless convention centers, or sports stadiums) fell to zero or worse. On top of all of that, the rise of ecommerce made large swathes of China's overbuilt brick-and-mortar retail space uncompetitive. Not willing to accept the prospect of going through a recession, and a Chinese relative view of truth that made them feel it was not necessary to mark assets to market, massive growth in credit was required to maintain lower and lower growth rates. Massive and still growing debts accumulated at the corporate and local government levels.

The Chinese also learned a lesson from the Japanese experience. Japan did not go through a sharp slow-down and chose instead to ignore the bad loans in the banking system and to go through their "lost decade." Growth slowed, but there was no social instability and no change in the basic government system. Both fac-tors appealed to the Chinese, and their policies this decade have been to follow the Japanese model. No mark-to-market, no sharp slowdown, no big write-offs. The Chinese financial system is mostly a closed system and China's foreign currency debt levels are manage-able. Therefore, China is unlikely to face a hard landing. However, the debt levels are so massive, the property overbuild so big, and the continued misallocation of capital unabated, making a soft landing also unlikely. China will most likely face a "long-landing." China will still have up cycles, but the trajectory is downward and increasing amounts of stimulus will be required for decreasing levels of returns.

One has to scratch their head and wonder why the Chinese leadership lacks the courage to make the nec-essary economic reforms to support future growth. Why allow the debt burden to grow to a level where it could threaten domestic stability? It is a reminder of how fortunate they were to have such visionary and long-term focused leaders as Deng Xiaoping and Zhu Rongji.

I do remain optimistic on China's economic prospects longer term. Chinese GDP per capita is still only around $9,000 versus roughly $50,000 for the US. China's population is around four times the size of the US. Mathematically, China only needs GDP per capita of one quarter the level of the US for the overall Chinese economy to equal the size of the US economy. It is inevitable that China will eventually surpass the US, as they will remain in the less challenging "technological catchup phase" for a long time. Additionally, unlike the Japanese, the Chinese are creative and can invent new ideas and products. China catching up to the US, however, is unlikely to happen as quickly as the Chinese would like.

In the short- to medium-term, China is facing much slower growth rates as they very slowly and haltingly reform their economy and financial system. Unfortunately, the current government is actually increasing the role of the state in the economy even though the lesson of the past seventy years was that the free market allocates capital far more effectively than the government. China will have to overcome some serious hurdles before they can catch the US.

CHAPTER 35

THE OUTLOOK FOR JAPAN

The outlook for Japan may not be as negative as their demographic trends would historically suggest, as improvements in automation are set to make much blue-collar employment obsolete. This is VERY bad news for the developing world.

The typical manufacturing pattern in Asia has been for low-end textile, toy, and other light industry jobs to move to low labor-cost countries. Over time, these countries moved up the value curve, manufacturing increasingly sophisticated products and eventually becoming competitive at higher-end electronics, autos, and machinery. This model started with Japan and then moved to Taiwan and Korea, and then to China and more recently is happening in Vietnam, Sri Lanka, and Bangladesh. The bad news is that this pattern is on track to change dramatically.

Improvements in automation technology are starting to hit an inflection point. Humans are marvelous machines with our keen eyesight, dexterous hands, strong muscles, and dynamic brains. The problem is that our hardware is basically set. Computers, on the other hand, continue to improve exponentially. Moore's Law highlighted how computer processing power doubles virtually every two years. This has led to huge improvements in artificial intelligence and machine learning.

Robots also continue to get stronger, faster, and more sophisticated, even learning to see with advances in vision sensor technology. For the more paranoid, scientists believe that the evolution of sight led to the Cambrian explosion and the biggest increase in the diversity of life on Earth. We can only wonder what impact machine vision will have on the future of robots.

The basic nature of factory automation is changing. In today's connected world, if an auto company's robot learns a superior process for doing an assembly task, that robot can teach the new process to other robots in any of that company's auto plants around the world. Machine learning is also developing the ability to test out nearly infinite variations to determine optimal designs and production processes. With improvements in sensor technology and robot vision, these virtual lessons can be tried out in the real world and then taught to all of the other robots in the same group. We already have robots making robots at factories in Japan, and now we'll have robots teaching other robots all over the globe. What this means is that until today, robots focused primarily on dirty or dangerous jobs such as welding, painting, or heavy lifting. But in the future, robots will be able to do functions such as assembly jobs that currently require human workers.

"The factory of the future will have only two employees, a man and a dog. The man will be there to feed the dog. The dog will be there to keep the man from touching the equipment."

—WARREN BENNIS

In such a world, Japan's literal interpretation of who is Japanese—and their subsequent demographic problem—may turn out to be a blessing in disguise. Maybe they had this plan all along? A falling population means Japan will have a declining dependence on imported energy, food, and other commodities. They also simply will not have a large young labor force to be displaced by factory automation. Japan can focus greater educational resources per pupil and thereby develop more scientists, engineers, and researchers that the future economy will require. Companies will be the major beneficiaries of this diversification and perhaps they will use their growing profit levels to hire and develop the remaining displaced workforce. I'm skeptical this will come to pass, but it's still possible. My expectation is that Japan, as a highly homogenous society, will embrace some type of universal basic income program, pursuing a more socialist course for wealth redistribution. The rest of the world will be watching as Japan shows what the future for an aging society looks like in the coming AI economy.

The reason I expect Japan to be relatively early to adopt a universal basic income system is that harmony is the top priority in Japan. With the shrinking population, there will be fewer people to support. Highly automated and robotized factories in Japan will also be highly profitable. Therefore, the natural solution will be for Japan to levy a robot tax on these companies and redistribute that money to the displaced working-age population, thereby supporting a stable and harmonious society. Given the Japanese emphasis on work and contribution to society, my expectation is that Japan's universal basic income system will be a defined minimum amount for everyone, with a government encouragement program that doubles or triples the salary a lower-wage worker receives. The government will also need to create social programs so that everyone has work opportunities.

Japan may turn out to be economically well positioned—but woe unto the developing world. The jobs that should be shifting from Japan and China to Southeast Asia, India, and many parts of Africa will get automated away. Factories will relocate to the US and Europe to get closer to end demand. We can already see this starting to happen with Nike and Adidas building new plants in the US and Europe, and for the first time in a quarter of a century, reversing the trend of offshoring production.

Japan will become a provider of a lot of the equipment

required for the future economy. I have a strong feeling that over the coming decades, much of human interaction will shift to the virtual world. Some online game companies already earn hundreds of millions or even billions of dollars catering to gamers in the virtual world. Virtual reality headsets are going to also improve dramatically in the next ten years as will online programs. People will increasingly be able to experience concerts, sporting events, speeches, parties, business meetings, and virtual reality games all in the comfort of their own homes. We probably will even vote and get our drivers' licenses (if we are one of the few that still wants to drive) all online in a virtual environment. Japan will be at a disadvantage in that their literal minds won't be suited for the abstract nature of a *Matrix*-like virtual world. But Japan would be well suited to provide the infrastructure for such a world, and once they do understand the new inventions and technological environment, their intuitive reasoning and dedication to excellence could lead to some interesting innovative companies in the virtual world.

Politically, I think we need to consider the possible remilitarization of Japan. As Benedict wrote after WWII, "Japan's motivations are situational. She will seek her place within a world at peace if circumstances permit. If not, with a world organized as an armed camp."[229] The samurai spirit still lurks in Japan. Samurai literally means "to serve." The samurai spirit can be seen in the *salary-*

229 Ruth Benedict, *The Chrysanthemum and the Sword*, 316.

man culture in Japan. *Salary-men* are the dedicated and extremely loyal salaried workers for Japanese companies. Like the samurai of the past with their dedication to their clan, the *salary-men* generally have lifetime employment and are loath to show disloyalty by switching companies. They live to serve their company and will sacrifice their health for their job and give their family secondary consideration relative to the needs of their company. There is a military-like sense of duty to their companies and this is a key factor for the strength and competitiveness of the Japanese economy.

The Japanese are also very hierarchical. Japan recognized the US as number one, and enjoyed the protection of the US nuclear umbrella. If that protection ever came into question, I have no doubt that Japan would move to remilitarize more aggressively. Japan already has one of the most advanced armies in the world. What I am implying is that Japan could develop an advanced nuclear arsenal and more advanced automated fighting capabilities to defend their place in the international order.

With their aging society, Japan would never again pursue imperial ambitions. But Japan could certainly take much more proactive steps to increase military power. If Japan perceived the Chinese to be the new number one globally, it would also not be out of the question for them to realign with China. The Japanese did not always look down on the Chinese. In the sixth and seventh centuries, they were so impressed with China they adopted as much of their culture as possible. The combination of Chinese human, industrial, and financial resources with Japanese technology, craftsmanship, and product innovation would be a potent combination. This is something the US needs to remain cognizant of looking forward. Though, I must say, that as one observes the contempt with which the Japanese and Chinese still hold each other, that no matter how rational an alliance may be, it remains highly unlikely.

CHAPTER 36

___

THE OUTLOOK FOR CHINA

My expectation is that China will eventually catch up economically with the United States. But it will take longer than the Chinese expect as they currently try to outgrow a bad debt problem by creating even more bad debt. Additionally, they have to deal with the negative impacts from the generation-defining trade war the US and China are entering. Obviously, China needs to change their underlying growth model and renegotiate a new (and more equitable) relationship with the US. Once China eventually learns these lessons, and makes the necessary painful adjustments, they will be poised to catch up with and even exceed the US.

I also have a strong conviction that China is pursuing a peaceful rise. Despite their desire for increased self-determination and leading influence in the Asia-Pacific region, the Chinese, by nature, are not expansionary empire builders. They merely want to be secure from invasion and for surrounding countries to be tributaries that properly kowtow to the Middle Kingdom. There will be tremendous tension as the US reacts and adapts to the rise of China, but I am optimistic that after this period of confrontation, we will eventually settle upon a stable bipolar equilibrium and the twenty-first century will be the US/China century.

When viewed from the outside, China looks like an economic juggernaut and the central government appears to be in total control. At the same time, their political system seems fragile and if economic growth slowed below 6 percent, political turmoil would arise.

When viewed from up close, however, it is clear that the Chinese central government has limited control over the provincial governments, who do not always follow government directives in terms of credit growth, low-return infrastructure projects, redundant manufacturing capacity, managing the rise of property prices, or pollution control. Xi Jinping is fighting so hard to accumulate power at the center specifically to reverse this trend. As for social stability, China withstood the starvation of tens of millions of people during the Great Leap Forward and the madness of the Cultural Revolution and, despite all of that, the Chinese Communist Party had no problem holding on to power. In this context, it is almost beyond belief that the Chinese people wouldn't have the sense, understanding, or tolerance to go through a normal economic down-cycle.

The Chinese economy is also not so strong as headline GDP numbers currently suggest. The balance sheets of many SOEs, local governments, and private companies in the overcapacity industries or sectors are terrible. The problems are: mountains of debts, large interest rate burdens relative to profits, troublesome working capital trends, un-factored environmental costs, and bleak prospects as demand shifts away from already overcapacity segments as the Chinese growth model slowly changes.

The fairly simple math of adding up China's annual trade surpluses along with the declines in Chinese foreign exchange reserves shows that capital flight over a twenty-four-month period across 2014 to 2016 was running at the pace of around a trillion dollars per year. That is a lot of money! One reason for the outflow of capital was the pursuit of better investment returns overseas. This was in part a reaction to the anti-corruption campaign Xi Jinping enacted when he took power in 2012, but capital flight in China was also the result of a closed society that doesn't protect individuals' rights. China is currently addressing the symptoms of this problem, but not the causes. China is also still overly reliant on stimulus spending in old economy sectors and an overheated property market to drive growth. Looking up close, China has some serious economic challenges.

I think we can already see the outcome for the Chinese economy over the next ten years or so. The government has no interest in marking assets to reality and taking big write-downs. This means China will continue to severely misallocate capital. Industries will remain overcapacity, suppressing prices and profit margins. Bad debts will continue to rise and increasing amounts of credit will be required for each new unit growth in GDP. China has a massive debt problem and despite efforts to slow down credit growth, the overall debt level continues to rise with no end in sight. China is choosing a long landing, so is in for a protracted period of slower growth and deflation. There will be some good areas for growth, particularly in the new economy, but growth in aggregate will be far slower than they've become accustomed to over the past thirty years. The trade/tech war with the US will exacerbate this slowdown.

China also has an enormous corruption problem given the emphasis on family over country which ultimately affects its economy. Chinese corruption has existed for millennia and that did not change with the Communist Party in charge. As the Chinese would say, they've changed soup, but not changed the medicine (换汤不换药). Basically, the government changed, but the underlying corruption problem is almost exactly the same. Officials at all levels feel they are entitled to leveraging their positions and authority to extract money from the system. Given the massive growth in the Chinese economy and increasing flows of money for corruption to tap into, the problem has become so big and resentment from the population so acute, the Communist Party, led by Xi

Jinping, had no choice but to address the problem. No doubt, much of Xi Jinping's anti-corruption efforts were politically motivated, but real progress was also made.

Even more worrisome is the looming health care disaster. Along with China's aging population, the country will also start paying the price for the awful degradation of their environment. Air pollution in China is horrific. Already the rate of lung, throat, stomach, and esophageal cancers are rising rapidly. With the combination of producing around half of the world's steel and cement, generating most of their power from burning coal, and the growth of the auto market at the rate of over 30 million units a year, air quality in China falls dreadfully short of the safe levels recommended by the World Health Organization. Furthermore, China has serious soil and water pollution problems.

If that weren't enough, food quality in China is severely compromised. Chinese food contains an array of problems from heavy metals in the rice, to low-quality and even reused gutter oils, to fake foods and unhealthy additives. In a frightening example of Chinese creativity, Chinese consumers have had to worry about not only melamine in milk or fake milk powder for babies, but also unscrupulous sellers of fake pig's ears,[230] fake eggs,[231]

230 "China Launches Investigation into 'Fake' Pigs' Ears," *The Telegraph*, May 16, 2012, http://www.telegraph.co.uk/news/worldnews/asia/china/9270069/China-launches-investigation-into-fake-pigs-ears.html.

231 "How to Identify Fake Chicken Eggs," *China Hush*, April 24, 2009, http://www.chinahush.com/2009/04/24/how-to-identify-fake-chicken-eggs/.

heavy metals in rice,[232] and even fake medicines.[233] On top of all of that, the Chinese have shifted from walking and bicycles to cars and subways. Exercise is down, and stress levels in such a fast-changing and over-competitive society have risen dramatically. Cancer, diabetes, and heart disease are growing at an epidemic rate.

There is also a perception that the Chinese government is fully in control of their economy and maybe has even developed some new superior growth model. The reality is different. The central government has a hard time getting local governments to follow their policies. In fact, it is due to this lack of central control that China has grown so fast.

China is more like a confederation of provinces. Each province wants to have their own power and steel plants, their own chemical factories, and their own auto and machinery plants. This has created a situation known as "the fallacy of composition." While it may have made sense at the time, when each province decided to separately build their own capacity, collectively it created a huge problem. This localization of resources led to higher-than-needed investment, which boosted growth as the extra capacity was built and ramped up, but created excess capacity and excess debt on top of that.

232 "'Cadmium Rice': Heavy Metal Pollution of China's Rice Crops," Greenpeace, April 24, 2014, http://www.greenpeace.org/eastasia/publications/reports/toxics/2014/cadmium-rice-heavy-metal/.

233 "China Arrests 1,900 in Crackdown on Fake Drugs," *BBC News*, August 6, 2012, http://www.bbc.com/news/world-asia-china-19144556.

Unfortunately, the central government in China is not the all-controlling economic monolithic power it is perceived to be.

The political history of China reflects power getting centralized by each new, strong leader and then this power slowly filtering out to the provinces. The center eventually loses control and China fragments again until a new dynasty emerges. The Chinese people dread these periods of disorder and uncertainty. The current dynasty started with Mao Zedong and his totalitarian grip on power. This loosened slightly with Deng Xiaoping and his authoritarian rule as he dismantled the cult of personality that Mao built up and shared power more broadly. Mao's title was the Leader of the Chinese People, whereas in his final years, Deng's only official title was Chairman of the Chinese Bridge Association. (He was an avid cards player.)

This loosened further to the consensus authoritarianism of Jiang Zemin and softened much more with the weak consensus authoritarianism of Hu Jintao. Xi Jinping has clearly modeled himself on Mao and is trying to restore power to the center and, so far, his policies appear to be moving China back in the right direction. Notably, Xi even adopted Mao's titles of "the Leader" and "the Chairman", something none of the leaders between Xi and Mao did. Xi has also declared himself president for life and is effectively the new emperor of China.

The Chinese Communist Party's control of their economy may not be as strong as perceived, but the party's grip on political power is not nearly as brittle as Western media suggests. There is an idea that if growth slows below 6 percent, then unemployment will rise, social instability will become widespread, and China could face political revolution. I suspect many international political pundits have seen the examples of South Korea and Taiwan where GDP per capita exceeded a certain level, and authoritarian governments transformed into democracies. I would caution against having this expectation for China. The civilization in China is 5,000 years old. Democracy is not part of the Chinese history, culture, or mindset. Unlike South Korea or Taiwan, China is not an ally dependent upon the protection of the US, so will not face many of the political pressures these countries felt.

Slower growth or student-led revolutions will not change the government in China. Only collapse of the Chinese Communist Party from within could lead to a new government. There are no signs that this will happen anytime soon. The uncertainty caused by a big economic slowdown would actually increase the people's support of the central government. (When I speak with Chinese citizens around the country, the complaints are *always* about the local government officials.) If China faced real discontent, they could always play the nationalist card vis-à-vis Taiwan or the disputed islands with Japan to get everyone back in line. There is an almost mythological belief that China will face big instability and the Communist Party will lose power in the next ten years. I've been hearing that for almost thirty years now and believe it will remain "ten years away" for at least the next fifty years or more. The US needs to accept the rise of China and build a better long-term relationship.

Despite all of their near-term challenges, in the long term China will catch up with and pass the US, and that is due to their sheer scale and their creativity. There is a perception in Western political and business circles that the Chinese are like the Japanese and lack the ability to create, and since the Chinese education system is based on rote learning, once the Chinese catch up with the developed world they will stagnate as they run out of areas to imitate. This view is mistaken. While it's true that the literal-minded Japanese are challenged to create, the Chinese are not literal thinkers and their lateral-reasoning process has proven quite creative in the past. As was mentioned earlier, China had the four great inventions of the ancient world: gun powder, the compass, paper making, and printing.

Let me give some recent examples of Chinese creativity. In August 2016, China launched the world's first quantum satellite, making China the first country to develop hack-proof telecommunication technology. Furthermore, China has the world's biggest supercomputer, the world's largest radio telescope. China has put a man in space and has landed a rover on the moon. They are building their own space station. They are leaders in mobile ecommerce and were the first to develop "pay with your face."[234] They are putting huge efforts into artificial intelligence (China is leading in speech recognition software),[235] and also leading the way in some areas of gene splicing and genetic enhancement.[236]

Think of the impact a person with a one-in-a-million talent has on the world. Given China's large population, there are about 1,400 such people in China. Increasingly, the Chinese system is finding and supporting these talents. They are not being lost to insufficient nutrition or wasting their talents on a farm somewhere. The Chinese system is still wholly inequitable and has many flaws, but the world should be prepared for more Chinese Elon Musks and Steve Jobs (and Jack Mas) to start emerging.

234 "8 Key E-Commerce Trends Coming Out of China," *Marketing*, June 4, 2017, http://www.marketing-interactive.com/8-key-e-commerce-trends-coming-out-of-china/.

235 Joe Milazzo, "How Baidu's Deep Speech 2 is Winning the Speech Recognition Game," *TutorMing Chinese for Business*, October 18, 2016, http://blog.tutorming.com/business/baidu-deep-speech-2-recognition-voice-command-china.

236 G. Owen Schaefer, "China May Be the Future of Genetic Enhancement," *BBC Future*, August 8, 2016, http://www.bbc.com/future/story/20160804-china-may-be-the-future-of-genetic-enhancement.

CONCLUSION

My dream in writing *Culture Hacks* was to help the US, Japan, and China to more deeply understand each other. The goal was to better promote peace and stability in the twenty-first century as the US and Japan rework their bilateral relationship, and both countries adapt to the rise of China. Specifically, I hope the US can learn to better communicate with the Japanese, recognize the profound differences between the Japanese and Chinese, and the importance of Japan in the Asian balance of power equation. Also, I want the US to learn to see China more realistically and to negotiate more equitable deals with verifiable safeguards in place to monitor Chinese pledges and promises. I also hope that China learns that they can out-negotiate most Americans, most of the time, but eventually this will come back to hurt Chinese interests. The Chinese have a long-standing philosophy to not let your fertile waters flow into neighbors' fields

(肥水不外流), but that going against this tradition and finding true win-win solutions will actually better serve China's long-term interests.

I'm optimistic that in a decade or two China, Japan, and the US will end up in stable and collaborative relationships. Clearer understanding of how each group thinks can help to mitigate many of the painful misunderstandings and miscalculations that will inevitably occur as the US and Japan adapt to the increasingly disruptive rise of China.

ACKNOWLEDGMENTS

I would like to thank my parents, who supported my going off to Japan and then to China with little money, no contacts, limited language skills, and no jobs lined up. They were skeptical, but supportive anyway. This book would have never existed without them. I would also like to thank my wife for patiently putting up with my manic research and writing style. She was also a consistent source of support, inspiration, and feedback. I'd like to also thank my kids. Writing a book took my time away from them. My teenage daughter inspired me with her kind advice to, "Give it up Dad, no one cares about your book." Which I translated from Gen Z language to mean "Good luck Dad, I'm really proud of the book you are writing!"

I'm also grateful to Tina Medina and Samantha Giles, two great editors that helped me to clean up my writing and to better craft the message. My sister Anne also helped with editing. Most of all, I'd like to thank master editor Emily Gindlesparger, who restructured the book, cut out the extraneous, and kept the message on point. Without all of their help, *Culture Hacks* would be far less readable. Of course, the responsibility for any mistakes or omissions rests with me.

Special thanks to Dave Asprey for helping to make me "bulletproof," to Terry Wahls for helping me to learn how to mind my mitochondria, and to Tony Robbins for helping a confused eighteen-year-old to find his way. I'd also like to thank all of the amazing friends I've made in Japan and China over the years. Without immersion and an open mind, I never would have learned to understand their uniquely unique cultures. I would also be remiss not to thank my company for generously allowing me to take a sabbatical to write this book. I missed the camaraderie of my colleagues dearly while I was away. And a special thanks to WHH, whose feedback and encouragement kept me going even when I wanted to give up.

ABOUT THE AUTHOR

RICHARD CONRAD grew up in Washington, D.C. and earned a double major in Engineering and Economics from Vanderbilt University. After graduation, Richard spent his twenties teaching himself Chinese and Japanese and eventually earned a master's degree in Economics as a local student at Fudan University in Shanghai, China. Richard later earned an MBA from the University of North Carolina at Chapel Hill and has worked for the last sixteen years for a large US money management firm researching, analyzing, and investing in Chinese and Japanese equities.

Made in the USA
Middletown, DE
09 July 2021

43871599R00265